WEATHER LORE
OF THE
ENGLISH COUNTRYSIDE

RED SKY AT NIGHT SHEPHERD'S DELIGHT?
--
WEATHER LORE OF THE ENGLISH COUNTRYSIDE

BY

PAUL J. MARRIOTT

Copyright © Paul J. Marriott
First Published by

Publishers of
History, Country and Biographical Books.
(Member of Independent Publishers Guild)
31 DASHWOOD RISE,
DUNS TEW,
OXFORD, OX5 4JQ
Tel. Steeple Aston (0869) 40615

First Published 1981

ISBN 0 9505730 5 1

All rights reserved. No part of this book may be reproduced or transmitted in any form or by any means, electronic or mechanical, including photocopying, recording or any information storage and retrieval system, without permission in writing from the Author and Publisher.

Reproduced from copy supplied
printed and bound in Great Britain
by Billing and Sons Limited and Kemp Hall Bindery
Guildford, London, Oxford, Worcester

INTRODUCTION

The two years taken in collecting, testing and editing this collection of English countryside weather lore has been both stimulating and exhausting. I have tried to embrace the scientific/academic end of the subject with the old country weather knowledge and blend together a readable but sound reference book. It contains nearly 1,900 adages covering all weather types from the famous "red sky at night, shepherd's delight," to the "ash before oak, you'll get a soak". 88 percent of these were star rated (the remainder being obvious statements). The chance of a weather saying being very good or excellent in the truth stakes was 14.6 percent or 1 in 7.

All old English county names are retained with Victorian and earlier sketches of birds, trees and flower motifs, to keep a country atmosphere in the book. No barometer maxims appear.

A star rating system is used for the reader as an instant assessment of the validity of each weather maxim. Also exhaustive tests were carried out on the sayings which appear in the format 96/169 (57). This example means that of 169 times the saying was tested 96 were correct or 57 percent of occasions were true. Further explanations can be seen at the beginning of the first chapter.

The data and techniques used in the tests are accounted for on pages 354-355. Briefly they cover nearly 37,000 daily airstream patterns of the U.K. from 1861-1971; monthly and seasonal temperatures for Central England 1698-1971 and rainfall for England and Wales 1727-1971; tree figures 1776-1935 and animal and crop records for 1866-1966.

References to occlusions, cold and warm fronts and warm sectors in the book are now generally accepted phrases which denote sharp changes between different airstreams.

I would like to express my sincere gratitude to all those concerned with this book, especially to Ray Pitts for his collection of West Oxon rook weather lore and H.A. Poskitt for many Yorkshire sayings. Acknowledgements are made to the Royal Meteorological Society for permission to use material from Richard Inward's 1898 collection of *Weather Lore*. If any acknowledgements have been omitted, then apologies are now rendered.

Finally all opinions expressed and test figures quoted in this book are entirely those of the author.

Paul J. Marriott
Duns Tew
Oxon
March 1981

CONTENT

Introduction	v
Explanation of Star Rating System	viii
January to December	1- 99
Moveable Feasts - Easter, Lent and Whitsuntide	100-105
Seasons and Annual Weather	106-122
Weekdays	123-128
Birds	129-165
Animals, Reptiles and Insects	166-201
Moon	202-213
Stars	214-216
Wind	217-241
Rain	242-251
Clouds	252-270
Thunderstorms and Cumulonimbus Cloud	271-276
Hail	277
Rainbow	278-282
Wild Flowers and Plants	283-295
Trees	296-305
Garden and Farm Produce	306-308
Sunset, Sunrise and Sun	309-318
Haloes	319-323
Sky and Air	324-326
Sound	327-329
Snow	330-334
Frost	335-340
Mist, Fog and Dew	341-346
Shepherd of Banbury	347-352
Bibliography	353
Explanation of Data used in the Test Figures	354-355
Index	356-376

STAR RATING SYSTEM AND TEST EXPLANATION

A large number of weather sayings are tested and all appear in the same form. For example 39/116 (34) means that the maxim was correct 39 times out of 116 or a 34 percent true rating. The star rating goes a stage further enabling the reader to make an instant assessment of each weather maxim - whether it is true or false. Of the 1,880 sayings 224 received no stars as they were obvious statements of fact. A star rating with no test results are the author's judgement. All percentages were taken to the nearest whole number.

Percentage in Test Result	Rating	Star Rating
1 - 16 percent	Very Poor	*
17 - 32 "	Poor	**
33 - 48 "	Fair	***
49 - 64 "	Good	****
65 - 80 "	Very Good	*****
81 -100 "	Excellent	******

JANUARY

January usually begins with a stormy period with the year's highest frequency for westerlies, lasting about two weeks - roughly 5-17th January with a peak date on the 8th. A quiet and frosty interlude normally follows with anticyclonic weather - about 18-24th, peaking 20-21st. However January returns to a stormy end as depressions cross England from the south-west - around 24th Jan-1st Feb, peaking on 31st Jan.

Froze Janiveer,
Leader of the year;
Mince pies in van,
Calf's head in rear.

The blackest month in all the year
Is the month of Janiveer.

An observation of the coldest and sometimes bleakest month of the year.

A favourable January brings us a good year. **

It depends on how one defines "a favourable January". A very cold and dry one can be suitable for lack of disease, since low temperature and a hard frost kills land virus and germs which will give sheep and cattle a good start to the year. On the other hand a mild dry January helps winter seeds for the grain farmer.

In Janiveer if the sun appear,
March April pay full dear. **

March in Janiveer,
Janiveer in March, I fear. **

These types of weather lore are all too common where the countryman believes in a compensating balance in weather. A sunny January has to be matched against a sunless March or April.

January

January warm, the Lord have mercy! ✷✷

*If grain grows in January, there
will be a year of great need.* ✷✷

*If birds begin to whistle in
January, frost's to come.*

*A January spring
Is worth nothing.* ✷✷

    The maxims mean that a warm January brings on plant growth which should be retarded by February and March frosts. The figures are tested for warm Januarys, hay and wheat from 1885 to 1966 giving poor results of 30 and 25 percent. The fourth maxim hails from Rutland. A mild January often leads to a mild February and March producing a better harvest than normal.

                                                              6/20 (30)
                                                               5/20 (25)

*Dry January, plenty of wine.
A wet January, a wet spring.* ✷✷✷

    More English vineyards were in operation in the medieval period than any other time showing the age of the maxim. The most important ingredient for growing grapes is warm excessive sunshine which is not forecast from a dry January. The second line contains little truth with a 36 percent correct result.

                                                               29/81 (36)

*Is January wet? — the barrel
remains empty.* ✷✷

January wet, no wine you get. ✷✷

*In January much rain and little
snow is bad for mountains,
valleys and trees.* ✷✷

*Much rain in January, no blossom
to the fruit.* ✷✷

    These similar sayings infer that a wet January will play havoc with winter seed, erasing topsoil and generally render-

January

ing disaster to farming. Certainly damage will be done and unless the rains continue into February and spring harvests will vary in quality.

Always expect a thaw in January.

A thaw is always experienced in January, although only slight ones occur in severe winters.

Fog in January brings a wet spring. ***

Fog is mainly connected with cold anticyclones or high pressure systems in winter (in summer they produce hot, hazy dry periods). The foggiest Januarys from 1861 to 1971 were compared with their corresponding springs but unfortunately only 42 percent were wet. 16/38 (42)

If there is no snow before January, there will be the more in March and April. **

Another compensating adage this time dealing with the balance of snow. Poor results evolved when tested against March and April above average snow from 1882 to 1974. 4/20 (20)

January freeze the pot by the fire,

A kindly, good Janiveer Freezes the pot by the fire.

As the day lengthens, So the cold strengthens.

These are well-established saws dealing with the coldest month of the year and are mainly pure observation and of little forecasting use. In the second maxim January daily temperatures start to slowly increase as daylight lengthens.

January

> *Jack Frost in Janiveer*
> *Nips the nose of the nascent*
> *year.*   ****

This rhyme refers to a cold January continuing into a cold February or "nascent" (beginning or young) part of the year. The persistence of similar monthly temperatures is one of the few true striking features to emerge from this book. Unfortunately it is only an evens chance that a cold January passes onto February.   54/110 (49)

> *Hoar frost and no snow is*
> *hurtful to fields, trees,*
> *and grain.*   **

> *When oak trees bend with snow in*
> *January, good crops may be*
> *expected.*   **

Sound advice here as hoar frost will injure seed and plant life at any time but a covering of snow will act as an insulator against frost and cold winds. The top line of the second adage refers to very deep snow. Snowy or very snowy Januarys 1885-1966 were tested with hay and barley figures. Low returns of 25 and 26 percent respectively occurred. In theory the insulated snow over seed should help towards a bumper harvest but with further months to go with varied weather in practice the picture is different.   10/39 (26)
     9/39 (23)

> *Thunder in January signifyeth*
> *the same year*
> *Great winds, plentiful of corn*
> *and cattle, peradventure.*   *

I suppose this very old weather lore was based on the idea that thunder, storms and great winds occurred together and if thunder erupted out of season in January the trend would continue.

> *Who in January sows oats*
> *Gets gold and groats;*

January

*Who sows in May
Gets little that way.*

An old-style farming maxim determining the best time to sow seed.

*January commits the fault and
May bears the blame.*   *

Again any extreme weather in January is supposed to have an effect on crops in May but really the only truth it contains is when applied as a metaphor to human affairs.

A warm January, a cold May.   ***

Another country balance lore with only satisfactory results.
21/49 (43)

*December frost and January flood
Never boded husbandman good.*

This weather sequence, especially a wet soggy January, plays havoc with cattle and seeding operations for the farmer or husbandman.

25 December to 5 January

*These twelve days are said to be
the keys of the weather for the
whole year.*   *

This is a pleasant thought, having each day ruling the corresponding months of the coming year. Similar results to those in the section 1-3rd January would be expected.

1 January

*Morning red, foul weather and
great need.*   *****

January

The above can be applied to any day of the year. For further reading turn to the chapter on sky colours.

> *If New Year's Day happen on a*
> *Saturday the winter will be mean,*
> *and the summer hot.* *

The day of the week measures time not weather in this North Riding of Yorkshire saw.

2 January

> *As the weather is this day so it*
> *will be in September.* *

No logic can be seen in this saying. The tested result of 11 percent, covering the temperature and rainfall of this day from 1861 to 1971 and the corresponding September, proves it.

12/105 (11)

1-3 January

> *The first three days of January*
> *rule the coming three months.* **

Low test values occur in this adage. 69/312 (22)

12 January

> *If on January the twelfth the*
> *sun shine, it foreshows much*
> *wind.* ***

Another saying which expects wind if the sun shines on this particular day - the results prove different. 25/57 (44)

13 or 14 January - St Hilary's Day

> *The coldest day of the year.* *

January

> *January the forteenth, Saint*
> *Hilary,*
> *Coldest day of the year.*   *

> *January the forteenth will*
> *either be the coldest or the*
> *wettest day of the year.*   *

Named after Hilarius, Bishop of Poitiers who died in 367 AD. The Anglican festival lies on the 13th but the second Yorkshire and third Hunts maxims refer to 14th January. This is the first of many fixed religious days that weather lore latches onto. Before clocks the countryman used natural times of the year such as harvest, start and end of seasons, first cuckoo call and so on, and also religious days. The three saws refer to this part of January as the coldest of the year. In fact the coldest night of the year at Kew and Greenwich (1841-1964) occurred in the last week of December (26-31st).

17 January - St Anthony's Day

> *After Saint Anthony's death there*
> *fell no rain from Heaven for*
> *three years.*   *

22 January - St Vincent's Day

> *Remember on Saint Vincent's Day,*
> *If that the sun his beams*
> *display,*
> *Be sure to mark his transient*
> *beam,*
> *Which through the casement sheds*
> *a gleam;*
> *For 'tis a token bright and clear*
> *Of prosperous weather all the*
> *year.*   *

St Vincent, born around Huesca in Spain and died from torture in 304 AD, became the patron saint of wine growers and drunkards, hence the connection in the third maxim. The mean-

January

ing of "prosperous weather all the year" was difficult to define as a mild wet year would suit fruit growers and not others. So average temperature and rainfall conditions were thought best and were tested for sunny 22nd Januarys covering 1861-1970, but as expected the results were as appalling as the saying.
21/280 (7)

> If the sun shine on January the
> twenty-second, there shall be
> much wind.   ***

> If Saint Vincent Day the sky is
> clear,
> More wine than water will crown
> the year.   **

Poor results occurred when excess wind blew on at least four days of the seven after a sunny 22nd January. One could nominate sun to shine on any day of the year and emerge with similar figures.
20/56 (36)

22 AND 25 JANUARY - ST VINCENT'S AND ST PAUL'S CONVERSION DAY

> If Saint Vincent's has sunshine,
> One hopes much rye and wine;
> If Saint Paul's is bright and
> clear,
> One does hope a good year.

25 JANUARY - ST PAUL'S CONVERSION DAY

> Saint Paul fair with sunshine
> Brings fertility to rye and
> wine.   ***

> Fair on Saint Paul's conversion
> day is favourable to all fruit.   **

> If Saint Paul's Day be faire and
> cleare,
> It doth betide a happy yeare;   **

January

But if by chance it then should rain,
It will make deare all kinds of graine;
And if ye clouds make dark ye skie,
Then neate and fowles this yeare shall die;
If blustering winds do blow aloft,
Then wars shall trouble ye realm full oft.   ***

If Saint Paul's Day be fair and clear, it indicates plenty; if cloudy or misty, much cattle will die; if rain and snow fall that day, it presages a dearth; if windy, it forebodes wars, as old wives do dream.   *

If the sun on Saint Paul's Day, it betokens a good year; if rain or snow, indifferent; if misty, it predicts great dearth; if thunder, great winds and death of people that year.   *

Saint Paul's Day, very good: a good yeare.   **

    Clouds on Saint Ananias's Day portend floods.   **

    This is St Paul's Conversion Day, sometimes called St Ananias Day after the Bishop of Damascus, who restored Paul's eye sight and baptised him after being blinded on the road to Damascus. Ananias died by being stoned in c70 AD. Most of the sayings concern a fair bright 25th January with a prosperous year - a stereotyped pattern for most of the saints' days. The fifth adage comes from Oxford.
    The 25th January was tested for mist, rain and fair weather. Wheat and hay figures are the annual yield per acre for England and Wales (1885-1966), weighted to arrest the acceleration in growth from c1948 due to the introduction of chemical fertilizers. The final yields were divided into three groups, poor, average and good. Cattle figures (1861-1971) were similarly grouped. The following poor results range from 14-37 percent.

January

Fair and sunny 25th January = good year. (Wheat) 14/44 (32)
                                            (Hay)   16/44 (36)
                                          (Spuds)   16/43 (37)
Rainy 25th January = poor grain and indifferent year.
                                    (Poor grain)   12/36 (33)
                         (Low number in cattle)   17/46 (37)
                         (Indifferent wheat)   9/36 (25)
Misty 25th January = great dearth. (Poor wheat)   3/14 (21)
                         (Low number in cattle)   3/22 (14)

26 January

> *If the weather be dry and bright
> on the twenty-sixth of January
> the year will generally be the
> same.* *

This North Riding (Yorkshire) maxim follows the pattern of the previous sayings. 7/53 (13)

26-31 January

> *The last twelve days of January
> ride the weather for the whole
> year.* *

Very like the lore covering 25th Dec - 5th Jan. Logically the same falsity and poor test outcome would apply.

FEBRUARY

After the early storms of February - 24 January to 1st February peaking 31st - comes a quiet anticyclonic period usually occurring 8-16th February reaching a maximum around the 13th giving cold, frosty and foggy weather. Another cold spell is experienced during 21-25th February peaking 22nd. A late cold stormy number of days - 26 Feb to 9 March peaking 1st - brings a northerly airstream (the time near the annual peak).

Februeer
Doth cut and shear.

Double-faced February.

There is always one fine week in
February.   ****

February, like other months, experiences fast changing weather. A couple of days of mild wet weather can quickly alter to a bitter cold easterly. The contrast is felt more during the winter months. The good result of 59 percent came from a test which searched for at least 7 dry days in February from 1861 to 1971.   66/111 (59)

Warm February, bad hay crop;   **
Cold February, good hay crop.   ***

All the months in the year
Curse a fair Februeer.

When gnats start in February,
the husbandman becomes a beggar.   **

If in February the midges dance
on the dunghill, then lock up
your food in the chest.   **

A February spring is not worth a
pin.

The first saw implies that in a warm February grass grows quickly and is receded by early spring frosts (bad results of 20 percent). The theory continues for cold Februarys and good

FEBRUARY

hay crops (final figure of 38 percent). In practice poor results show little faith in the adages. The third Cornish saying reiterates the first maxim. Gnats and midges dancing again refer to warmth and disaster for the husbandman. 3/15 (20)
5/13 (38)

Isolated fine days in February are known in Surrey as "weather breeders", and are considered as certain to be followed by a storm. ********

The fact that this Surrey saying restricts fine weather to only one day greatly increases the odds for sudden storms to follow.

*February singing,
Never stints stinging.*

A real tongue-twister meaning that a mild February ("singing") always has days of sharp frosts never limiting its sting.

If bees get out in February, the next day will be windy and rainy. *******

Whenever the bees get about at this time (February), we are certain to get wind and rain the next day. *******

February rain is only good to fill ditches.

*February fill the dykes,
Weather either black or white.*

*February fill dyke, be it black or be it white;
But if it be white, it's better to like.*

February

February fill ditch,
Black or white, don't care which;
If it be white,
It is the better to like.

February fill dyke;
March lick it out.

February fill dyke
With what thou dost like.

February fill the ditch,
Black or white we don't care
which.

Rain in February is worth as
much as manure.

One of the most famous of English weather lore. White refers to snow and black means rain. Unfortunately most people fail to grasp the real meaning. Basically it is a command by the farmer wanting February to fill the dykes (in East Anglia) and ditches elsewhere with rain or snow. The latter is more preferable as it gives insulation against sharp frosts and cold winds. The maxims do *not* mean that February always fills dykes. The first adage hails from France and is included to show the wide coverage of this famous saying. Hampshire provides the home for the seventh saw. Please note the subtle differences in all of the weather lore.

When it rains in February, all
the year suffers. **

This applies to the annual crop to suffer, not the year's weather. Wet soggy topsoil ruins corn seed.

In February if thou harvest
thunder,
Thou will see a summer's
wonder. *

Thunder in February or March,
poor sugar maple year. *

February

The first saying is similar to the January saw about thunder. A "summer's wonder" is supposed to occur because thunder in February is out of season. Not enough occasions happened to test the saw.

> *When the cat in February lies in
> the sun, she will creep behind
> the stove in March.* ****

> *When the north wind does not blow
> in February, it will surely come
> in March.* *****

The first part proclaims a warm February will be followed by a cold March. When tested only a 49 percent result emerged. The second part gives a very good 69 percent figure but before accepting this a 70 percent value also occurs when the saw is changed to include a northerly in February. The great annual maximum in northerlies happens in spring with a gradual build up in February and March. 21/43 (49)
31/45 (69)

> *February makes a bridge, and
> March breaks it.* **

The building of a bridge in February means a bridge of ice or a very cold period followed by a mild March thaw which will "break" the bridge. The test result was poor. 22/107 (21)

> *Fogs in February mean frosts in
> May.* *

There is little meaning in this saw. Certainly high pressure areas will produce fogs in February (also frost) and sometimes night ground frost in May but that is as far as the connection goes - no continuous sequence through March and April occurs. Poor results of 12 percent evolved. 5/41 (12)

> *For every thunder with rain in
> February there will be a cold
> spell in May.* *

February

Another piece of wild weather lore containing no truth.

If February gives much snow
A fine summer it doth foreshow.   **

A favourite balance saw - a snowy February will produce a fine summer. Cold reality begs differently.   9/30   (30)

If February brings no rain
'Tis neither good for grass nor   ***
grain.   **

A dry February (look at the February fill dyke maxims for pleas of water or snow) is supposed to be the husbandman's nightmare. But there are further months to go before harvests which often have favourable weather improving the crop. The low results say that the various harvests were good.

    (Hay) 11/30 (37)
    (Wheat) 7/30 (23)
    (Barley) 7/30 (23)

A warm day of February is a
dream of April.

Taken literally, a warm February day when one is near the end of winter must feel easily like a foretaste of April spring.

There will be as many frosts in
June as there are fogs in
February.   *

By now it should be plainly obvious that high pressure areas can contribute to February fogs and frosts in later months but are unconnected in sequence. Therefore testing would prove unsatisfactory and time wasting.

Violent north winds in February
herald a fertile year.   ***

February

The theory that a cold snap in February brings forth warm weather to produce good harvests is incorrect. Hay and wheat returns showed 47 and 33 percent. 14/30 (47)
10/30 (33)

1 February - St Bridget's Day

Bridget's feast-day white,
Every ditch full.

In Ireland the first day of February is named after St Bride or St Brigid who was born c450 AD probably in Louth or Armagh and died c520. Snow falling on this day or any other in February does not always signify that a great depth has accumulated.

2 February - Candlemas Day

The most prolific day of the year for weather lore. By the mid-5th century the day was celebrated with lighted candles to commemorate Simeon's comment about Jesus as "a light to lighten the gentiles". Also on this day candles are thrown away to end Christmas.

Snow at Candlemas
Sign to handle us.

At Candlemas
Cold comes to us. ✱✱

The first hails from Rutland. Tests on the second showed no favouritism to cold weather falling on the 2nd.
33/108 (31)

Candlemas Day! Candlemas Day!
Half our fire and half our hay.

On Candlemas Day
You must have half your straw
and half your hay.

FEBRUARY

They mean that when one is halfway through winter one should have stored half the season's fuel, hay and straw.

> *On Candlemas Day*
> *The good goose begins to lay.*
>
> *If it neither rains nor snows on*
> *Candlemas Day,*
> *You may straddle your horse and*
> *go and buy hay.*
>
> *If Candlemas Day be fine and*
> *clear,*
> *Corn and fruit will then be*
> *dear.* ∗∗

The second adage comes from Lincs. The test used poor grain harvest figures, but achieved sad results.   11/34   (32)

> *If Marie's purifying daie,*
> *Be cleare and bright with sunnie*
> *raie,*
> *Then frost and cold shall be*
> *much more*
> *After the beast than was before.* ∗∗∗
>
> *When on the Purification the sun*
> *hath shined,*
> *The greatest part of winter*
> *comes behind.* ∗∗
>
> *If it be bright and clear on*
> *February the second there will*
> *be a long continuance of cold*
> *wintry weather.*

Candlemas Day or the Purification of the Virgin Mary has various forecasts to make. The first maxim receives 47 percent and the third hails from Yorkshire.   21/45   (47)

> *You should on Candlemas Day*
> *Throw candle and candlestick*
> *away.* ∗∗∗

February

Candlemas Day is when candles should be thrown away to denote the end of Christmas.

> *As far as the sun shines in on*
> *Candlemas Day,*
> *So far will the snow in afore*
> *old May.*   *
>
> *As far as the sun shines in at*
> *the window on Candlemas Day, so*
> *deep will the snow be ere winter*
> *is gone.*   *
>
> *On Candlemas Day, just so far as*
> *the sun shines in,*
> *Just so far will the snow blow*
> *in.*   *

More ridiculous weather balance lore.

> *The hind had as lief see his wife*
> *on the bier,*
> *As that Candlemas Day should be*
> *pleasant and clear.*   *

A very odd maxim. Possibly the meaning is as follows - a hind in this case is a farm workman; the phrase "had as lief" means to do one thing or another and a bier is a movable frame on which coffins are placed. Since this line comes first one therefore must assume that if a farm labourer's wife dies on 2nd February it will be "pleasant and clear". What a morbid saying!

> *If Candlemas Day be mild and gay,*
> *Go saddle your horses, and buy*
> *them hay;*
> *But if Candlemas Day be stormy*
> *and black*
> *It carries the winter well on its*
> *back.*   ****

February

> If Candlemas Day be gay and bright,
> Winter will have another flight.   ***
> But if Candlemas Day brings clouds and rain,
> Winter has gone and won't come again.   ****

> If Candlemas be fine and clear,
> We've half the winter to have or more.   ***
> But if Candlemas be cold and wet,
> A little more winter we shall get.   ***

Probably the most famous and important of the Candlemas proverbs. The last part contains good results (57 percent) for a wet cloudy 2nd Feb continuing in the main for the rest of the month. The third maxim from Kennington (Berks) produces only average results.   31/54 (57)
4/9 (44)

> After Candlemas Day the frost will be more keen,
> If the sun then shines bright, that before it hath been.   ***

> On Candlemas Day, if the thorns hang a-drop,
> Then you are sure of a good pea crop.   **

> Sow or set beans in Candlemas waddle.

Sussex provides the first saw. The second is an example of sowing bean seeds by the moon - "waddle" means the moon's wane.

February

*If a storm on February the
second, spring is near; but if
that day be bright and clear,
the spring will be late.* ★★
★★

*If it snows on February the
second, only so much as may be
seen on a black ox, then summer
will come soon.* ★

*If on February the second the
goose finds it wet, then the
sheep will have grass on March
the twenty-fifth.* ★★

*When drops hang on the fence on
February the second, icicles will
hang there on March the twenty-
fifth.* ★★★

*When drops hang on the fence on
February the second icicles will
hang there on March the fourteenth.* ★★★★

The long saw has little to offer in fact. The connection of 25th March with 2nd Feb is Mary. The former is St Mary's or Lady Day and latter the Purification of the Virgin Mary. Poor results of 10 percent refer to snow on 2nd Feb followed by an early summer. Also ice after a wet 2nd Feb boasted 46 percent. The second maxim from North Riding (Yorkshire) contains surprisingly good figures of 63 percent.   1/10   (10)
27/59   (46)
35/56   (63)

*When the wind's in the east on
Candlemas Day,
There it will stick 'till the
second of May.* ★

Easterlies total from 7 to 15 days over the 95-day period from 2nd Feb to 2nd May.   0/9   (0)

*When Candlemas Day has come and
gone,
The snow lies on a hot stone.*

February

This is particularly true when referring to ground temperatures now at their lowest. This allows a snow covering to melt only slowly during the daytime. Besides at night warm daytime stone or concrete surfaces rapidly cool to freezing temperatures.

A windy Christmas and a calm Candlemas are signs of a good year. *

There were only a small number of occasions to test but one would expect a negative result.

If the sun shines on Candlemas Day, We shall have snow in May. *

This hails from Kennington, Berks, but is totally false.
4/43 (9)

Candlemas shined, on the winter's behind. *

Most fine Candlemas Day proverbs refer to more of winter to come - this one is different.

6 February - St Dorothea's Day

Saint Dorothea gives the most snow. *

In a quick survey over 1875-1975 the risk of snow was marginally higher for January and February than December and March. To give an actual day for the deepest snowfall seems too brash. Any time during Dec-March, a severe snowstorm could occur.

7-14 February - Buchan's First Cold Spell **

This is known as Buchan's First Cold Period. Dr Alexander Buchan, once Secretary of the Scottish Meteorological Society,

February

established in 1867, to his own satisfaction, 6 cold and 3 warm periods during the year in Scotland. His fame came after his death when in 1928, Lord Desborough presented a bill for fixing Easter's date in Parliament. The suggested Easter date coincided with Buchan's Second Cold Period (11-14 April). The bill was defeated but public interest was aroused. In the following year, by sheer chance, the 9 Buchan periods were nearly all correct so his name became a household word - popularity he did not deserve. 7-14th February was tested for average temperature from 1861 to 1971. Poor results of 28 percent show unreliability in the spell. Infact if Buchan had called the period a warm spell he would have increased the result to 50 percent.

31/111   (28)

14 February - St Valentine's Day

Saint Valentine,
Set thy hopper by mine.

To Saint Valentine, the spring
is a neighbour.

St Valentine's Day was named after two saints. One was a Rome priest decapitated c269 AD and the other a person, who saved a patient from an incurable disease, also beheaded in c273 AD. In medieval times birds were believed to pair probably leading to the sending of "valentines". The two weather saws render as milestones in the old farming calendar. A hopper was a machine for spreading seed.

Mid-February

Winter's back breaks about the
middle of February.   *

On reflection one would have thought that the beginning of March would be more the time for breaking "winter's back".

22 February - St Peter's Day

If cold on Saint Peter's Day,
it will last longer.   *****

February

The saying proves to be an excellent one. On average a cold St Peter's Day lasts about 5½ days in the test, coinciding with the cold snap normally found at the time of the year (see the start of the chapter).   41/55   (75)

> *The night of Saint Peter shows*
> *what weather we shall have for*
> *the next forty days.*   *

Unfortunately this saw is the first of many saint day ones with 40-rain days occurring afterwards. It is likely that they have a common origin with Noah's flood. The test result fails dismally.   0/106   (0)

24 February - St Matthias' Day

> *Saint Matthias,*
> *Sow thy leaf and grass.*

This is the husbandman's old style date for first sowing.

> *If it freezes on Saint Matthias'*
> *Day, it will freeze for a month*
> *together.*   *

Another miserable result.   0/43   (0)

> *Saint Matthias breaks the ice;*   *
> *If he finds none, he will make*   **
> *it.*

A warm 24th February following an icy spell and a very cold 24th following a non-icy period yield poor figures of 11 and 20 percent respectively.   5/45   (11)
     9/46   (20)

> *Saint Matthy*
> *All the year goes by.*

February

*At Saint Mattho
Take thy hopper and sow.*

*Saint Matthie
Sends sap into the trees.*

28 February - St Romanus' Day

*Romanus bright and clear
Indicates a goodly year.*   *******

    Further old time expressions to date the beginning of farming chores. When tested for wheat and hay low 35 and 33 percent results evolved.   16/46 (35)
      15/46 (33)

MARCH

March normally starts with a cold stormy period (21st Feb to 9th March, peaking on 1st) where the northerly almost reaches its annual spring maximum. This is followed by a very quiet time in the middle of the month with early spring anticyclones (12-19 March, peaking 13-14th). Finally a return to cold stormy weather is experienced (24-31 March, maximum 28th) with another predominance of northerlies.

March, many weathers.

March many weathers rained and blowed,
March grass never did good.

In beginning or in end
March its gift will send.

March yearns the lammie
And buds do form,
And blows through the flint
Of an ox's horn.

These maxims are all a testimony to the varied weather to be expected in March. The last saw hails from Northumberland.

A peck of March dust is worth a king's ransom.	***
A peck of March dust is worth an earl's ransom 'when do vall and thornen leaves.'	***
Dust in March is worth a king's ransom.	***
March dust on an apple leaf Brings all kinds of fruit to grief.	***
A bushel of March dust is a thing Worth the ransom of a king.	***

MARCH

*A bushel of March dust on the
leaves is worth a king's ransom.*   ***

*A peck of March dust and a
shower in May,
Makes the corn green and the
meadows all gay.*   ***

*The March wind causes dust and
the wind blows it about.*

 These are some of the most famous of English weather sayings with the second from Dorset, third from Kennington in Berks and fourth hailing from Herefordshire. Basically they are promising that any dry March is suitable in the soil preparation and sowing of spring cereal and vegetable seed. Also a very wet soil after a wet February would be dried by a dusty March. On the other hand a wet March would cause chaos with heavy topsoil.

*March dry, good rye;
March wet, good wheat.*   **

 This Suffolk saying differs from others especially in the second line. Most other wet March maxims are supposed to produce poor harvests. Poor results of 19 percent occur.

               6/31   (19)

*Better to be bitten by a snake
Than to feel the sun in March.*

*March grows,
Never dows.*

*March flowers
Make no summer bowers.*   **

*March damp and warm
Will the farmer much harm.*   **

*A damp rotten March gives pain
to farmers.*   **

 The first maxim originates in Wilts and the second from

MARCH

Yorkshire. All basically imply that a wet or wet and warm March bring on plant life too quickly which is often checked by late spring frosts. Also spring seed has too muddy a soil for a firm beginning. The poor results apply to the last two saws.
Wheat 3/14 (21)
Spuds 6/14 (43)

A wet March makes a sad August.   ***

*March water is worse than a
stain on a cloth.*   ***

However agreeable the theory might seem in practice the results are bad. Later months with their varied weather will influence, to a great extent, the final crop state.
Wheat and spuds 12/31 (39)

*The March sun raises, but
dissolves not.*

The above saw refers to the weak sun of March having enough heat to raise mist or fog into low cloud but lacking enough energy to dissolve or evaporate it. A late June sun could quickly tackle the complete clearance of dense fog.

*March, black ram
Comes in like a lion and goes
out like a lamb.*   **

*March comes in with an adder's
head and goes out with a
peacock's tail.*   **

March snow hurts the seeds.

Presumably "black ram" is similar to a black sheep referring to the oddity and variation in March's weather. Of course ram is used to rhyme with lamb. To come "in like a lion" or "adder's head" refers to March beginning stormy with gales (54 percent result). A "lamb" and "peacock's tail" means March ends quietly and serene (19 percent correct). Normally March comes in and goes out like a lion. A lion start to be followed by a lamb ending produced only 22 percent.   60/111 (54)

March

                                                                                        21/111 (19)
                                                                                         13/60   (22)

> *March comes in like a lamb and*
> *goes out like a lion.*   ****

This reverses the previous two adages, but receives a better combines test result of 56 percent.   14/25 (56)

> *As March hasteneth all the*
> *humours feel it.*

I think this means that as one goes through March experiencing its extreme weathers one can liken it to the human good, bad or ill humours.

> *A dry March, a wet April, a dry*
> *May and a wet June,*
> *Is commonly said to bring all*
> *things in tune.*   ***

This rare pattern of dry, wet, dry and wet months only occurred once in 1935 during the period 1885-1971. In that year good wheat and barley harvests and a poor hay crop happened.

> *A windy March and a rainy April*
> *will make a beautiful May.*   *

> *A windy March foretells a fine*
> *May.*   *

Conditions gave a disastrous result.   2/19 (11)

> *March wind and May sun*
> *Make clothes white and maids dun.*

The combination of March wind and May sun is supposed to induce good drying weather for clothes and sun-tan for young ladies.

MARCH

Fogs in March, frost in May.   *

*So many mists in March you see,
So many frosts in May will be.*   *

*As many mistises in March, so
many frostises in May.*   *

These sayings (the third one hails from Wilts) are similar to one in the February chapter. The same meteorological reasons apply and the results are very poor.   6/46 (13)

*As many days of fog in March, so
many days of frost in May, on
corresponding days.*   *

This Hampshire maxim is even more daring expecting corresponding monthly days to experience March fog and May frost. Even worse results emerge with only 7 percent.   3/46 (7)

*So many frosts in March, so many
in May.*   *

Another hopelessly incorrect adage. More frosts occur in March than May by virtue of its earliness in the year.

*Mists in March bring rain,
Or in May frost again.*   **

Only the top line is tested - that after a foggy or misty day the following one will have rain. Poor figures evolved.
58/289 (20)

*March winds and April showers
Bring forth May flowers.*

*March search, April try;
May will prove if you live
or die.*

MARCH

The first is the most famous saying of the two, both having similar meanings.

> *A dry March, a wet April, and*
> *cool May*
> *Fill barn, cellar, and bring*
> *much hay.* ✱✱

Only three years during 1888-1971 fulfilled the maxim's conditions - all with poor crop harvests.

> *As it rains in March, so it*
> *rains in June.* ✱✱

The test was executed by comparing the three rainfall categories (dry, average and wet) of March against those of June from 1727 to 1971. Bad figures emerged. 79/245 (32)

> *Fog in March, thunder in July.* ✱✱✱

A ridiculous saying with poor results. 4/10 (40)

> *As much fog in March, so much*
> *rain in summer.* ✱✱

This was tested with high frequencies of March fogs having wet summers. This proved similar in content and result to the previous saw. 14/49 (29)

> *A wet March makes a sad harvest.* ✱

A "sad August" is taken as a wet and cold month but the only sad occurrence is the results. 17/80 (21)

> *As much dew in March, so much*
> *fog rises in August.* ✱

March

This is a weather and 6-month balance maxim. As one would expect the test proved fatal.   13/111   (12)

> *A frosty winter and a dusty*
> *March, and a rain about Averil,*
> *Another about the Lammas time,*
> *when the corn begins to fill,*
> *Is weel worth a pleuch o'gowd,*
> *and a'her pins theretill.*   ***

> *In March, and at all seasons of*
> *the year when the judges are on*
> *circuit and there are criminals*
> *to be hung, storms prevail.*   *

This Lincolnshire saying escapes the author's comprehension although itself is a fascinating piece of weather lore.

> *In March is good graffing, the*
> *skilful do know,*
> *So long as the wind in the East*
> *do not blow:*
> *From moon being changed, 'till*
> *past be the prime,*
> *For graffing and cropping is very*
> *good time.*

> *A dry March never begs its*
> *bread!*   **

> *A March without water,*
> *Dowers the hind's daughter.*   **

The idea of a dry March producing a good wheat harvest is fine for the early stages of crop growth but weather in later months determines the end product. It is opposite in meaning to the earlier Suffolk saw. The last maxim probably means that a bumper harvest from a dry March will increase the hind's (farm labourer) wages enabling him to afford a dowry for his daughter.

March

> *March buys winter's cloak and*
> *sells it three days afterwards.*   ****

A simply marvellous saying stating that a spell of cold weather in late winter is always short. The excellent results showed that on 78 percent of occasions the cold nip lasted under 4 days.   230/296 (78)

> *When it thunders in March, one*
> *may say alas.*

Presumably March thunder means heavy showers which in turn could erode away top soil and harm young root crops.

1 March - St David's Day

> *Upon Saint David's Day*
> *Put oats and barley in the clay.*

The traditional saint's day for early spring sowing.

2 March - St Chad's Day

> *Saint David and Chad,*
> *Sow pease good or bad.*

> *David and Chad,*
> *Sow peas good or bad;*
> *If they're not in Benedick,*
> *They had better stop in the*
> *ricke.*

Another early-style sowing day. St Chad was born in Northumbria, became Abbot of Lastingham in North Yorkshire and died of the plague there in c672 AD. Benedick refers to St Benedict's Day on 21st March.

1-3 March

> *First comes David, then comes*
> *Chad,*

March

> *And then comes Winneral as though*
> *he was mad.*   ✳✳✳
> *White or black*   ✳✳
> *Or old house thack.*

    Here we have three saints, St David on 1st, St Chad on 2nd and St Winnold on 3rd, which were milestones in the old weather calendar. White means snow and black rain, as in the February filldyke set of sayings. House thack refers to house thatch and Winneral being mad means stormy. The windy results in the test of three days comes out best.

        Windy 55/110 (50)
        Snow   16/110 (15)
        Rain   39/110 (35)

Late February and Early March

> *Whenever the latter part of*
> *February and beginning of March*
> *are dry, there will be a*
> *deficiency of rain up to*
> *Midsummer Day.*   ✳

    Midsummer Day is the 24th June.   2/14 (14)

11-28 February and 1-10 March

> *If the eighteen last days of*
> *February be*
> *Wet, and the first ten of March,*
> *you'll see*
> *That the spring quarter and the*
> *summer too,*
> *Will prove too wet, and danger*
> *to ensue.*   ✳

    This saw produces terrible results.   0/111 (0)

1-10 March

> *If the first ten days of March*
> *are cold and rainy, so will the*
> *spring and summer be.*   ✳✳✳

March

There was only one year (1916) when all 10 days were cold and wet. If one takes 5 days or more as cold and wet then 40 percent of the following spring and summer seasons continued this pattern. 4/10 (40)

10 March

*If it does not freeze on the
tenth, a fertile year may be
expected.* ***

*Mists or hoar frosts on this day
betoken a plentiful year, but not
without some diseases.* ***

All very disappointing figures.

Above freezing	= good wheat	14/46	(30)
on 10th March.	= good hay	16/46	(35)
Misty on	= good wheat	9/17	(53)
10th March.	= good hay	7/17	(41)
Hoar frost	= good wheat	15/35	(43)
on 10th March.	= good hay	10/35	(29)

17 March - St Patrick's Day

*Saint Patrick's Day, the warm
side of a stone turns up, and the
broad-back goose begins to lay.*

19 March - St Joseph's Day

*Is't on Saint Joseph's Day clear,
So follows a fertile year.* ***

Another balance saying with grim results.

Wheat	15/48	(31)
Hay	19/48	(40)

21 March - St Benedict's Day

Saint Benedict,

March

> *Sow thy peas or keep them in thy rick.*
>
> *Whatever the weather is on March the twenty-first that weather will continue until twenty-first of June.*   *
>
> *Where the wind is at twelve o'clock on the twenty-first of March, there she'll bide for three months afterwards.*   *

This means that one should sow peas on 21 March - if left later then a failure would occur. This is another old spring equinox milestone adage. The second saw hails from Yorkshire and third originates in Surrey and Hants. Terrible test results apply to the last two weather sayings.   0/106   (0)

Vernal Equinox - About 21 March

> *When the wind blows from the north-east, a uniformly dry quarter during the week of the vernal equinox, it is an all but unfailing guide to the general character of the ensuing season.*   **

The test was confined to a north-easterly on the 21st to see if a dry week then occurred (26 percent) or a dry season (16 percent).   5/19   (26)
    3/19   (16)

20-27 March

> *If a storm arise from the east on or before the spring equinox or if a storm arise from any point of the compass about one week after the spring equinox the summer is generally dry four out of five times.*   ***

March

> *If a storm arise from the south-west or west-south-west on or just before the spring equinox summer is generally wet four out of five times.* ******

These three saws with their confident high forecast success rate are not confirmed in the tests.

Eastern storm around 20 March	9/27	(33)
Any storm 25-27 March	15/47	(32)
SW or WSW storm 19-21 March	5/16	(31)

25 March - St Mary's or Lady's Day

> *Is't on Saint Mary's bright and clear,*
> *Fertile is said to be the year.* *******

Again poor results on a saint's day.

Wheat	18/44	(41)
Hay	15/44	(34)

29-31 March - The Borrowing Days

> *The last three days of March are called the Borrowing Days; for as they are remarked to be unusually stormy, it is feigned that March has borrowed them from April to extend the sphere of his rougher sway.* *******

> *March borrows of April*
> *Three days, and they are ill;*
> *April borrows of March again*
> *Three days of wind and rain.* ******

> *The warst blast comes in the borrowing days.* *******

> *March borrowed of April, April borrowed of May,*
> *Three days, they say:*
> *One rained, and one snew,*
> *And the other was the worst day that ever blew.* *****

MARCH

March borrowed from April.
Three days, and they were all ill:
The first of them is wan and weet,   ***
The second is snaw and sleet,   **
The third of them is a peel-a-bane,   **
And freezes the wee bird's neb to
the stane.

High winds on these days, a dry
summer to follow.   ***

March does from April gain
Three days, and they're in rain,   **
Returned by April in's bad kind,
Three days, and they're in wind.   ***

The fourth saying hails from Staffs. The basic meaning of Borrowing Days is the stormy period which often occurs at the end of March and extends into April. So March "borrows" the first three days of April to extend March. The reverse is also true when April lengthens its beginning. However in reality all test figures are unsatisfactory.

                 First saying   48/111   (43)
                 Second saying   25/111   (23)
                 Fifth   saying = 1st April   41/107   (38)
                                = 2nd April   18/104   (17)
                                = 3rd April   23/104   (22)
                 Sixth   saying   17/42   (40)
                 Seventh saying = Rain   33/111   (30)
                               = Wind   13/33   (39)

APRIL

Usually April experiences a cold stormy period in the middle (10-15th, peaking 14th) of the month with the annual maximum of Northerlies. A similar weather type is repeated from 23rd to 26th peaking on 25th.

A dry April
Not the farmer's well.
April wet
Is what we should get.

April showers bring summer flowers.

April showers bring forth May flowers.

An April flood carries away the frog and his brood.

In April Dove's flood is worth a king's good.   ***

Moist April, clear June.   **

April wet, good wheat.   ***

April rains for men, May for beasts.

Although it rains, throw not away thy watering pot.

April has thirty days, and if it rained on thirty-one, no harm would be done.

All of these sayings refer to wet Aprils. With temperature now high enough and rainfall more or less plentiful continual crop growth is assured. The fifth maxim originates in Derbyshire where the river Dove is situated. The eighth saw means that a rainy April is good for corn and a wet May for grass

April

crops. The results for the latter can be seen in the May chapter. The last saw implies that April rain is welcome, that sowing is completed and young crops need water. The poor test figures of 17 percent refer to the sixth saying.   14/80 (17)

A cold April
The barn will fill.   **

April cold and wet fills barn and
barrel.   *

April wears a white hat.

The belief here is that a cold April, although temporary stunting growth, will bring mild and wet weather the following months and produce a good wheat or barley harvest.

         A cold April = Wheat and barley   8/34   (24)
         A cold and wet .. = ...   2/13   (15)

A sharp April kills the pig.   ***

This intriguing snippet alas receives poor figures when tested with the number of pigs in England and Wales 1866-1966 (specially weighted) of 33 percent.   11/33 (33)

April snow breeds grass.

Snow in April is manure; snow in
March devours.

Till April's dead
Change not a thread.

Changeable as an April day.

April weather,
Rain and sunshine, both together.

True observations of the changeable weather to be experienced in April.

April

Plant your 'taturs when you will,
They won't come up before April.

Whatever March does not want April
brings along.

What March will not
April brings always.

Both applicable to the two varied weather months of March and April.

April for me, May for my master.

After warm April and October, a
warm year next.   ✱✱✱

No real truth in this adage.   16/49   (33)

Thunderstorm in April is the
end of hoar frost.   ✱✱✱

When April blows his horn,
'tis good for hay and corn.   ✱

Thunder in April,
Floods in May.   ✱✱✱

"Blows his horn" in the second saw means thunder but emerges with unsatisfactory results.   2/13   (15)

1 April - All Fool's Day

If it thunders on All Fool's Day
It brings good crop of corn and
hay.   ✱

So few cases occur here that no test was instigated.

April

1-3 April

> *If the first three days in April*
> *be foggy,*
> *Rain in June will make lanes*
> *boggy.* ✱✱

    I'm afraid this Huntingdonshire saying falls on stony ground.   2/10 (25)

6 April - Latter Lady Day

> *On Lady Day the latter*
> *The cold comes on the water.* ✱✱

    This does *not* mean that water temperature of our rivers and coast reaches its annual minimum (which occurs in February and March) but refers to the supposed cold weather (result of 29 percent) expected around 6th April.   32/109 (29)

Late March or Early April

> *There are generally some warm*
> *days at the end of March or*
> *beginning of April, which bring*   ✱✱✱✱
> *the blackthorn into bloom, and*
> *which are followed by a cold*
> *period called the Blackthorn*
> *Winter.* ✱✱

> *Beware of the Blackthorn Winter.* ✱✱

> *Tis always cold when the black-*
> *thorn is in bloom. The blossom*
> *generally appears in March.* ✱✱

    These are famous weather sayings. The Blackthorn flowers on average on 30 March in S.W. England through to 4th April in S.E. England, 9th in Midlands and later as one goes further north. The period to test for cold weather during the "Blackthorn Winter" was 6-12th April (centred around the Midland's flowering date of 9th). The first maxim refers to a warm spell in late March and early April which was tested 27 March to 5

April

April. Average figures of 53 percent were returned for three or more consecutive warm days. Similar conditions were applied to the 6-12th April for a cold spell falling *after* a warm 27 March to 5 April - only 31 percent emerged. The Blackthorn Winter occurring in its own right failed miserably on 21 percent.

```
                                             59/111  (53)
                                             18/59   (31)
                                             23/111  (21)
```

11-14 April - Buchan's Second Cold Spell   **

The Blackthorn Winter is sometimes extended beyond 6-12th April which nicely slots into Buchan's second cold spell, but when tested proves to be false.   34/111 (31)

23 April - St George's Day

> *When on Saint George's rye will hide a crow, a good harvest may be expected.*
>
> *At Saint George's the meadow turns to hay.*

Two old-style farming sayings which are perfectly true.

> *Saint George cries "Goe!"*
> *Saint Mark cries "Hoe!"*

Presumably on St George's Day crops and vegetation grow quickly and on St Mark's weeding and hoeing are the order of the day. St Mark's Day is 24th April.

25-28 April

> *If from the twenty-fifth to the twenty-eighth of April the full moon come with serene nights and no wind (at which time the dew commonly falls a great plenty), the ancients, from*

April

> *their experience, held it
> certain that the crops of grain
> would suffer.* ******

    Unfortunately the full moon occurred only once during 25-28 April in the tested years 1959-71. Regardless of the moon, nights of heavy dew can form at any random time in April.

MAY

Often a pleasant month. Usually the period 29 April to 16 May attracts Northerly airstreams alternating with some anticyclonic intervals - the Westerly being at its annual minimum. 21 - 31 May is recognized for its fine dry weather with anticyclones and Southerlies predominating.

The merry month of May.

This mainly refers to May Day and maypole activities and similar celebrations during the month.

A hot May makes a fat churchyard.   *

For a warm May
The parsons pray.   *

These old adages, like their winter counterparts, prophesy death (mainly of the old and young) caused by mild Mays which are supposed to bring on disease. Weighted death figures per 1,000 head of population for Oxford were tested covering April to June with very poor results.   1/13 (8)

Blossoms in May
Are not good, some say.

Flowers in May, fine cocks of
hay.   *****

These are sayings referring to mild winters and springs which accelerate blossoms or flowers to appear early in May. The same process is supposed to occur with hay in June. Logically the results should be very good and indeed are with a 70 percent correct rating.   16/23 (70)

The month of May seeks warmth

MAY

> *to exchange for bread.*   ***

This confirms the previous adages.

> *If May will be a gardener, he*
> *will not fill the granaries.*   ***

> *Dry May brings nothing gay.*   **

> *A dry May is followed by a wet*
> *June.*   ***

A dry May is bad for grain crops - a mixture of warmth, sun and rain is ideal. Little confidence was held for the third saying which is born out with poor results for all three.

```
           First saying  = Wheat    5/12  (42)
                         = Barley   6/12  (50)
          Second saying  = Wheat    8/23  (35)
                         = Barley   6/23  (26)
                  Third saying      27/82 (33)
```

> *March wind and May sun*
> *Makes clothes white and maids*
> *dun.*

The combination of spring wind and sun is supposed to be helpful in drying clothes and sunburning the gentle sex.

> *When May is dry, the following*
> *September is apt to be wet.*   ***

No relationship can be established here.   29/81 (36)

> *Many thunder storms in May,*
> *And the farmer sings "Hey!*
> *hey!"*   ****

> *The more thunder in May, the less*
> *in August and September.*   ****

MAY

    These two adages have surprisingly good results. Close conditions and heavy rain associated with thunderstorms would help crop development. The first set of figures refer to six or more thunderstorms in May.   5/8 (63)
                                                                                                              4/7 (57)

May damp and cool fills the barns
and wine vats.   ****

A May wet
Was never kind yet.

A May flood
Never did good.

A shower of rain in May
Is worth a load of hay.   ***

A wet May
Makes a big load of hay.   ***

A wet May
Makes a lang-tailed hay.   ***

A rainy May marries peasants.   ***

Rain in May makes bread for the
whole year.   ***

    The fourth saw hails from the Kentish Weald; fifth from West Shropshire and sixth from Whitby, North Yorkshire. Varied results appear throughout, the highest with 62 percent from barley in the first maxim. The seventh saw possibly means that peasant smallholders would normally own a small number of cows instead of a large acreage of wheat which is supposed to benefit from a wet May.   First saying = Wheat 6/13 (46)
                                                                                   = Barley 8/13 (62)
                                                                     Fifth saying 11/24 (46)

Betwixt April and May if there
be rain,
'tis worth more than oxen and
wain.   ***

MAY

The hay figures are good.   Hay   16/29 (55)
                                             Wheat   7/29 (24)

> *For an east wind in May 'tis*
> *your duty to pray.*   ****
>
> *A windy May makes a fair year.*   *

These two maxims tend to differ in meaning. An Easterly wind in May is always dry which can be said to persist to play havoc with crop growth.

> *A cold May is kindly,*
> *And fills the barn finely.*   ***
>
> *A cool May and a windy*
> *Barn filleth up finely.*   ***
>
> *A cold May and a windy*
> *A full barn will find ye.*   ***
>
> *A cold May is good for corn and*
> *hay.*   **
>
> *Cold May brings many things.*
>
> *Cold May enriches no one.*
>
> *Cool and evening dew in May*
> *brings wine and much hay.*   *
>
> *If May be cold and wet, September*
> *will be warm and dry, and vice*
> *versa.*   *
>
> *Frost in May*
> *Frost in September.*   *

Berks, Hants and Wilts provide the ninth adage. A minimum of 17 days in May with a good wind was used as a basis for some of the tests. Nearly all figures are disappointing. The last two weather balance saws follow the usual poor return pattern.

                         First saying = Wheat 10/29 (34)
                                       = Barley 12/29 (41)

MAY

Second saying	= Hay	9/16	(56)
	= Wheat	7/16	(44)
Fourth saying	= Wheat	3/14	(21)
	= Hay	4/14	(29)
Seventh saying		2/14	(14)
Eighth saying		2/17	(12)
"Vice-versa"		2/25	(8)
Ninth saying		0/18	(0)

A snow storm in May
Is worth a waggon load of hay.   *

The reasoning behind the saying is baffling.   2/11   (18)

He who sows oats in May
Gets little that way.

The latest for sowing spring oats used to be February to March in the South and April in Northern England.

Those who bathe in May
Will soon be laid in clay;
They who bathe in June
Will sing a merry tune;
They who bathe in July
Will dance like a fly.

Presumably this is a reflection on the water temperature in relation to man's bathing capabilities.

A swarm of bees in May
Is worth a load of hay;   *****
A swarm of bees in June
Is worth a silver spoon;   ****
But a swarm in July
Is not worth a fly.   ***

Towards the end of May or beginning of June it becomes favourable for bee swarming. The saying means that early colonies will collect surplus pollen for beekeepers and late ones will not gather sufficient food to survive.

May

> *Shear your sheep in May,*
> *And shear them all away.*

If sheep are sheared too early in May after which a real cold snap is still likely survival problems occur. The usual time for sheep shearing is in the warmer months of June/July.

> *Go and look at oats in May,*
> *You will see them blown away;*
> *Go and look again in June,*
> *You will sing another tune.*

Sound old-style advice the farmer used.

> *Be it weal or be it woe,*
> *Beans blow before May doth go.*

Good or bad, one should always expect a few days of strong wind in May.

> *What April cannot do*
> *May will do all day.*

The May sun is stronger and warmer than in April and can disperse fogs quicker and help plants grow faster.

> *May makes or mats the wheat.*

A cold or warm and wet May can make or dull (mat) wheat.

1 May - St Philip's and St James' Day

> *Hoar frost on May the first*
> *indicates a good harvest.*   ***

Little can be expected from this maxim.   12/27   (44)

49

May

> *The later the blackthorn in*
> *bloom after May the first, the*
> *better the rye and harvest.*   *

A late blackthorn bloom depends on previous seasons and the present May weather.

8 May

> *If on the eighth of May it rain,*
> *It fortells a wet harvest, men*
> *sain.*   **

Since harvest for grass is in June and cereals in any of the three months July to September only June and September were tested. Poor results prevail.   June harvest   12/46   (26)
Sept harvest   15/46   (33)

9-14 May - Buchan's Third Cold Spell   ***

Hopeless results for the so-called Buchan third cold spell (see index for remaining spells).   47/111   (42)

11-13 May - St Mamertius', St Pancras and St Gervatius' Day

> *Who shears his sheep before*
> *Saint Gervatius' Day loves*
> *more his wool than his sheep.*   **

These three saints' days are known as the "Three Icemen", but like the previous cold spell, are a myth.   97/333   (29)

Middle of May

> *In the middle of May, comes the*
> *tail of the winter.*   **

The "middle of May" was taken as 11-20th. The results are based on the *number* of cold days in the period. The highest frequencies of cold days were 9, 12, 15 and 19th. There is no continuous cold spell but individual days of low temperature.
    323/1110   (29)

MAY

17-19 MAY - ST DUNSTAN'S DAY (19 MAY)

> *Saint Dunstan was a brewer and*
> *was sold to the devil who*
> *blighted all apple trees from*
> *the seventeenth to the nineteenth*
> *of May. Hence the cold blast*
> *which usually comes about this*
> *time.* **

St Dunstan's Day (19th May) showed the highest total of cold days in the three-day period. The test was carried out in the same way as the previous saying. 102/333 (31)

17-23 MAY

> *Storms from the east or south-*
> *east, between the seventeenth*
> *and twenty-third of May,*
> *indicate a wet summer.* ***

This saw promised much but cold reality proved otherwise. The 39 percent refers to wet summers after a storm from the East or Southeast occurs on at least two days. The 37 percent similarly applies to a minimum of four days. 12/31 (39)
3/8 (37)

19-21 MAY

> *Easterly winds on May the*
> *nineteenth to the twenty-first*
> *indicate a dry summer.* ***

This adage might prove fruitful but unfortunately only 4 years of the tested 111 supplied a cold spell 19-21 May.

> *Franklin's frost strikes on*
> *nineteenth, twentieth or*
> *twenty-first of May.* **

This Devon adage states that a frost occurs on at least

one of these three days. The unknown gentleman called Franklin has probably remained forgotten because of the falsity of the maxim - certainly the 27 percent result bears this out.

89/333 (27)

24 May - St Urban's Day

Saint Urban drives his mother from the fire.

Urban brings summer.

Hopefully by now all night frosts have ceased and warmer weather has arrived, so "mother" can venture outside instead of remaining by the fire.

End of May

Cast ne'er a clout 'till May be out.

'till May out leave not off a clout.

"May" refers to the month and *not* the May blossom.

JUNE

The most frequent weather pattern affecting England during June is a stormy one. Usually during 1-4 June the first wave of cool stormy summer weather occurs with frequent cyclonic disturbances. Fortunately a dry spell 5-11th, peaking on the 7th, with anticyclones helps to change the trend. However the 12-14th is usually associated with a second phase of wet cool stormy weather followed by the third and final onslaught from about 20th into early July with a very noticeable return of the Westerlies.

When it is hottest in June, it will be coldest in the corresponding days of the next February. *

The result speaks for itself. 5/113 (4)

*Mists in May and heat in June
Bring all things into tune.* ****

*Mist in May, heat in June,
Make the harvest come right soon.* ****

If June be sunny harvest comes early. ****

*A calm June
Puts the farmer in tune.* ****

*Calm weather in June
Sets corn in tune.* ****

There is no doubt that a calm or warm June which would give plenty of night-time dew could combine and help towards an acceleration in crop and plant growth.

JUNE

A dry May and a leaking June
Makes the farmer whistle a
merry tune. ****

A dry May and a dripping June
Bring all things into tune. ****

The combination of a dry May and wet June gives good results (57 percent) for barley. The second maxim hails from Bedfordshire.
            Wheat 3/7 (43)
            Barley 4/7 (57)

A cold and wet June spoils the
rest of the year. ***

A wet June makes a dry September. **

A leak in June brings harvest
soon. ****

A leaky May and dry June keep a
poor man's head abune.

A leaking June brings harvest
soon. ****

June damp and warm
Does the farmer no harm. ****
A good leak in June
Sets all in tune.
A drip in June
Brings all things in tune. ****

Cornwall gives rise to the second saw. Even though wet weather brings a crop to a certain growth level, warmth and sunshine are also much-needed ingredients.
           Second saying 25/79 (32)
  Sixth saying = Wheat/hay (lines 1 and 2) 3/6 (50)
      = Wheat/hay (rest of rhyme) 11/20 (55)

Wheat or barley 'll shoot in
June
If they bain't no higher'n a
spoon.

June

This West Somerset saying would be true if the June weather had large amounts of sunshine, rainfall and warmth.

*In the hay season, when there is
no dew, it indicates rain.* *****

Unfortunately this saw has not been tested but doubtless very good results would emerge. The reasoning is obvious - dewless nights are associated with moderate to fresh winds with or without low cloud. These are often the forerunners of rain. The only exception is with a very dry night (low humidity) accompanied by a breeze.

*If north wind blows in June,
good rye harvest.* **

Rye is a rugged crop which can grow in almost any soil and under any diverse weather conditions.

*A swarm of bees in June is
worth a silver spoon.* ****

*A swarm of bees in June is not
worth a silver spoon.* **

Mainly included as an example of two maxims with completely opposite meanings. Refer to the May section for the complete bee verse.

As June, so next January. **

This saw is basically a half-yearly comparison test between June and January. Unfortunately temperature only scores 20 percent and rainfall 43. 54/273 (20)
83/194 (43)

Early June

When the wind goes to the west

June

> *early in June, expect wet
> weather 'till the end of August.* ✱✱

The first summer storms normally begin in early June and often with Westerly winds, but for the pattern to continue till the end of August occurs only on a few number of occasions.

20/69 (29)

8 June

> *If it raineth on the eighth of
> June a wet harvest men will see.* ✱✱

Testing the extreme months of the harvest period, June and September, one arrives at poor results.   June 12/41 (29)
Sept 11/41 (27)

11 June - St Barnabas Day

> *On Saint Barnabas
> Put a scythe to the grass.*
>
> *Rain on Saint Barnabas' Day
> good for grapes.*   ✱
>
> *Barnaby bright, Barnaby bright,
> The longest day and the shortest
> night.*
>
> *Barnaby bright
> All day and no night.*
>
> *Saint Barnabas mow your first
> grass.*

Joseph Barnabas was born in Cyprus and died about 80 AD. June is the hay harvest month and farmers always used St Barnabas Day as the time to commence scything grass.

15 June - St Vitus' Day

> *If Saint Vitus's Day be rainy
> weather,*

June

> *It will rain for thirty days
> together.*   *

> *Oh! Saint Vitas, do not rain,
> so that we may not want barley.*

> *If Saint Vitas's Day be rainy
> weather,
> It will rain for forty days
> together.*   *

St Vitus or St Guy was a martyr from the 4th century AD and is the protector of epileptics. Here we have another of the rainy saints' days but this time expecting 30 wet days to follow instead of 40. The results apply to the first and third saws.   0/41 (0)

21 AND 24 JUNE

> *June the twenty-first, summer
> begins; June the twenty-fourth
> Midsummer Day.*   *

Extremely poor figures emerge here.   1/111 (1)

> *If the cuckoo does not cease
> singing at midsummer, corn will
> be dear.*   ***

Cuckoos usually remain till July/August before they migrate. Unfortunately no records of the last-heard cuckoo are available

23 JUNE - MIDSUMMER'S EVE

> *Camomile flowers or St John's
> Wort gathered on St John's Eve
> and hung up in the house will
> provide protection against storms.*   *

> *If it rains on Midsummer Eve,
> the filberts will be spoiled.*   *

The first maxim is true of many flowers that afford protection against storm and thunder. The plant chapter provides

JUNE

many examples of this. Nuts (filberts) being spoilt by rain on this eve is pure myth.

24 JUNE - ST JOHN'S OR MIDSUMMER'S DAY

Before Saint John's Day we pray for rain; after that we get it anyhow.

Rain on Saint John's Day, and we may expect a wet harvest. ✱✱

Previous to Saint John's Day we dare not praise barley.

If Midsummer Day be never so little rainy, the hazel and walnuts will be scarce, corn smitten in many places; but apples, pears, and plums will not be hurt. ✱✱ ✱✱✱

Rain on Saint John's Day, damage to nuts. ✱✱

*Cut your thistles before Saint John,
You will have two instead of one.*

*Never rued the man
That laid in his fuel before Saint John.*

If a cuckoo sings after Saint John's Day the harvest will be late. ✱✱✱✱

The first saw was obviously originated by an extreme pessimist although contains the seeds of truth. The ancient day was one of the milestones of the old farming calendar, even before it became a Christian saint's day. The range of subjects it covers in weather lore is a testament to its great age. Infact a type of rye called St John's Day or Midsummer Rye was introduced being a rugged crop grown in the most inferior soil and under extreme weather conditions. The fourth maxim has the horrible phrase "never so little rainy" which is interpreted

June

as meaning extreme rainfall. Only the corn part is tested.

Second saying	12/42	(29)
Fourth saying = Wheat	10/31	(32)
= Barley	11/31	(35)

27 June

> *If it rains on June the twenty-
> seventh, it will rain seven
> weeks.*   *

Another example of meaningless weather lore.   0/45   (0)

29 June - St Peter's Day

> *If it rains on Saint Peter's Day,
> the bakers will have to carry
> double flour and single water;*   ***
> *if dry, they will carry single
> flour and double water.*   ***

This of course means that a wet 29 June will produce little wheat and a dry St Peter's Day plenty of wheat. However both tests came up with unsatisfactory results.

Wet 29 June	13/33	(39)
Dry 29 June	20/50	(40)

> *Peter and Paul will rot the
> roots of the rye.*

Presumably this refers to rain on both St Peter's and St Paul's Day (25 January).

29 June - 4 July - Buchan's Fourth Cold Spell   ***

Again another of the fatal Scotsman's cold weather periods which gains a meagre 44 percent accuracy rating. (Refer to the index for all 9 Buchan periods).   49/111   (44)

JULY

The usual weather of July begins with the late June Westerlies and storms for the first week. Then follows a warm mid-July period 10-24th. The last week 23-30th July continuing into August normally suffers a return to thundery, cyclonic weather. The highest annual mean daily temperatures are reached at the end of July into August.

No tempest, good July,
Less the corn but look ruely.

A valid observation of corn, now reaching maturity, which would be flattened by any violent summer thunderstorm - especially in the last week of July.

When the sun enters Leo, the
greatest heat will then arise.   *

The sun enters Leo on 24 July. The "greatest heat" was tested as the year's highest temperature to fall during 24-28th - poor results of 4 percent arose. Just for warm weather to occur in this period during this notoriously wet time only 6 percent was conjured up.   5/124   (4)
                                                                    7/111   (6)

In July
Shear your rye.

In July
Some reap rye;
In August,
If one will not, the other must.

Further old-style farming rhymes covering rye.

A shower of rain in July, when
the corn begins to fill,

JULY

*Is worth a plough of oxen, and
all belongs theretill.*

*Much thunder in July injures
wheat and barley.*

These are more subtle observations than first meets the eye. A shower means rain and sunshine - the perfect weather blend for July corn. The second maxim mentions thunder which means heavy or violent showers which can flatten whole fields of corn with terrific downdraughts of rain and hail.

As July so the next January. **

No truth emerges when comparing similar rainfalls of July and January with 39 percent and temperature offering 21 percent.
96/244 (39)
58/273 (21)

*Whatever July and August do not
boil, September cannot fry.*

Culinary metaphors explaining that the excessive heat of the summer months of July and August is reduced in power when September comes along.

*When the months of July, August,
and September are unusually hot,
January will be the coldest month.* ***

Normally January is the coldest month of the year occurring on 43 percent of occasions. After a hot summer it only increases to 45 percent.   5/11 (45)

*A swarm of bees in July is not
worth a butterfly.* ***

A pretty saying meaning that a late July bee swarm would collect very little pollen to produce honey for the beekeeper.

July

> *As the days begin to shorten*
> *The heat begins to scorch 'em.*

The days begin to shorten in July and although one would expect a slight decrease in the sun's heat the year's highest mean daily temperatures occur in late July. So the crops would be scorched. The maxim's counterpart can be seen in the January section.

> *The English winter ends in July*
> *and begins in August.*

A pessimistic piece of weather lore that must have been formulated during a wet, cold miserable late July day when the summer looked as if it would never begin.

1 July

> *If the first of July be rainy weather,*
> *It will rain more or less for four weeks together.*   *

There is absolutely no truth in this adage.   2/40   (5)

First Friday in July

> *The first Friday in July is always wet.*   ***

As expected the result is unsatisfactory.   49/111   (44)

2 July – St Mary's Day

> *If it rains on Saint Mary's Day,*
> *it will rain for four weeks.*   *

Another disastrous result.   0/52   (0)

3 July to 11 August – The Dog Days

July

>*As the dog-days commence, so
they end.* *

>*If it rains on the first dog-day,
it will rain for forty days after.* *

>*Dog-days bright and clear
Indicate a happy year;
But when accompanied by rain,
For better times our hopes are
vain.*

>*July, to whom, the dog-star in
her train,
Saint James gives oysters and
Saint Swithin rain.*

The Dog Days are the 40 days during which the Dog star, Sirius, rises and sets with the sun. The general country belief was that it added heat to the sun. I'm afraid there is no truth in the adages. First saying 7/111 (6)
Second saying 0/57 (0)

10 July

>*If it rains on July the tenth,
it will rain for seven weeks.* *

This saying never works. 0/52 (0)

12 July

>*To the twelfth of July from the
twelfth of May
All is day.*

This weather saying must date before 1752 when the present style calendar was introduced (on 2nd September 1752). Then 11

JULY

days were added so the 3rd Sept. became the 14th. This would put the old 12 June around the summer solstice or the longest day in today's calendar. Hence an equal period either side of this date would constitute a time when "all is day".

14 July - St Processus' and St Martin's Day

*If it rains on the feast of
Saint Processus and Saint Martin,
it suffocates the corn.*

The Norfolk adage is correct in saying that any heavy rain in July could seriously damage corn.

12-15 July - Buchan's First Warm Spell   **

Further bad figures for Buchan's first warm spell. (Refer to index for the remaining spells.)   25/111   (23)

15 July - St Swithin's Day

*If about Saint Swithin Day a
change of weather takes place,
we are likely to have a spell
of fine or wet weather.*

*If Saint Swithin weep, that
year, the proverb say,
The weather will be foul for
forty days.*   *

    Saint of the soakers.   *

*Saint Swithin's Day if it do
rain
For forty days it will remain.
Saint Swithin's Day on it be
fair
For forty days t'will rain
nae mair.*   *

*How, if on Saint Swithin's
feast the welkin lours,*

July

> *And every penthouse streams
> with hasty showers,
> Twice twenty days shall clouds
> their fleeces drain,
> And wash the pavements with
> incessant rain.*   *

> *In this month is Saint Swithin's Day,
> On which if that it rain they say,
> For forty days after it will
> Or more or less some rain distil.*   *

> *Saint Swithin is christening
> the apples.*

St Swithin's Day is the most famous of the saints' days for weather lore, still held very dearly and stubbornly believed in. Unfortunately a different story emerges when the facts are checked. The majority of the sayings concern a wet St Swithin Day followed by 40 similar ones. However there is an exception in the first saw. Swithin, who was an Anglo Saxon bishop of Winchester c852-c862 AD, originated the rain legend by wishing to be buried in a churchyard where rain from the church eaves might fall upon his grave. When he was removed to Winchester Cathedral on 15 July 971 it poured for 40 days (15 July to 23 August) or so legend has it.

During 1861-1971 none of the sayings became true but an average of 21.1 raindays out of the 40 were independantly wet after a wet 15 July. Similarly 20.8 dry days occurred after a dry 15 July. Identical results were observed by Mirrlees in 1929 and Brazell in 1968.

                       Wet 15 July then wet for 40 days   0/55   (0)
                       Dry .. .. .. dry 0/55   (0)

> *All the tears that Saint Swithin
> can cry
> Saint Bartlemy's dusty mantel
> wipes dry.*   ****

This is interesting since St Bartholomew's Day is the 24th August 41 days after. It is a sudden dry ending to the supposed 40-day wet spell. Results are average.   28/55 (51)

July

20 July - St Jacob's Day

> *Clear on Saint Jacob's Day,*
> *plenty of fruit.*   *

> *If it rains on Phillip's and*
> *Jacob's Day, a fertile year may*
> *be expected.*   *

More nonsensical pieces of weather lore. Philip's Day refers to the 1st May.

20 July - St Margaret's Day

> *So much rain falls about this*
> *day that people often speak of*
> *"Margaret's Flood".*   ***

The figure of 43 percent suggests nothing special about rain on this day.   46/107 (43)

22 July - St Mary Magdalen's Day

> *Alluding to the wet usually*
> *prevalent about the middle of*
> *July, the saying is: "Saint*
> *Mary Magdalen is washing her*
> *handkerchief to go to her*
> *cousin Saint James' fair."*   ***

The results are barely satisfactory - anyhow the middle of July is often frequented by a warm period (10-24th).
    21/56 (37)

25 July - St James' Day

> *Till Saint James' Day be come*
> *and gone,*
> *You may have hops and you may*
> *have none.*

Ancient country-style weather lore.

AUGUST

The thundery, cyclonic weather of late July normally continues into the first week of August. The most dramatic change, after a mixed weather pattern for mid-month, is the beginning of the late August or first storms of autumn. 20-30th August covers this weather type with a peak on 28th.

Dry August and warm
Doth harvest no harm.

Extreme weather in the form of strong gales, thunderstorms or heavy rain is a great disadvantage to a mature crop. Hence quiet late summery-type conditions are most welcome.

So many August fogs, so many
winter mists.   *

After the fiasco of the poor results from the saws dealing with fogs in March, frosts in May and the like, one suspects that this adage will be closely related.

A fog in August indicates a
severe winter and plenty of
snow.   *

This old saying is similar to the fog lore of March. The basis is the belief that August anticyclones, causing the fog, will continue as a trend into winter. By then frost, low temperatures and fog will be the norm. Little truth is born from the results.   3/19   (16)

When the dew is heavy in
August, the weather generally
remains fair.   ***

The first sentence is certainly true. To produce heavy dew at night the most favourable conditions needed are clear skies

August

and a calm wind which are often associated with anticyclones and fair weather. August thunderstorms are on the decline after the summer July maximum but still remain frequent. The last part of the maxim possesses no real truth with 44 percent.

                 8/18 (44)

As August, so the next February. **

Another balance saw of August's weather against February's with hopeless results of 34 percent for rainfall and 19 percent for temperature.

                 83/244 (34)
                 52/273 (19)

A rainy August
Makes a hard bread crust. ****

Heavy rain should have an effect on the final wheat crop yield. There is slight evidence for this in the 55 percent rating.

                 15/27 (56)

None in August should over the
land, in December none over the
sea.

It is assumed this proverb applies to fog which is a rarity inland in August but common over the sea and coastal waters. The reverse is true in December.

It is always windy in barley
harvest; it blows off the heads
for the poor.

A poetic ditty, possibly with a religious flavour, forgiving the stormy weather in August, which causes barley damage, by compensating the needy poor.

1 August - Lammas or Loaf-Mass Day

After Lammas corn ripens as

August

much as by night as by day.

1-7 August

*If the first week in August
is unusually warm, the winter
will be white and long.* ✱✱

A compensating saw with disastrous test figures.
4/20 (20)

6-11 August - Buchan's Fifth Cold Spell ✱✱✱

Again consistent with results from the other Buchan periods (refer to other Buchan periods for their dates in the index).
50/111 (45)

12-15 August - Buchan's Second Warm Spell ✱✱

Disastrous results for Buchan's second warm spell.
26/111 (23)

15 August - St Mary's (Assumption) Day

*On Saint Mary's Day sunshine
Brings much and good wine.* ✱

Another silly maxim of the type where one day's weather decides the fate of a year's crop.

24 August - St Bartholomew's Day

*If this day be misty, the
morning beginning with a hoar
frost, the cold weather will
soon come, and a hard winter.* ✱

*At Saint Bartholomew
There comes cold dew.* ✱✱✱

August

*Bartholomew
With the heavy dew.*   ***

*If Saint Bartlemy's Day be fair
and clear,
They hope for a prosperous
autumn that year.*   **

*As Saint Bartholomew's Day, so
the whole autumn.*   **

*Thunderstorms after Bartholomew's
Day are more violent.*   **

   The usual connection with St Barthomew's Day is dew. Although still summer the nights are becoming longer with minimum temperatures lower. The extra cooling period allows more dew to form which consequently delays harvesting in the morning until the sun is strong enough to evaporate it. In the first saw hoar frosts are rare in August let alone on the 25th so no investigation could be held, even so the result would have been poor. Prosperous autumn in the fourth saying can mean wet or dry depending on the country business it involves, but both offer poor returns. The fifth adage was tested by taking the general airstream of the day and comparing its temperature and rainfall categories with following autumn. Poor results.

                  Fourth saying = dry autumn   9/53 (17)
                              = wet autumn 11/53 (21)
                           Fifth saying 18/109 (17)

SEPTEMBER

The most frequent weather pattern associated with September is the three dry periods known as the "Old-wives summer" which in turn are followed by wet stormy days. The dry spells normally occur 7-10th, 16-21st and 30th as travelling anticyclones move east across the U.K. into the Continent. The most common time for gales and depressions is around the 24th.

> *When September has been rainy, the following May is generally dry; and when May is dry, the following September is apt to be wet.* ******

Only the first part is tested. Conclusions for the second half can be seen in the May chapter.   24/75 (32)

> *September rain is much liked by the farmer.*
>
> *September rain good for crops and vines.*

Crop maturity and land preparation for winter ploughing are helped by September rain which has the distinction of coming in short periods.

> *If the storms in September clear off warm, all the storms of the following winter will be warm.* *****

A storm or depression crossing the country clearing "off warm" refers to it taking a track across Scotland or further north so as to avoid the full force of its cold rear northerly winds. The trend of cyclonic movement in high latitudes might continue into October but no longer.

SEPTEMBER

*When a cold spell occur in
September and passes without a
frost, a frost will not occur
until the same time in October.*   *

Although not tested the saying fails because of dates. To assume that one weather type occurs exactly one calendar month after a cold September spell is pure folly. In fact a cold September spell is no guarantee to any following weather sequence.

*Thunder in September indicates
a good crop of grain and fruit
for next year.*   ***

Nonsensical saw supported by bad test figures.
                Wheat, barley and oats   6/15   (40)

*September blows soft till the
fruit's in the loft.
November take flail, let ships
no more sail.*

*Dry mild September will make
cellars full of good ale.*

Countrymen hope September will be a quiet month without the full blast of gale force winds (notable in November) to ruin late harvesting.

*Many haws, many sloes,
Many cold toes.*   *

*A heavy crop of berries foretells
hard weather ahead.*   *

This is the time-honoured period when people firmly believe that a plentiful crop of red berries or haws prophesy a severe winter to follow. This is based on the myth that nature provides an abundance of berries for birds to eat and survive the cold winter. Pleasant weather lore, but in truth a surplus of berries is the result of good growing seasons in the previous year. The poor result bears this out.   3/16   (19)

September

> *September dries up wells and* ✱✱
> *breaks down bridges.* ✱✱✱

This means that after a summer flood or drought, September often continues the sequence putting in the finishing touches. In reality there is little evidence.

Dry September 9/42 (21)
Wet September 31/84 (37)

> *Stooks leave to stand for three Sundays.*

This Yorkshire (North Riding) old farming maxim refers to a stook or a number of sheaves (usually 6 to 12) of grain stacked for drying. The stook is angled to face the prevailing wind and positioned to catch the maximum amount of sunshine. The period they are left depends on the location and weather conditions. The suggestion of a minimum of 14 days (three Sundays) in the saying is probably correct.

> *The harvest late, garden stuff good and cheap; honey, flax and hemp abundant.*

True farming facts from the North Riding of Yorkshire.

1 September

> *Fair on September the first,*
> *fair for the month.* ✱✱

Another fable that has fallen by the wayside.

12/53 (23)

8 September

> *As on the eighth of September,*
> *so for the next four weeks.* ✱

A completely useless maxim. 0/111 (0)

September

14 September - Holycross or Holyrood Day

> *If dry be the buck's horn*
> *On Holyrood morn,*
> *Tis worth a kist of gold;*   ***
> *But if wet it be seen*
> *Ere Holyrood e'en,*
> *Bad harvest is foretold.*   **

This Yorkshire adage is pleasant when read but disagreeable in result.   Dry 14/41 (34)
                                                                     Wet 12/38 (32)

Mid-September

> *There are generally three*
> *consecutive windy days about*
> *the middle of September, which*
> *have been called by the Midland*
> *millers the windy days of barley*
> *harvest.*   *****

This maxim was tested for three consecutive windy days during the period 11-20th September (mid-month). The peak was 12-15th (refer to beginning of this chapter). The result obtained a high rating of 66 percent.   73/111 (66)

15 September

> *This day is said to be fine six*
> *years out of seven.*   ****

To obtain a dry 15th September 6 times out of 7 times is to do so on 86 percent of occasions. When tested the figure returned was 55 percent.   58/105 (55)

19 September

> *If on September the nineteenth*
> *there is a storm from the south,*
> *a mild winter may be expected.*   *

September

This Derby saying, like the majority of daily weather maxims, falls flat upon its face.   1/10   (10)

Autumn Equinox - About 21 September

A quiet week before the autumn equinox and after, the temperature will continue higher than usual into winter.   **

A well-established high pressure system rapidly changing to stormy conditions is the normal weather sequence around the time of the autumn equinox. The test gave only a rating of 21 percent.   5/24   (21)

20-22 September

These three days of September rule the weather for October, November and December.   *

Another "key days" maxim ruling future monthly weather, in this case the early days of the autumn equinox commanding October to December. The temperature and rainfall of each day's airstream were tested against their corresponding month. Only 10 percent were correct.   33/318   (10)

21 September - St Matthew's Day

St Matthee,
Shut up the bee.

St Matthew
Brings on the cold dew.   ***

Matthew's Day bright and clear
Brings good winde   **

Saint Matthew,
Get candlesticks new.
Saint Mathi,
Long candlesticks buy.

September

> *St Matthew brings the cold rain
> and dew.*   *

Most of the St Matthew Day rhymes are concerned with the approach of cold weather and the first ground and air frosts of autumn.
      Cold dew   50/106 (47)
      Cold rain 4/106 (4)

> *A southerly wind on September
> the twenty-first indicates that
> the rest of the autumn will be
> warm.*   **

Only a very few examples of a Southerly wind on this day occurred so the saw could not be tested.

29 September - St Michael's Day (Michaelmas)

> *So many days old the moon
> is on Michaelmas Day, so
> many floods after.*   *

> *If Michaelmas brings acorns,
> Christmas will cover the fields
> with snow.*   **

> *Michaelmas rot
> Comes ne'er in the pot.*

> *A dark Michaelmas, and a light
> Christmas.*   **

> *If Michaelmas Day be fair, the
> sun will shine much in the winter;
> though the wind in the north-
> east will frequently reign long,
> and be very sharp and nipping.*   **   ***

This set of diverse poetic sayings are difficult to test apart from the last one.
    Fair 29 September then a sunny winter 12/46 (26)
    Fair 29 September then NE'ly in winter 18/55 (33)

September

There is a superstition about examining the oak apples on the twenty-ninth of September, and auguries are inferred from their condition.

Weather and other prophecies are made from the condition of oak apples on this day (Oak Apple Day is 29 May).

OCTOBER

Normally the third Old-wives summer dry period at the end of September continues into early October (till 4th). Then it becomes stormy 5-12th peaking 8-9th, returning to quiet anticyclonic weather in mid-month 16-20th, peaking on 19th. The see-saw pattern continues when the late autumn rains and storms appear 24 October to 13 November peaking on 29th.

*Dry your barley in October,
Or you'll always be sober.*

If barley is not properly dried then malt and consequently liquor are not available, so the farmer will always be sober.

There are always nineteen, some say twenty-one, fine days in October.   *

This Kent saying is untrue.
                19 fine October days   10/94   (11)
                21   ..   ..   ..   3/94   (3)

Much rain in October, much wind in December.   **

Another maxim with poor results.   10/34   (29)

When it freezes and snows in October, January will bring mild weather; but if it is thundering and heat-lightening, the weather will resemble April in temper.   ****

    **

The first part is a balance saw which surprisingly works with 64 percent results. Poor figures greet the second part.

OCTOBER

                                                                                7/11 (64)
                                                                               2/9   (22)

> *If October brings heavy frosts and winds, then will January and February be mild.*   *

> *If October brings much frost and wind, then are January and February mild.*   *

Similar balance sayings with little to offer.   4/33 (12)

> *Now that it is October, don thy woolly smock.*

    Certainly by the time October comes frost will be becoming more frequent.

> *A warm April and October, a warm year next.*   ***

    An unusual blend of a mild April and October (6 months apart) forecasting a warm year to follow.   16/49 (33)

> *Warm October, cold February.*   **

Another balance maxim with no truth.   10/58 (17)

> *For every fog in October a snow in winter, heavy or light according as the fog is heavy or light.*   *

    This type of pedantic weather lore has entered the realms of fiction.

October

*A large number of foggy days in
October indicates a hard winter.* ✻✻

Based on the theory that October anticyclones producing fogs will persist into winter to give very cold weather.
6/36 (17)

*If in the fall of the leaves in
October many of them wither on
the boughs and hang there, it
betokens a frosty winter and
much snow.* ✻✻✻

*If the oak wears its leaves in
October you may expect a hard
winter.* ✻✻✻

Dry quiet weather in October allows leaves to stay on the trees. For the test 13 or more anticyclonic days in a dry Oct were checked against any following cold winter. The results were unsatisfactory.
9/27 (33)

*Full moon in October without
frost, no frost till full moon
in November.* ✻

Warm cloudless weather in October hardly lasts into November.

*If the October moon appears
with the points of her crescent
up, the month will be dry, if
down, wet.* ✻

This is a famous saying with no scientific basis. The moon is shaped like this because of its odd elliptical orbit around the Earth catching the sun's light.

*If the deer's coat is grey
in October there will be a
severe winter.* ✻✻

October

> *If the hare wears a thick coat
> in October, then lay in a good
> stock of fuel.*   *

> *If foxes bark much in October
> they're calling up a great
> deal of snow.*   *

> *The Carrion Crow
> Creeping back again
> With October wind and rain.*

The Carrion Crow is involved in partial migration but the remainder of the family are residential. The maxim emphasizes October's storms aptly illustrated by the Crow.

> *As the weather in October, so
> it will be in the next March.*   **

Rainfall (27 percent) and temperature (20 percent) figures showed little comparison.   66/244 (27)
55/273 (20)

> *A good October and a good blast,
> To blow the oak, acorn and mast.*

The average periods of October's stormy and windy weather can be seen at the beginning of the chapter.

> *If there is thunder in October,
> January will be wet.*   ***

One cannot see the reasoning behind this saw.   3/9 (33)

29 September and 16 October - St Michael's and St Gallus' Day

> *If it does not rain on Saint
> Michael's and Gallus, a dry
> spring is indicated for the
> next year.*   **

October

> *If it does not rain on Saint*
> *Michael and Gallus*
> *The following spring will be*
> *dry and propitious.* ★★

Weather lore incorporating two saints' days.   11/34   (32)

18 October - St Luke's Day

> *Saint Luke's little summer.* ★★★

> *There is often about this time*
> *a spell of fine, dry weather,*
> *and this has received the name*
> *of Saint Luke's little summer.* ★★★

> *An Indian Summer often occurs in*
> *October or November.*

This is one of the most famous English weather sayings and is adamantly believed by countrymen. However the figures tell a different story. The period 15-21st October was tested for dry sunny weather. Also a minimum of three days allowed for a "little summer" to occur. A 31 percent chance of this happened when the 18th was one of the three days. The 41 percent result refers to any consecutive three-day period happening during 15-21st. In fact the driest days were the 18 and 19th which also coincide with our Indian summer (strictly an Indian summer is a lengthy dry sunny spell from late Sept. into November). The name is probably derived from the N. American Indians who relied on a similar fine spell in late autumn for harvesting. The third saying proves it.   34/111   (31)
   45/111   (41)

28 October - St Simon's and St Jude's Day

> *This day was anciently*
> *accounted as certain to be* ★★★
> *rainy.*

These figures give an evens chance of rain on 28 October.
   52/108   (48)

October

*On Saint Jude's Day
Then oxen may play.*

*On Saint Simon and Saint Jude
winter approaches at a gentle
trot.*

The first month of winter (December) is very near and the end of October could easily feel colder weather. However the result of 44 percent for a cold 28th Oct was nothing special.
47/108   (44)

NOVEMBER

The late autumn storms and rains usually continue until 13th, peaking 9-12th. In mid-month one sees a brief quiet foggy anticyclonic interlude covering 15-21st peaking 18-20th. The return in late Nov and early Dec to unsettled rainy weather is the first of the early winter storms. These are almost certain to occur 24 Nov through to 14 Dec with two separate maximums on 25 Nov and 9 Dec.

> *When in November the water*
> *rises, it will show itself*
> *the whole winter.*   ***

November rains replace the dry soil of the previous summer. Also with the drop in evaporation loss drains and well levels soon rise. Unfortunately the rains do not continue over winter.

30/81   (37)

> *October and November cold indicate*
> *that the following January and*
> *February will be mild and dry.*   *

There is no relationship here.   0/15   (0)

> *If there's ice in November that*
> *will bear a duck,*
> *There'll be nothing after but*
> *sludge and muck.*   **

The saying was tested for a mild wet winter.   9/52 (17)

> *Ice in November*
> *Brings mud in December.*   *

Further hopeless test figures.   4/52   (8)

November

*A cold November, a warm
Christmas.*   ***

A 41 percent result tells the usual story.   14/34 (41)

*A cold November signifies a
cold winter.*   ****

This has an evens chance of being correct.   53/106 (50)

*Thunder in November, a fertile
year to come.*   *

One can see no logic in this maxim.   0/6 (0)

*As November, so the following
March.*   **

Unfortunately the comparison of rainfall (35 percent) and temperature (15 percent) proves to be useless.   85/244 (35)
   41/273 (15)

*If the November goose bone be
thick, so will the winter
weather be.*   *

Another dainty morsel to whet the appetite of fiction lovers.

*When the hoar-frost is first
accompanied by easterly
winds, it indicates that
the cold will continue a
long time.*   ***

These figures are based on the cold continuing for at least three days. They are disappointing since Easterlies should normally prevail at this time.   9/27 (33)

November

1 November – All Saint's Day (Hallowmas)

> *Farewell, thou latter spring;*
> *Farewell, thou All Hallow'n*
> *summer.*   **

    In this Shakespeare quote the period 30 Oct to 1 Nov was tested for a dry spell. Only 18 percent were totally dry and any two consecutive day dry spell won a 32 percent rating. The 31st was by far the driest.   20/111 (18)
                                                                   35/111 (32)

> *If on All Saints' Day the beech*
> *nut be found dry, we shall have*
> *a hard winter; but if the nut*   *
> *be wet and not light, we may*
> *expect a wet winter.*   **

    Here a dry mild October was tested for a severe winter (13 percent) and a wet month against a wet winter (29 percent).
                                                                   4/32 (13)
                                                                   23/80 (29)

> *If ducks do slide at Hallowtide,*
> *At Christmas they will swim;*   ***
> *If ducks do swim at Hallowtide,*
> *At Christmas they will slide.*   ***

    Little to recommend this adage. The duck rhyme applies to sayings in most winter months.
                Icy 1st Nov. then wet Xmas   20/46 (43)
                Wet .. ..   .. icy ..   18/50 (36)

> *On the first of November if the*
> *weather hold clear,*
> *And end of wheat sowing you do*
> *for this year.*

Old-style farming lore.

November

Early November

When you see gossamer flying,
Be sure the air is drying.

Gossamer is the web of a small spider often spun on foliage. This light mass of thread will float in calm air or spread over grass. Gossamer literally means "goose summer" referring to early November (11th Nov is St Martin's "little summer") when geese were eaten - the time when gossamer was plentiful.

Late October to Early November

If the latter end of October
and beginning of November be
for the most part warm and
rainy, then January and
February are like to be
frosty and cold, except after
a very dry summer. **

Unfortunately this famous "Shepherd of Banbury" balance saying number 25 is untrue. 2/7 (29)

10 November - St Martinmas Eve

Where the wind is on Martinmas
Eve, there it will be through
the coming winter. *

The weather on Martinmas Eve is
an index to the barometer for
some two or three months forward. *

The first saw originates in Atherstone, Warwicks, and the second hails from the Midlands. Both are hopeless. 0/106 (0)

11 November - St Martin's Day
(Martinmas or Hollandtide)

NOVEMBER

> *If ducks do slide at Hollantide,*
> *At Christmas they will swim;*   ***
> *If ducks do swim at Hollantide;*
> *At Christmas they will slide.*   ***

A familiar period representing St Martin's summer - similar to October's St Luke's summer. The adage reverts to a well-known theme relating icy weather to wet and the reverse. As one would expect the results are poor.

                 Icy 11th Nov. then wet Xmas   16/43   (37)
                 Wet .. .. .. icy ..   20/47   (43)

> *If it is at Martinmas fair, dry*
> *and cold, the cold in winter*
> *will not last long.*   ****

This saying is supposed to show the trend of the next winter, unfortunately it does not succeed.   11/22   (50)

> *When the wind is in the quarter*
> *from the south-south-west at*
> *Martinmas, it keeps mainly to*
> *the same point right on to the*
> *old Candlemas Day, and we shall*
> *have a mild winter up to then*
> *and no snow to speak of.*   *

> *If the wind is in the*
> *south-west at Martinmas, it*
> *keeps there till after*
> *Candlemas, with a mild winter*
> *up till then and no snow to*
> *speak of.*   **

The two maxims are similar with the second coming from the Midlands. In this 96-day period the S.W. quadrant ranges from 10 to 27 days. The first part up to Candlemas has a 0 percent rating and a mild winter renders 24 percent.   0/29   (0)
                                                          7/29   (24)

> *Wind north-west at Martinmas,*
> *severe winter to come.*   *

NOVEMBER

This Huntingdonshire saw is another pointer to the following winter's weather, but with disastrous results. 2/17 (12)

> *Expect Saint Martin's summer,*
> *halcyon days.* ✱✱

> *Saint Martin's summer lasts*
> *three days and a bit.* ✱✱✱

Here we have the first real reference to St Martin's summer, mentioned by Shakespeare in the first maxim. Both were tested along similar lines to St Luke's summer (18 October). The period chosen was 8-14th Nov. The 24 percent refers to three consecutive dry days including the 11th. 35 percent involves any three consecutive dry days in the week period. Unfortunately St Martin's summer is a myth - even the date with the highest total number of dry days was the 10th. 26/110 (24)
39/110 (35)

> *If the wind is south-westerly*
> *at Martinmas,*
> *It keeps there till after*
> *Christmas.* ✱

The Midlands provide the first saying, but both are extremely misleading. 0/106 (0)

> *If Saint Martinmas ice can*
> *bear a duck,*
> *The winter will be all mire*
> *and muck.* ✱✱✱

Another icy/wet duck theme with little truth. 19/43 (44)

6-13 NOVEMBER - BUCHAN'S SIXTH COLD SPELL ✱✱

A further disastrous result which completes the set of cold spells. (Refer to index for the rest of Buchan's spells.)
31/110 (28)

November

21 November

*As November the twenty-first,
so is the winter.* *

Each airstream's temperature and rainfall categories occurring this day were checked for similar combined results in winter. Only 9 percent was returned.   10/108 (9)

22 November

*Wherever the wind is at
midnight before Deddington
Fair,
There it will stay till the
end of the year.* *

This refers to Oxfordshire's old Deddington Martinmas Fair held on this day. Very poor figures emerged.   0/106 (0)

23 November - St Clement's Day

Saint Clement gives the winter. *

St Clement was St Peter's third successor in Rome and died c100 AD. Identical testing was carried out as on the 21st Nov.
  17/106 (16)

25 November - St Catherine's Day

*As at Catherine foul or fair,
so will be the next February.* ***

St Catherine was born in Alexandria and is the patron saint of grinders, millers and spinners.   36/106 (34)

Late Autumn

*Flowers in bloom late in autumn
indicate a bad winter.* *

NOVEMBER

A balance maxim which was tested for a very mild November and a severe winter to follow.   5/54   (9)

> *If October and November be*
> *snow and a frost, then January*
> *and February are like to be*
> *open and mild.*   *

The Shepherd of Banbury's 26th adage but is completely untrue.   0/44   (0)

DECEMBER

On average the early winter storms and rains continue into December till about 14th, peaking around 9th. A quiet frosty period occurs usually 18-24th, peaking 19-21st with frequent South and East winds. A most reliable weather trend is when the old year sees a dramatic change to storms bringing a post-Christmas thaw 25 Dec to 1st January, peaking 28th. Here cyclonic and Westerly winds are most predominant.

> *Thunder in December presages fine weather.*   **

First Sunday in December

> *If it rains on this Sunday before Mass, it will rain for a week.*   *

A religious weather saying related to the day of the week and unlikely to have any sound weather reasoning. Refer to the chapter on weekdays and Sunday's weather.

3-14 December - Buchan's Third Warm Spell   ****

At last a good result for one of Buchan's 9 periods. This ties in with the early winter cyclonic storms which produce mobile depressions and mild Westerlies. A 60 percent rating confirms this. (Refer to index for other Buchan spells.)

                                                                                67/111   (60)

13 December - St Lucy's Day

> *Lucy light, Lucy light, The shortest day and the longest night.*

Refer to the sixth adage of 21st December.

December

21 December - St Thomas' Day

> *Look at the weathercock on Saint Thomas' Day at twelve o'clock, and see which way the wind is, for there it will stick for the next lunar quarter.* *

St Thomas was the "doubting apostle".   8/111 (7)

> *Frost on the shortest day is said to indicate a severe winter.* **

This Lancashire saying is a combination of frost occurring on the winter solstice and its hopeful inspiration to the rest of the winter. But alas the test contains terrible results.
    8/44 (18)

> *If it freeze on Saint Thomas' Day, the price of corn will fall; if it be mild, the price will rise.* *** ***

The price of corn was measured as wheat being abundant or scarce in the following year's crop, but ratings are low.

    Frozen 21st Dec. = good wheat   14/35 (40)
    Warm   ..   .. = bad   ..   17/44 (39)

> *If the ice will bear a goose before Christmas, it will not bear a duck after.* **

> *If ice will bear a man before Christmas, it will not bear a mouse afterwards.* **

The goose and duck theme produces another low rating.
    5/22 (23)

December

> *Saint Thomas grey, Saint Thomas grey,*
> *The longest night and the shortest day.*

This is a statement of fact.

Before Christmas

> *Sharp frosts before Christmas mean much rain afterwards.*   **

Similar themes failing miserably.   20/87 (23)

25 December - Christmas Day and Night

The weather lore for Christmas is prolific, being the most significant religious event of the Christian year. It must be emphasized that the following saws in this sub-section deal with Christmas Day and Night only.

> *A clear and bright sun on Christmas Day fortelleth a peaceable year and plenty; but if the wind grows strong before sunset, it betokeneth sickness in the spring and autumn quarters.*   ***

This first saw offers little hope.   16/40 (40)

> *If the sun shine through the apple tree on Christmas Day, there will be an abundant crop in the following year.*   *

> *If windy on Christmas Day, trees will bring much fruit.*   *

December

It is difficult to believe that one day's weather will influence the following year's fruit crop.

If it snows during Christmas Night, the crops will do well.   *

Snow on Christmas Night, good hop crop next year.   *

Presumably this means that snow covering young seeds will be protected from cold blasts and sharp frosts by the snow's insulation properties. Only five incidents of snow were found to fall on Christmas Night, so could not be tested, even so poor results would be inevitable.

If Christmas Day on Thursday be,
A windy winter ye shall see;
Windy weather in each week,
And hard tempest strong and thick,
The summer shall be good and dry,
Corn and beasts shall multiply;
The year's good for lands to till,
Kings and princes shall die thy skill.   *

If Christmas Day on Monday be,
A great winter that year you'll see.   *

If that Christmas Day should fall
Upon Friday, know we all
At winter season shall be easy,
Save great winds aloft shall fly.   *

When certain weekdays coincide with Christmas Day and are then used as a basis for weather forecasting one might as well relate the number of pints of beer the author drinks on Christmas Day to the weather of the following spring.

December

*A dull Christmas Day with no
sun bodes ill for the harvest.* *******

Reaffirmation using test figures of the falsity of this weather saw. 15/41 (37)

24-26 December

Reference to *Christmas* in English weather lore must be treated as the whole of Christmas and not the two specific times of Christmas Day and Night, in the previous sub-section. It must also be remembered that the modern Christmas includes Boxing Day which was originally one of the four holidays that bank employees took due to the Bank Holiday Act of 1871. Soon after, Boxing Day was observed as a Public Holiday. So at the time of the *Christmas* weather lore, Boxing Day did not exist. The author has chosen 24-26th Dec as a reasonable period for the "old-time" Christmas.

*A green Christmas makes a fat
churchyard.* ******

Another enjoyable maxim. Green Christmas of course means a mild wet period when green foliage temporarily grows. A fat churchyard is the fatal effect of this on old and young people. The results are poor in fact a severe cold Christmas was the major weather cause in "killing off" people through hypothermia. The 25 percent rating was based on January to March deaths and a mild Christmas. 2/8 (25)

*A green Christmas brings a
heavy harvest.* ******

Disappointing results for this Rutland maxim. 10/32 (31)

*At Christmas meadows green,
at Easter covered with frost.* *****

*Christmas in snow, Easter in
mud;* *****

DECEMBER

> *Easter in snow, Christmas in mud.*   *

The fact that Easter is a movable feast gives no weather credence to these two sayings, only a religious connection.

> *Light Christmas, light wheat-sheaf;*   *
> *Dark Christmas, heavy wheat-sheaf.*   *

The meaning of light and dark refers to a full and new moon.

> *Christmas wet, empty granary and barrel.*   ***

An unreliable adage.   9/25 (36)

> *If at Christmas ice hangs on the willow, clover may be cut at Easter.*   ***

A pleasant saying meaning that a cold Christmas will eventually turn the winter mild and wet accelerating early clover growth to be cut in the spring (Easter). In reality there is little truth.   7/21 (33)

> *If Christmas finds a bridge, he'll break it;*   *
> *If he finds none, he'll make it.*   ***

To find a bridge and break it means dry weather will be followed by torrential rain or vice-versa. There is a similar maxim in the September chapter. Tested for Christmas (3 days) and afterwards (27-29th) with poor results.

                  Dry Xmas = wet 27-29th   1/29 (3)
                  Wet   .. = dry   ..   13/33 (39)

> *If the beech shows a large bud*

December

> *at Christmas a moist summer
> will probably follow.*   ***

A mild Dec is tested for a wet summer.   16/48 (33)

> *Thunder during Christmas week
> indicates that there will be
> much snow during the winter.*   *

Very few cases arose. Anyway it is difficult to understand the relationship between thunder and snow.

28 December - Childermas or Holy Innocent's Day

> *If it be lowering and wet on
> Childermas Day there will be
> scarcity; while if the day be*   **
> *fair it promises plenty.*   ***

The usual bad returns. Scarcity is taken as loss in crops but the usual poor results prevail.

                     Wet 28th Dec. = scarce harvest   12/47 (26)
                     Dry ..   .. = plentiful ..   13/38 (34)

31 December

> *If New Year's Eve night wind
> blows south,
> It betokeneth warmth and
> growth;*   ***
> *If west, much milk and fish in
> the sea;*   ***
> *If north, much cold and storms
> there be;*   *
> *If east, the trees will bear
> much fruit;*   **
> *If north-east, flee it man
> and brute.*   ***

The last day of the old year is supposed to determine the weather of the new. Winter and spring were combined with temp-

December

erature and rainfall categories. Only South, West and North winds on 31st were tested with poor returns; not enough cases occurred with an Easterly.

South wind	5/11	(45)
West ..	4/11	(36)
North ..	0/6	(0)

November and December

Thunder and lightning early in winter or late in fall indicate warm weather.   *******

Not enough data found to research any test.

Late December

If the old year goes out like a lion, the new year will come in like a lamb.   ******

Although December often ends like a lion (meaning roaring gales), the new year to follow like a lamb (quiet weather) seldom occurs. Refer to the March chapter for a similar theme.

12/68 (18)

MOVEABLE FEASTS

Easter

All the Christian movable (i.e. no fixed calendar date) feasts are commanded by Easter Day (Sunday) which can fall from 22 March to 25 April. Today Easter covers four days Good Friday, Saturday, Sunday and Monday. The latter was introduced as a bank holiday in 1871. Periodically a series of bad Easters with wet cold weather experienced under the fluctuating date system, has provoked Parliament to pass laws to give Easter a fixed date. In 1928 such a proposal was observed for Easter Sunday to fall on the second Sunday in April. (Refer to the 7-14th February in that month's section for further information.)

Using this fixed day a comparison was made using temperature and rainfall figures from 1829-1928. Two facts emerged; that on average the later the date of Easter the better the weather and that there was no weather advantage for a fixed or movable Easter.

Shrove or Pancake Tuesday

So much as the sun shineth on Pancake Tuesday, the like will shine every day in Lent.   *

When the sun is shining on Shrovetide Day, it is meant well for rye and peas.   *

Lent, lasting for 40 days, begins on Ash Wednesday. The main difficulty in testing weather lore associated with movable feasts was the hard-slogging job of working their dates during the years 1861-1971. All of the sayings showed nothing.

Thunder on Shrove Tuesday foretelleth wind, store of fruit, and plenty.   *

Lent

Ash Wednesday

> *Wherever the wind lies on Ash Wednesday, it continues during all Lent.* ✱

> *As Ash Wednesday, so the fasting-time.* ✱

Both maxims were completely false.   0/94   (0)

Lent (40 Days from Ash Wednesday)

> *Dry Lent, fertile year.* ✱✱

When applied to wheat a 25 percent rating is returned.
                                            7/28   (25)

> *Never come Lent, never come winter.*

Presumably this Herefordshire adage means that a late Lent during April is into spring but a late cold snap can still occur.

Palm Sunday

> *If the weather is not clear on Palm Sunday, it means a bad year.* ✱✱

Another bad saying where one day's weather rules the year's crop.   10/35 (29)

> *From whatever quarter the wind blows on Palm Sunday, it will continue to blow for the greater part of the coming summer.* ✱

Easter

    This Hampshire saw is poppycock.   0/94   (0)

Holy or Maundy Thursday

> *Fine on Holy Thursday, wet on*
> *Whit Monday; fine on Whit*   **
> *Monday, wet on Holy Thursday.*   ***

A Huntingdonshire saying which produces sad figures.
    Fine on Holy Thursday wet on Whit Monday   16/53 (30)
    Fine on Whit Monday wet on Holy Thursday   20/58 (34)

> *If a piece of hawthorn is*
> *gathered on Holy Thursday*
> *and kept in the house it*
> *will never be struck by*
> *lightening because:*
> *Under a thorn*
> *Our Saviour was born.*

Quaint piece of weather lore with religious connotations. Similar thunder/lightning saws can be found in the plant chapter.

Good Friday

> *Rain on Good Friday,*
> *foreshadows a fruitful*
> *year.*   ***

The result speaks for itself.   11/33 (33)

Easter Day (Sunday)

> *A wet Good Friday and a wet*
> *Easter Day*
> *Makes plenty of grass, but*
> *very little hay.*   **

> *A wet Good Friday and a wet*
> *Easter Day*

Easter

*Makes plenty of grass, but
little good hay.* ✱✱

Leicester supplies the second saying but both follow the usual false pattern. 5/23 (22)

*If the sun shines on Easter Day,
it shines on Whit Sunday
likewise.* ✱✱✱

One wouldn't expect this to be true. 23/51 (45)

*A good deal of rain upon
Easter Day
Gives a good crop grass,
but little good hay.* ✱✱

*If it rains on Easter Day,
There shall be good grass
but very bad hay.* ✱✱

Both saws, the first one hails from Herts, look more sensible at first glance with rain around late March or April bringing on grass in June, but results state otherwise.
Poor hay 11/35 (31)

*Such weather as there is on
Easter Day there will be at
harvest.* ✱

The general airstream flow for Easter Day was tested for August and September harvests. Aug. harvest 16/88 (18)
Sept. .. 13/88 (15)

Easter (4 Days)

Late Easter, long, cold spring. ✱✱✱

This Sussex maxim involving a late Easter provides a poor result. 11/30 (37)

Easter

> *Past Easter frost,*
> *Fruit not lost.* ✸✸✸

Not entirely true, especially if an early Easter (late March or early April) occurs when frost is still feasible to attack fruit blossom.

> *Easter come early, or Easter*
> *come late,*
> *Is sure to make the old cow*
> *quake.* ✸✸

This Herefordshire saw refers to cold weather implying that when Easter comes along it will always be cold. Not true.
20/63 (32)

> *Easter in the snow, Christmas*
> *in mud,* ✸
> *Christmas in snow, Easter in*
> *mud.* ✸

This is pure myth.

Pastor Sunday

> *If it rains on Pastor Sunday,*
> *it will rain every Sunday until*
> *Pentecost.* ✸

Applied to the five Sundays until Pentecost and tests show a 3 percent chance of success.
1/38 (3)

Ascension Day

> *As the weather on Ascension Day,*
> *so may be the entire autumn.* ✸✸

Another saying stuffed with nonsense.
23/89 (26)

Easter to Whitsuntide

Whitsuntide

*If fair weather from Easter to
Whitsuntide, the butter will be
cheap.* ✱✱

This relates to cheap or abundant amounts of butter which in turn means excess cow's milk. This is connected with plentiful grass caused by high rainfall in June and July. July rainfall was tested but with poor results. 24/85 (28)

Corpus Christi

*If it rains on Corpus Christi
Day, the rye granary will be
light.* ✱

Another maxim where one day's weather rules a year's rye harvest.

Whitsunday

*Whit Sunday bright and clear
Will bring a fertile year.* ✱✱✱

*If Whit Sunday bring rain, we
expect many a plague.* ✱✱✱

Whit Sunday wet, Christmas fat. ✱✱✱

I'm afraid no truth can be found in these saws.
19/49 (39)

Pentecost - Whitsuntide

*Strawberries at Whitsuntide
indicate good wine.* ✱✱✱

*Rain at Pentecost forbodes
evil.*

Whitsuntide is Whit Sunday plus a few days.

SEASONS

Spring

*A late spring
Is a great blessing.*

A late spring never deceives.

A late spring certainly helps crops after a cold start, but sometimes its nett effect is felt too late.

*Better late spring and bear
than early blossom and blast.*

This applies to fruit growers. Early blossom will often be checked by late winter frosts. So it is better to be over the major frost period in a late spring and accept a below average blossom and fruit harvest.

*If the spring is cold and wet, then
the autumn will be hot and dry.* ✸✸

A neat balance saying for spring and autumn, but in reality has little to offer.   7/32 (22)

A wet spring, a dry harvest. ✸✸

Again little to offer.   August harvest   29/84 (35)
                            Sept.   ..   25/84 (30)

*In spring a tub of rain makes a
spoonful of mud.* ✸✸
*In autumn a spoonful of rain makes
a tub of mud.* ✸✸✸

Spring

If this maxim means that in spring the soil water evaporation is greater than in autumn - hence a large spring rainfall would leave little in surface mud, then it is correct. However it could also mean a heavy spring rainfall would be followed by a dry period and vice-versa in the autumn. For testing a high or low month's rainfall was checked for the correct rainfall in the following month in spring and autumn. Poor results emerged.
                Wet spring month followed by dry   75/231 (32)
                Dry autumn ..   ..   .. wet   83/241 (34)

The spring is not always green.
The spring although often sunny can be cold and dull. Crops and plants only grow when continual hourly temperatures are above about 6°C (43°F).

Thunder in spring
Cold will bring.   **
Spring thunderstorms only indicate that heavy showers are about at that time.   12/39 (31)

First thunder in spring - if in the south, it indicates a wet   *
season; if in the north, a dry
season.   *
The same sentiments apply as in the previous adage - the direction is a misfit.

Early thunder, early spring.   ***
Test figures show this to be incorrect.   5/12 (42)

Lightning in spring indicates a
good fruit year.   **
One would have thought that this maxim would follow the usual trend of poor results.

Spring

> *If there's spring in winter, and*
> *winter in spring.*
> *The year won't be good for anything.* ****

There is some truth in as much that a warm winter can accelerate seed which is often checked or ruined by cold spring frosts.

> *Long winter and a late spring are*
> *both good for hay and grain, but* *****
> *bad for corn and garden.* ***

The hay results are marvellous with 73 percent but the bad corn harvest only yields 45 percent. 8/11 (73)
5/11 (45)

> *The spring she is a young maid,*
> *who does not know her mind.*

A reminder that spring from March to April possesses some of the most variable weather of the year.

> *Spring is here when you can tread*
> *on nine daises at once on the*
> *village green.*

A lovely poetic saying which is appealing and very true.

> *A dry spring - a rainy summer.* **

This balance saw is unfortunately incorrect. 24/81 (30)

> *Early blossoms indicate a bad*
> *fruit year.* ****

Indicating that an early spring with good fruit blossoms will be tragically affected by late spring frosts, adding up to a bad fruit year.

Summer

> *Generally a moist and cool summer*
> *portends a hard winter.* ✱✱

This Bacon balance saw has poor results.   11/42 (26)

> *A wet summer almost always precedes*
> *a cold, stormy winter.* ✱✱

> *The summer be rainy, the following*
> *winter will be severe.* ✱✱

Note that these two sayings relate only to a wet summer.
 14/82 (17)

> *Midsummer rain*
> *Spoils hay and grain.*

Midsummer rain is often of the violent thundery type and the cold down draughts associated with these hail showers can ruin hay and flatten grain fields.

> *Happy are the fields that receive*
> *summer rain.*

Opposite in meaning to the previous adage. When summer rain is gentle it is often warm and this combination is good for a reasonably fast growth rate.

> *A dry summer never made a clear peck.* ✱✱

Meaning a dry summer produces a low crop yield or weight (peck) because of lack of rain. Warmth, sun and rain are the perfect weather blend for a bumper crop. The results are poor. Summer weather is only a part of the long 9-month growth of a winter crop. 9/33 (27)

Summer

A dry summer never begs its bread. ✱✱

This Somerset maxim has an opposite meaning to the previous saw.   7/33   (21)

Who so hath but a mouth
Will never in England suffer drought.

This means that although long dry summer droughts occur once every decade or so (remember 1959, 1975 and 1976!) eventually autumn or late summer rains return.

Drought never bred dearth in England.

Similar to the preceding maxim where a drought never really lasts long enough to starve people to death in this country.

A very hot and dry summer is sometimes followed by a severe winter. ✱✱

The classic example of one extreme season balancing another. Notice the word "sometimes" has crept in, but even so only a 23 percent success is assured.   6/26   (23)

An English summer, two hot days
and a thunderstorm.

A real pessimistic version of an English summer - sometimes correct. One feels total agreement especially on holiday when all it does is bucket down with rain.

After a famine in the stall,
Comes a famine in the hall. ✱✱

A famine in England begins in the
horse-manger. ✱✱

The first adage refers to a bad hay crop in the first line and poor corn harvest in the second. The chance of two such harvests in succession is 23 percent. The last saying refers to a poor hay yield.   6/26   (23)

SUMMER

One swallow does not make a summer. ✲✲✲✲

Summer goes with the swallows. ✲✲✲✲

The first is a gorgeous famous saying repeated in the bird chapter. True swallow migration often sees the lonely leaders arriving first in the country - it's a few days later when the main flocks arrive that one hopes the warmer weather has come. The second maxim marks the end of summer for a countryman as the swallow seeks warmer climes.

In summer a fog from the south, ✲✲✲
warm weather; from the west, rain. ✲✲✲

A summer fog is for fair weather.

Grey mists at dawn,
The day will be warm.

These three maxims are placed together because it is felt that all too often people believe summer fog/mists presage a dry warm day. The crux is to determine the *type* of fog or mist occurring in the morning. Poor visibility originating after a clear calm night will quickly evaporate and clear. Fog and mist caused by a change of air mass say to a warm moist airstream, often remains all day in summer.

A cool summer and a light weight
in the bushel. ✲✲

Poor test figures show that winter and spring weather are also important seasons in the final crop success or failure.

Wheat 12/34 (35)
Barley 10/34 (29)

A mild, wet winter always follows
an unproductive summer. ✲✲✲

"Unproductive" means poor harvest. The best result was for a mild wet winter to follow a poor hay harvest.

Wheat 10/24 (42)
Barley 11/28 (39)
Hay 14/27 (52)

Summer

*T'is not the husbandman but the
good weather that makes the corn
grow.*

Although the husbandman has special skill and knowledge, the weather ruled the success or failure of farming - even today with modern machines and land chemicals.

*The greater the haze, the more
settled the weather.* ✱✱✱✱✱

Summer haze, especially when thick, is the sign of a temperature inversion above the ground (usually below 2,000ft). These are associated with anticyclones which in turn can be related to quiet dry summer spells. In the test haze guaranteed at *least* three settled days on 71 percent of occasions.

```
At least three dry days    201/283  (71)
  ..    ..  four    ..  ..  171/283  (60)
  ..    ..  five    ..  ..  150/283  (53)
```

Winter is summer's heir. ✱✱

The balance saw was tested with equal temperature and rainfall categories to be persistent in each season.

```
Temperature   45/273  (16)
Rainfall      70/254  (28)
```

What summer gets, winter eats. ✱✱

The maxim means that summer's weather will produce the opposite effect in winter. Again temperature and rainfall categories were tested.

```
Temperature   32/214  (15)
Rainfall      43/169  (25)
```

Autumn

Clear autumn, windy winter; ✱✱
Warm autumn, long winter. ✱✱

Only the second line was tested with poor figures.
                21/111 (19)

Autumn

> *A wet fall indicates a cold and
> early winter.* ******

Again poor results here.   Cold winter   17/80   (21)
                                               Early ..   10/80   (13)

> *Much fog in autumn
> Much snow in winter.* *******

A "see-saw" maxim which follows the usual pattern.
                                                                     3/7   (43)

> *Thunder in the fall indicates a
> mild, open winter.* *****

An illogical adage with a bad outcome.   2/14   (14)

> *Short harvests make short addlings.*

The Yorkshire saw is obvious but earthy.

> *If during the autumn, the winds
> have been mainly from the South-
> east, or if the temperature has
> been lower than usual, it generally
> rains a great deal about the end
> of the year.* *******

The end of the year was selected as   26-31st December (6 days) but results showed little.

                       4 days out of 6 wet   19/36   (53)
                       5 ..   .. .. 6 ..   10/36   (28)
                       6 ..   .. .. 6 ..   7/36   (19)

> *A hot and dry summer and autumn,
> especially if the heat and drought
> extend far into September, portend
> an open beginning of winter, and
> cold to succeed towards the latter
> part of the winter and beginning
> of the spring.* ******

Winter

This balance saw from the ancient pen of Bacon sounds full of promise but that's all. 2/10 (20)

> *If on the trees the leaves still hold,*
> *The coming winter will be cold.* ★★

A saw with similar cousins in the October and November chapters.

Winter

> *Winter never died in a ditch.*

Even though a winter, say by the middle of February, has been favourably mild it can still rapidly turn cold and snowy until real spring arrives.

> *Winter finds out what summer lays up.* ★★

It is difficult to know whether winter experiences the type of weather that summer saves for the future.

> *Abundant wheat crops never follow a mild winter.* ★★★★

This is really a good result but is against reasoning as a mild winter should bring on winter wheat and even an average spring shouldn't affect its abundant crop potential.
29/41 (71)

> *A green winter makes a fat church-yard.* ★★

Refer to the Christmas section in the December chapter for a full meaning.

> *When there is a spring in the winter, or a winter in the spring, the year is never good.* ★★★★

Winter

Similar to an adage in the spring section.

> *Summer in winter, and a summer's
> flood,
> Never boded an Englishman good.* ✱✱✱✱

Excess weather of this type plays havoc with growing nature.

> *A warm and open winter portends a
> hot and dry summer.* ✱

Classic balance saw from Bacon's pen, but offering only a 10 percent success rating.   5/48 (10)

> *One fair day in winter makes not
> birds merry.*

One fair day in winter, impersonating the false beginning of spring, often catches birds out of their normal winter singing and feeding habits.

> *A fair day in winter is the mother
> of a storm.* ✱✱✱

It is always difficult to define a "fair" day; it is one of those loose adjectives like nice. But the author used it as meaning a clear dry sunny warm or hot day with a slight or moderate breeze. The test figures are not really any good.
Storm to follow "fair" day within 24 hours   36/121 (30)
.. ..   48   ..   55/121 (45)

> *An unusually fine day in winter is
> known as a 'borrowed' day, to be
> repaid with interest later in the
> season, known also as a 'weather-
> breeder'; and by sailors as a 'fox'.* ✱

The terms "borrowed day" and "weather breeder" occur in other periods of the year. Excellent weather lore poetry but poor in the truth stakes.

Winter

> *When winter begins early, it ends*
> *early.*   ✱✱✱

This is also untrue with a 46 percent result.

                                                                                                        25/55   (45)

> *An early winter,*
> *A surly winter.*

> *An early winter is surely winter.*

It is interesting to note that a difference of one letter in "surly" and "surely" completely changes the meaning. An early cold frosty or snowy winter in November is the most dangerous to a farmer.

> *Winter thunder,*
> *A summer's wonder.*   ✱✱✱

> *Winter thunder*
> *Bode's summer's hunger.*   ✱✱✱

Two balance maxims. Extracting winter thunder out of the June and July summer is supposed to help towards a warm sunny summer or abundant crop. Unfortunately the meaning falls by the wayside. (Refer to the February chapter for similar adages.)

                                      Wheat and barley   3/9   (33)
                                      Hot/dry summer   4/9   (44)

> *Winter thunder and summer flood*
> *Never boded an Englishman good.*   ✱✱✱

Any extreme weather conditions such as flood and thunder play havoc for the husbandman.

> *Winter thunder,*
> *Poor man's death, rich man's hunger.*   ✱✱
> *Winter thunder,*
> *Rich man's good and poor man's*
> *hunger.*   ✱✱

The saying is supposed to mean that winter thunder is good for fruit and bad for corn.

Winter

> *Sudden frosts in winter, after*
> *rain,*
> *Soon bring back more rain again.* ✱✱✱

Apparently this does not always happen in fact only on 47 percent of occasions.   38/81 (47)

> *When the Winter Solstice (about 21*
> *December) has not been preceded*
> *nor followed by the usual storms,*
> *the following summer will be dry*
> *at least 5 times out of 6.* ✱✱

Usually 18-24th December has a quiet frosty period peaking 19-21st, around the winter solstice. Storms normally occur *before* 18th and *after* 24th. The test applies to 15-27th Dec. where times were viewed when no more than 2 days of gales blew. In the saying 5 out of 6 dry summers followed or 83 percent but the test only came up with 25.   4/16 (25)

> *As the days grow longer,*
> *the storms grow stronger.* ✱

As daylight starts to grow longer from late December the storms do grow stronger but a quiet period usually reigns in February. In March the gales return but from April into summer and autumn this saying is totally false.

> *After a frosty winter there*
> *will be a good fruit harvest.* ✱✱✱

> *If the drop do freeze in the*
> *cup of the blum*
> *Surely there will be no plums.* ✱✱✱

These two sayings are contradictory.

> *A winter fog*
> *Will freeze a dog.* ✱✱✱✱

Winter freezing fog is the coldest of the year. It is often associated with an anticyclone producing extremely low temperatures. And of course freezing fogs are notorious for producing

Winter

rime deposits which with temperatures of -5 to -12°C prove the point.

> *Under water, dearth;*
> *Under snow, bread.* ****
>
> *Under water famine, under snow bread.* ****

This again is the explanation of snow affording an insulation for plant life, seeds etc, against frost and cold winds. Water or rain will freeze, kill or rot vegetation.

> *Too fine a winter will swamp the summer.* **

Another balance saw with poor results. 5/24 (21)

> *A good winter brings a good summer.* *
>
> *A good winter, a good summer.* *

It is difficult to know the dubious meaning of good winter and summer in these two maxims. A warm wet winter is good to some and not others. In the end a good winter and summer was defined as one with average temperature and rainfall.
1/21 (5)

> *A persistently hazy atmosphere in winter is a sign of cold raw weather.* *****

A true saying that needs no testing. The majority of winter hazy conditions imply long dry days around anticyclones. The winter anticyclones differ from the summer ones in as much that they experience extreme frost and really cold conditions tending to worsen as the hazy days continue.

> *Expect the frost to increase in severity, and the weather to become drier and crisper, if, in winter, the wind veers from north-west to north-east.* *****

Winter

The results are very good and are tested on dry clear days under winter conditions at least two days after a North Easterly has set in. The cases for NW to NE winds are short-lived often occurring with depressions traversing Southern England or the English Channel and hence this part of the saying is false. 34/50 (68)

> *A wet autumn followed by a mild*
> *winter is the forerunner of a dry,*
> *cold spring.* *

> *A moist autumn with a mild winter*
> *is followed by a cold and dry*
> *spring, retarding vegetation.* *

An exact set of figures which look impressive but in reality are untrue. 1/12 (8)

> *Predict fog in autumn and winter*
> *when (1) the sky is clear (or*
> *clears) at sunset; (2) there is no*
> *more than a mere breath of wind;*
> *(3) when the air is fairly damp.* *****

All true. Here we have the basic ingredients for fog formation. I like the "not more than a breath of wind", if it was calm then only shallow fog patches would form. A light wind is needed to produce the turbulence to mix the fog so it becomes widespread. This country adage is indeed very shrewd.

Year

> *A dry year never starves itself.*

Presumably this means there are clear nights with dew to help in the annual moisture total.

> *After a wet year a cold one.* **

Poor figures emerge here. 4/19 (21)

Year

     Wet and dry years come in triads.   *
A fanciful idea that pays poor dividends.   1/19   (5)

     A snow year, a rich year.   **

     Snow year, good year.   **

     A snow year is a good year.   **

Seeds and vegetation are insulated against frost and bitter winds by snow in the winter half-year.   Barley   9/32   (28)
                                                                                     Hay   13/32   (41)
                                                                                      Wheat   8/32   (25)

     A good nut year, a good corn year.   *

     A good hay year, a bad fog year.   *
Again the significance of this saw is baffling.
                                                                                    6/38   (16)

     A pear year,
     A dear year.   ****

     A cherry year,
     A merry year.   ****

     A plum year,
     A dumb year.   ****

     In the year when plums flourish
     all else fails.   ****

The second adage originates from Kent and the third from Devon. Plums are hardiest of all stone fruit and apart from being susceptible to damage by spring frosts can live in all varieties of weather. Hence the poor harvests of other fruit crops. Cherry is one of the earliest to begin so an abundant year signifies a mild wet spring, good for most crops.

Year

*A serene autumn denotes a windy
winter;
A windy winter, a rainy spring;
A rainy spring, a serene summer;
A serene summer, a windy autumn;
so that the air on a balance is
seldom debtor to itself.* **

*Spring. Slippy, drippy, nippy.
Summer. Showery, flowery, bowery.
Autumn. Hoppy, croppy, poppy.
Winter. Wheezy, sneezy, breezy.* *****

A wonderful brief description of the year's seasons.

*Extreme seasons are said to occur
From the 6th to the 10th year of
each decade, especially in alternate decades.* **

Extreme seasons were added to each decadal year. The most frequent year for extreme seasons was the 2nd (ie say 1891, 1901, 1911 and so on) followed in order by 10th, 3rd, 9th, 1st, 4th, 6th, 8th, 5th and 7th year. From the maxim the 6th to 10th years are supposed to have the bulk of extreme seasons which of course is untrue. Alternate decades are also a folly.

*The first 3 days of any season
rule the weather of that season.* *

Another "keys of the season" type saw where the weather on the first three days of any season dictates the following three month's weather. Similar maxims prove useless when tested.

*The general character of the
weather during the last 20 days
of March, June, September or
December will rule the following
seasons.* **

The saw looks promising but a quick glance at the results shows little confidence in it.

Year

```
Last 20 days of March  = spring   63/245   (26)
 ..   ..  ..  .. June  = summer   54/245   (22)
 ..   ..  ..  .. Sept. = autumn   90/245   (37)
 ..   ..  ..  .. Dec.  = winter   48/244   (20)
```

*A year of grass – good for nothing
else.*

This means a year of excess rain, and although crops need rain, too much is disastrous.

*There can never be too much rain
before mid-summer.*

Rain is always needed from April to June when crops begin to accelerate in growth.

*The harvest depends more on the
year than on the field.*

Like all things, farming was dependant on the random effects of the English *weather* rather than soil consistency.

A windy year is an apple year.   ✱✱✱

WEEKDAYS

There is no logical reason why a day of the week should affect the weather. Nearly all results bear this out. The wettest weekday (figures for Teddington Oct 1953 to Sept 1968) is Thursday (with 47.9 percent chance or rain) then Saturday (44.8) followed by Wednesday (44.4), Friday (43.7), Sunday (43.4), Tuesday (42.7) and finally Monday (41.5) falling perfectly as the recognized washing day. The order can be reversed for the driest days of the week. Thursday as the wettest is appropriate as it stems from the Scandinavian Thor - the god of thunder.

WEDNESDAY

When the sun sets clear on Wednesday, expect clear weather for the rest of the week.   ****

Wednesday clearing, clear till Sunday.   *

These two maxims are similar with surprisingly good results for the first one of 58 percent.   63/109 (58)
1/16 (6)

THURSDAY

*On Thursday at three
Look out, and you'll see
What Friday will be.*   **

This Devon saw can be applied to any day.

FRIDAY

*Friday's a day as'll have his trick,
The fairest or foulest day o' the wik.*   ****

Weekdays

*Friday is the best or worst
day of the week.*   ****

As the Friday, so the Sunday.   ***

*If on Friday it rain
Twill on Sunday again;*   ***
*If Friday be clear
Have for Sunday no fear.*   **

*If the sun sets clear on a
Friday, it will blow before
Sunday night.*   **

The relationship between Friday and Sunday may have been influenced by the Christian Good Friday and Easter Sunday. The first adage hails from Shropshire and shows Friday to be the 4th wettest and 3rd driest weekday with figures to prove it. The third saying was tested on similar airstreams for both days. Poor results for the fourth and fifth saws occur.

Wettest Friday	342/783	(44)
Driest ..	441/783	(56)
Third saying	41/177	(23)
Wet Friday then dry Sunday	33/77	(43)
Dry .. .. wet ..	25/99	(25)

Saturday

*There is never a Saturday
without some sunshine.*   *

*There is never a Saturday in
the year
But what the sun it doth appear.*   *

The sun appears on 44 Saturdays out of a 100.

*Saturday change, and Sunday
full,
Is always wet, and always wull.*   ***

A Northants saw, not particularly true.   14/36 (39)

WEEKDAYS

SUNDAY

> *If it rains on Sunday before*
> *Mass, it will rain all week.*   *

> *Rain afore church*
> *Rain all the week, little or*
> *much.*   *

> *Sunday clearing, clear till*
> *Wednesday.*   **

Low ratings for this adage.   3/14 (21)

> *Saturday's moon, Sunday seen*
> *The foulest weather there ever*
> *hath been.*   *

Too ridiculous to contemplate (see Moon chapter).

> *If sunset on Sunday is cloudy,*
> *it will rain before Wednesday.*

A safe obvious bet. Once the weather trend becomes changeable with Westerlies and depressions bringing rain fronts across the UK, the chance of rain, even within two days, is very high. So whether the cloudy sunset appears on Monday, Thursday or Sunday, the consequence is factual.   57/76 (75)

> *When it storms on the first*
> *Sunday in the month, it will*
> *storm every Sunday in the*
> *month.*   *

The last phrase refers to the remainder of Sundays in the month.   2/21 (10)

Weekdays

> *The last Sunday in the month
> indicates the weather of the
> next month.*   *

Usual pattern of useless test figures.   6/44   (14)

> *A wet Sunday, a fine Monday,
> wet for the rest of the week.*   *

This saw from Winchester has little to offer.   3/21   (14)

Any Day

> *A misty morning may have a fine
> day.*   ***

It all depends on the type of mist - whether valley, hill or frontal. (Refer to the fog/mist chapter.)

> *Too bright a morning breeds
> a lowering day.*   *****

This is absolutely correct. A brilliant clear morning inland with excellent visibility always occurs with a cold polar airstream which is often potentially unstable or showery. So as the temperature of the day increases shower clouds form (cumulus) and rain showers often occur in afternoon/evening.

> *When there are three days cold,
> expect three days colder.*   ***

One would expect this saying to be true with cold weather persisting but surprisingly only 38 percent are correct.
    107/282   (38)

> *·A warm and serene day, which
> we say is too fine for the
> season, betokens a speedy
> reverse.*   ***

Any Day

A similar saw with ratings can be seen in the winter section.

> *A blustering night, a fair day.*   ***

> *For morning rain leave not your journey.*   ***

These two should have an evens chance. Blustery nights can continue throughout the next day and equally can abate to produce fine gentle weather.

> *A bad day hath a good night.*   ***

This is really only true with daytime showers which frequently cease inland overnight. This of course is mainly due to the falling night temperature allowing little energy to produce them.

> *Twilight looming indicates rain.*   ***

Twilight looming indicates a cloudy or overcast sky after sunset or before sunrise. It hints at a certain amount of cloud or mist/fog. The question is what type of cloud is capable of producing wet or dry conditions.

> *A day in England is generally much like the one before.*   **

This is a test of persistence of weather which is probably the best forecasting tool for this country. It is certainly better than chance conjecture. Results were based on the same type of airstream for two consecutive days.   234/729 (32)

> *Between the hours of ten and two*
> *Will show what the day will do.*   ****
>
> *Between twelve and two*

Any Day

You'll see what the day will do.   ****

*A cloudy morning bodes a fair
afternoon.*   **

    The second adage is Cornish. They contain a large amount of truth. They are subtle and hint of the situation where cumulus or cottonwool clouds form during the morning and by two o'clock (afternoon), which is the usual time of maximum temperature, one can decide by the cloud depth the severity of the showers, if any at all. Also mist, fog or low cloud can be decided to clear or remain by 1400 hours depending on the state of the sky and time of year. For example in winter if fog has not dispersed by early afternoon it will remain all day. Unfortunately the passage of rain belts is not really affected by the time of day.

*A wet morning may turn into a
dry afternoon.*

    It's the use of the word "may" which renders the saw as useless.

BIRDS

In west Oxfordshire at the morning bird chorus if they begin and then stop after ten minutes, then resume ten to fifteen minutes later, the day will be unsettled. If they continue throughout the chorus the day will be more settled. **** ****

If the birds be silent, expect thunder. ****

This first West Oxon saying has the ingredients of truth. Around dawn more birds sing than any other time of the day often lasting 20 to 40 minutes. Daylight is an important factor affecting bird-song. Therefore if dark heavy clouds hang around morning twilight, the dawn chorus of birds can be late or intermittent. Often rain and storms follow such an overcast beginning to the day. The opposite is also often true.

The second saw could be correct as a thunder cloud (see cloud chapter under cumulonimbus cloud) often darkens the daylight, of great consequence in bird song.

If birds begin to whistle in the early morning in winter, it bodes frost. **

In west Oxfordshire if birds play tag in the air, it is a sign of unsettled, thundery weather. ***

If birds that dwell in trees return eagerly to their nest, and leave their feeding grounds early, it is a sign of storms. **

If birds return slowly to their nest, rain will follow. **

Blackbird

If small birds seem to duck and wash in the sand, it is held to be a sign of coming rain. **

When summer birds take their flight, summer goes with them. ***

Land birds are observed to bathe before rain. **

The second West Oxon lore is most probably connected with bird behaviour. Bacon wrote the third law.

Blackbird

When blackbirds sing from the tree tops a fine day is promised but from bottom branches, beware. ***

If a blackbird sings with its tail straight down it is "waiting to shoot the water off". *

One of our most beautiful songsters with numerous voice facets. His warning cry of "pink, pink" and long continuous note at dusk are examples. In the last saw there seems to be no connection between tail down and forthcoming rain. The Blackbird often vocalizes with erratic up and down tail movements.

CROW

CRANE

> *Whenever migrating birds, especially the cranes, take flight earlier than usual, a cold winter may be expected.* *

This is a rare migrant to England from Scandinavia.

CROW

> *When crows go to the water, if they beat it with their wings, throw it over them, and scream, it foreshows storms.* *

> *The continual prating of the crow, chiefly twice or thrice quick calling, indicates rain and stormy weather.* *

> *If the crow hath an interruption in her note, like hiccough, or croak with a kind of swallowing, it signifies wind and rain.* *

CROW

The wicked crow aloud foul weather threats.   *

If starlings and crows congregate together in large numbers, expect rain.   *

The hoarse crow croaks before rain.   *

One crow does not make a winter.   ***

    Bacon penned the first maxim leading the way to the many sayings concerning the Crow. Its most frequent weather asset is its voice, normally a hoarse "kaaah", usually repeated three times in succession. Although the Carrion Crow is a solitary bird it will gather in family parties in summer and in large roosting flocks in autumn and winter. The last saying is difficult to understand. Although the Carrion Crow is involved in partial migration it basically remains in this country (see a similar saying connecting Swallows and summer).

CUCKOO

In East Riding of Yorkshire a cuckoo's frequent calling is a sign of rain.   **

Cuckoo

There seems to be no relationship between the Cuckoo's famous call and following rain except for the rain and strong wind theme, common in bird weather lore.

> *When the cuckoo comes to the bare thorn,*
> *Sell your cow and buy your corn;* **
> *But when she comes to the full bit,*
> *Sell your corn and buy your sheep.* ***

> *Bad for the barley, and good for the corn,*
> *When the cuckoo comes to an empty thorn.* **
> *If the cuckoo sings when the hedge is brown,*
> *Sell thy horse and buy thy corn.* **
> *If the cuckoo sings when the hedge is green,*
> *Keep thy horse and sell thy corn.* **

The first and second (Shropshire) sayings are subtle and need to be explained. The male Cuckoo mainly arrives in the second or third weeks of April from its winter quarters in Africa. This time is the normal start of spring and the countryman has blended the cuckoo's arrival and spring together in the rhymes. "Bare thorn" and "empty thorn" refer to a late start to spring; "hedge is brown" is the beginning of an average season and "full bit or "hedge is green" an early spring. Now the state of the season has been established related forecasts are made for following harvests. A good or bad grass harvest in June will affect sheep, horses and cows since this is their basic food. So to "sell your cow" means a poor grass harvest and "buy your sheep" applies to good grass or hay. The barley and corn harvests in August and September are similarly treated. In precis, early spring brings a good grass but poor corn harvest. Average springs forecast bad grass but good corn harvest and late springs allow bad grass but good corn to follow. The six possibilities were tested, all with poor results.

Early spring = good hay harvest   9/20   (45)
Early spring = poor wheat harvest   6/20   (30)
Average spring = bad hay harvest   7/20   (35)

Dotterel

```
Average spring = good wheat harvest      5/20   (25)
Late spring = good wheat harvest         2/15   (13)
Late spring = bad hay harvest            5/15   (33)
```

> *If a cuckoo can be penned up in*
> *an enclosure of hedges and trees,*
> *to prevent it flying away, then*
> *summer will never end.*   *

Country weather lore believed that if a Cuckoo brought fine weather and was penned or imprisoned in a bush or hedge it was a guarantee to keep the fine conditions. Over a dozen English place names include the word Cuckoo - Cuckoo Bush Hill in Gotham, Notts, which may refer to this ancient activity.

Dotterel

> *When dotterel do first appear,*
> *It shows that frost is very near;*   *
> *But when the dotterel do go,*
> *Then you may look for heavy snow.*   **

This Wiltshire saying applied to the times when these members of the Plover family were widespread throughout England. Now less than 100 pairs nest here arriving in May and leaving in October.

Duck

If ducks or drakes do shake and flutter their wings when they rise, it is a sign of ensuing water.   *

When ducks are driving through the burn,
The night the weather will take a turn.   *

If a breast bone of a duck be red, it signifyeth a long winter; if white the contrary.   *

Divers and ducks prune their feathers before a wind; but geese seem to call down the rain with their importunate cackling.   *

If ducks and geese fly backwards and forwards, and continually plunge in water and wash themselves incessantly, wet weather will ensue.   *

Fieldfare

The fourth maxim hails from Bacon's pen which like the rest contains little fact. The lore about breastbone colouring can be related to a similar one in the Goose section.

Fieldfare and Redwing

Larger than usual flocks of fieldfare or redwings indicate very cold weather and a long, hard winter.   *

The huge flocks of Fieldfare and Redwing appearing from September to April (winter visitors from Northern Europe) have no connection with forecasting weather. When a severe winter occurs the large numbers are vastly reduced.

Finch

When the finch chirps, rain follows.   *

Domestic Fowl

If fowls huddle together outside the henhouse instead of going to roost, there will be wet weather.   *

Domestic Fowl

If fowls grub in the dust and clap their wings, or if their wings droop, or if they crowd into a house, it indicates rain.

    If fowls roll in the sand,
    Rain is at hand.

Hennes resorting to the perche or rest covered wyth dust declare rayne.

If the cock moult before the hen,
We shall have weather thick and thin;
But if the hen moult before the cock,
We shall have weather hard as a block.

    If cocks crow late and early,
    clapping their wings unusually,

Guinea Fowl

> *rain is expected.*   *

> *If the cock crows during a downpour it will be fine before night.*   *

> *If the cock goes crowing to bed,*
> *He will certainly rise with a*
> *watery head.*   **

> *Days lengthen a cock's stride*
> *each day after Christmas.*

> *Pea-fowl utter loud cries before*
> *a storm, and select a low perch.*   **

There is probably little truth in all of the Domestic Fowl sayings. The seventh maxim originates in Devon and the penultimate one provides another way of saying that daylight has passed its shortest span and is now lengthening.

Guinea Fowl

> *The guinea fowl called the 'comeback' in Norfolk, is regarded as an invoker of rain. It often continues clamorous throughout the whole of the rainy days.*   *

> *Guinea-fowls squall more than usual before rain.*   *

This bird was introduced into England in 1550 for domestic usage but is now on the decline.

Water Fowl

> *Water-fowl meeting and flocking together, but especially seagulls and coots flying rapidly to shore from the sea or lakes, particularly if they scream, and playing on the dry land, foreshow wind; and this is more certain if they do it in the morning.*   ****

Goose

If the feathers of water-fowl be thicker and stronger than usual, expect a cold winter. *

Among East Coast folk there is a pretty belief, very widely held, that in May, when the sea-fowl are hatching out on the saltings, providence checks the spring tides so that they do not rise high enough to interfere with the birds. These they call by the appropriate name of "bird tides". *

The widely held view that Sea Gulls and Sea Fowl fly inland to shelter from gales and storms raging at sea may contain a certain amount of truth. Fish would be more difficult to acquire in rough seas, and today with water pollution and lack of natural food, many Sea Fowl have taken to feeding and nesting well inland from their coastal habitat. The last East Coast saw is quaint showing one of the many appealing facets of bird weather lore but unfortunately the saying contains fiction not fact.

Goose

Goose

*When the goose-bone, exposed to
air, turns blue, it indicates
rain; when it retains its colour,
expect clear weather.* *

*Breast-bone of goose to dark-
coloured after cooking, no
genial spring, and vice versa.* *

*The whiteness of a goose's breast-
bone is superstitiously thought to
indicate the amount of snow during
winter.* *

*The goose and the gander
Begin to meander;
The matter is plain,
They are dancing for rain.* *

*Geese flying out to sea is a
sign of good weather.* ***

*Early arrival of winter migrants
such as ducks, geese and swans,
indicate very cold weather and
a long hard winter.* **

The first three maxims (the second hails from Lincoln) deal with the colouring of the Goose's breastbone when exposed to air. It states that a dark colour provides harsh weather and a light colour proclaims mild conditions. It is difficult to find the exact connection and is probably lost in time. Possibly the breaking of the "wish-bone" of Domestic Fowl has some relationship. Migratory Geese usually arrive in October.

Marsh Harrier

*The marsh harriers, or dunpickles,
alight in great numbers on the
downs before rain.* **

The saying refers to the Marlborough Downs in Wiltshire.

Heron

When a heron stands melancholy on the sand it only denotes rain.

A heron, when it soars high, so as sometimes to fly above a low cloud, shows wind; but kites flying high show fair weather.

When the heron or bittern flies low, the air is gross and thickening into showers.

Herons in the evening flying up and down, as if doubtful where to rest, presages some evil-approaching weather.

Jackdaw

*If the heron stand melancholy on
the banks, it portends rain.*   *

*If the heron cry in the night as
she flies, it presageth wind.*   ***

    The first Bacon and fifth saying presumably refer to the Heron's usual role of waiting in silence ready to strike with its sharp bill at fish, frogs or water vole. Its preying stance is to rest on one leg with half-closed eyes, hunching its head between its shoulders. The Heron high or low in flight does not seem to have any pre-knowledge of weather.

Jackdaw

*When three daws are seen on St
Peter's vane together,
Then we are sure to have bad
weather.*   *

St Peter's church, like the saw, comes from Norwich.

Kingfisher

*A dead kingfisher hung up by the
legs even inside a house is said
to turn its beak to windward.*   *

KINGFISHER

A foolish but interesting saying.

MAGPIE

For anglers in spring it is always unlucky to see single magpies; but two may always be regarded as a favourable omen. And the reason is, that in cold and stormy weather one magpie

Magpie

alone leaves the nest in search of food, while the other one remains sitting with the eggs or young ones; but when two go out together, it is only when the weather is mild and warm, and favourable for fishing. *

Magpies flying three or four together and uttering harsh cries predict windy weather. *

When Magpie eggs are incubating it's the lonely female that stays on the nest (for about 21 days in April or May). After this both parents are seen flying together during the 28-day feeding period of their young. So in April to June the pattern is naturally set for single or pair Magpies proving there is no relationship with cold or mild weather. From the second saw the only time the bird is seen in threes or fours is when it partakes in ceremonial gatherings - otherwise they fly alone or in pairs.

Martin

When martins appear winter has broken. ****

No killing frost after martins. ****

Moorhen

> *Martins fly low before and
> during rainy weather.*   ***

    The Sand Martin arrives at the end of March, the House Martin not till the end of April. Winter is nearly over by mid-April but not all frosts. Apart from frost hollows, like Rickmansworth in Herts, which can have night ground frosts nearly the whole year through, May is the last month for general frost. If killing frosts mean severe air frosts then the second is true.

Moorhen

> *When moorhens fly at night to a
> distance from their usual water,
> and utter discontent cries
> during their flight, expect rain.*   ***
>
> *When moorhens build their nests
> high above water it is the sign
> of a wet summer and vice versa.*   *

The last maxim is similar to one in the Swan section.

Owl

Owl

In England the owl's calling heralds hailstorms. *

The screeching owl indicates cold or storm. *

If owls hoot at night expect fair weather. *

The whooping of an owl was thought by the ancients to betoken a change of weather, from fair to wet, or wet to fair. But with us, the owl when it whoops clearly and freely, generally shows fair weather, especially in winter. *

An owl hooting quietly in a storm indicates fair weather, and also when it hoots quietly by night in winter. *

If owls scream during bad

Peacock

> *weather, there will be a change.* *
>
> *The dirt-bird sings, and we shall have rain.* *

There is little or no truth in the Owl's hoot or cry leading to ensuing weather. The famous screech is from the Barn Owl; the eerie hoot (mentioned in the third Bacon saying) comes from the Short and Long-Eared Owl but more probably from the Tawny Owl. The Little Owl was only introduced into Northants in the late 19th century so can be discounted as Owl bird weather lore is much older. As most Owls are nocturnal hunters they are frequent night callers producing hoots and shrieks which are connected with hunting and anger at breeding time - not weather.

Parrot

> *Clamorous as a parrot against rain.* *
>
> *Parrots whistling indicate rain.* *
>
> *It is said that parrots and canaries dress their feathers and are wakeful the evening before a storm.* *

These saws relate to the caged or domestic Parrot. Shakespeare was responsible for the first one.

Peacock

> *When the peacock loudly bawls, Soon will have both rain and squalls.* ***
>
> *If peacocks cry in the night, there is rain to fall.* ***
>
> *The strutting peacock yawling 'gainst the rain.* ***
>
> *When the peacock's distant voice you hear, Are you in want of rain?* ***

Pheasant

> *Rejoice, 'tis almost here.*
> *And with his voice prognosticates*
> *all weathers.*   ✱

    The Peacock calls throughout the day and night. When dark it has a frightening voice which, like the Green Woodpecker, can be heard louder in a strong wind often prevailing before rain. It seems unusual that the four sayings apply to the call and not the Peacock's famous fan of bright coloured feathers so striking when fully displayed.

Pheasant

> *If pheasants roost late in*
> *evening and are up with the sun*
> *in the morning, a good day is*
> *promised but if early to perch*
> *and to feed, the weather will*
> *break up.*   ✱✱✱

    Known to have been in England for over 900 years, this most colourful of birds (the cock Pheasant), unfortunately has only one piece of weather lore.

Pigeon

Pigeons wash before rain.   *

Doves or pigeons coming later home to the dove house in the evening than ordinary, is a token of rain.   ****

If pigeons return home slowly, the weather will be wet.   ****

These maxims are common to many bird species. There may be a plausible link with weather. In Pigeon racing it was observed that faster return times occurred on cloudless days. The Pigeon was using the sun for navigating and positioning, but on a cloudy day when a layer obscured the sun above the bird's flight level, slow times prevailed and sometimes even loss of life. In the last saying a Pigeon late in returning to the medieval dovecote would have miscalculated possibly because of increase in cloud cover, often a forerunner of rain.

Plover

Raven

When the plovers fly high and
then low, making their plaintive
cry, expect fine weather.   ****

Similar in meaning to the Rook weather lore.

Raven

If a raven stalks about, it only
denotes rain.   *

When the crow or rayen gapith,
agaynst the sonne, in somer,
heate foloweth.   *

Ravens, when they croak continuously,
denote wind; but if the croaking is
interrupted or stifled, or at longer
intervals, they show rain.   *

When ravens sit in the sun, expect
fine weather to last.   *

Robin

If ravens croak three or four times and flap their wings, fine weather is expected.   *

If a raven is observed in the morning soaring round and round at a great height and making a hoarse croaking sound the weather will be fine.   **

If the raven makes several different cries in winter, it is a sign of a storm.   *

The first and third prophesies are from the prolific pen of Bacon. The Raven, the largest of the Crow family, used to be a familiar common bird in this country but has now been driven to South-West and Northern England, Wales and Scotland. It is renowned for deep croaking or "pruk-pruk-pruk" but more for its flying acrobatics. In spring Raven pairs tumble in the air, rolling sideways, nosediving and even flying upside-down. Unfortunately there seems to be no relationship between the Raven's antics and his prowess as a weather forecaster.

Robin

*If the robin sings in the bush,
Then the weather will be coarse;*   ***

Robin

If the robin sings on the barn,
Then the weather will be warm. ★★

On a summer evening, though the weather may be in an unsettled state, the robin sometimes takes his stand on the topmost twig or housetop singing cheerfully and sweetly - a primose of succeeding fine days. Sometimes, though dry and warm, he may be seen melancholy, chirping and brooding in a bush, or low in a hedge: this promises the reverse of his merry lay and exalted station. ★★★

If robins are seen near houses, it is a sign of rain. ★

Robins indicate the approach of spring. Long and loud singing of robins in the morning denotes rain. Robins will perch on the topmost branches of trees and whistle when a storm is approaching. ★ ★ ★★

Robins sing from hedge or bush, storms are near; when they sing in the open, good weather is expected. ★★★

The above weather lore is mainly confined to the Robin singing in high trees and barns delivering us future warmth (although the fifth saw has the opposite meaning) or chirping in low branches predicting rain or cold weather. One must remember both the male and female Robin look very similar uttering their famous "tic, tic", "tsweee" or "tsit" throughout the year (except in July when moulting) mainly in territorial defence. However there is a time in mid-winter, when most of the Robin weather lore applies, certainly in the first East Anglian saying, when the female hunts the male. While the cock sings in the high trees, the hen remains in the undergrowth hoping to be accepted as a mate after a few weeks. Although there seems to be little connection between the Robin and weather, one cannot help but feel joyful and friendliness towards the bird when he suddenly appears with his distinctive redbreast.

Rook

I'm sure the countryman would wholeheartedly agree with the choice of the Robin as Britain's national bird.

Rook

When birds of long flight, rooks, swallows, or others, hang about home, and fly up and down or low, rain may be expected.   ✱✱✱

When rooks seem to drop in their flight, as if pierced by a shot, it is said to foreshadow rain.   ✱✱✱✱

This 'tumbling' of rooks is amongst the best-known signs of rain in places where those birds are found.   ✱✱✱✱

*When rooks fly sporting high in air,
It shows that windy storms are near.*   ✱✱✱

If rooks stay at home, or return in the middle of the day, it will

Rook

rain; if they go far abroad, it will be fine.   *

It is believed in some parts of Yorkshire that when rooks congregate on the dead branches, there will be rain before night; if they stand on the live branches, the day will be fine.   * *

Rooks will not leave their nests in the morning before a storm.   ***

If rooks feed in the streets of a village, it shows that a storm is near at hand.   *

If rooks or blackbirds sit on the top-most branches looking in one direction (mainly in afternoons) for long periods, bad weather can be expected from that direction.   *

If rooks fly low, it means rain; if they feed busily and hurry about together, a storm is likely; if they sit about on fences, or dart down and reel about, expect wind.   *

If rooks fly from their nests in a straight flight around dawn, a dry day will occur.   ****

If rooks twist and turn on leaving their nest, rough weather is approaching, if they stay by their nest, screaming raucously, gales are on the way.   **** *

When rooks are late leaving the rookery in the morning and hurry about feeding on the roadside, it will rain.   ***

High rook nests mean a good summer.   *

Rook

Rook weather lore is prolific and varied with the fifth maxim hailing from Devon. Their very advanced communial life has been the foundation for much country belief, such as the supposed Rook parliaments and Rook circles sitting in judgement on criminal Rooks. Complete understanding of Rook's social rules is lacking. Certainly the "peck order" or the hierarchy position where the highest in the social order eats first is comprehended (probably evolution has allowed the strongest to survive in times of food shortage. The real reason for the Rook's autumn tumbling, twisting and diving display in free air is unknown. The sixth Yorkshire maxim about dead and live branches is intriguing, probably an older non-meteorological origin to it. The seventh saying originates in Cornwall; eighth from Durham and the remainder hail from West Oxon. With his famous continuous tree-top "cawing" in the rookeries and acrobatic aerial display no wonder much Rook weather lore has emerged.

This famous West Oxon saw about rookeries positioned high in trees foretelling a good summer is of course based on the myth that the Rook can foresee no storms or gales which would demolish the nests. The truth is different. Rookeries are normally permanent features and a pair of Rooks use the same nest each year adding material and repairing it. If winter gales did destroy the rookery then new nests would be sited where tree branches were strongest whether high or low.

Seagull

Seagulls in the field indicate a storm from the south-east. *

Sea-mews early in the morning making a gaggling more than ordinary foretoken stormy and blustery weather. *

When sea-mews appear in unwanted numbers, expect rain and high south-west winds. *

Seagull, seagull, sit on the sand;
It's never good weather when you're on the land. ****

The Sea-Mew is a general name meaning Gull. Strong onshore

Seagull

gales often make Sea-Gulls venture inland for food, indeed some Gulls remain there most of their life.

Skylark

When larks fly high and sing long, expect fine weather. ****

Field-larks congregating in flocks indicate severe cold. *

When larks rise before they sing at dawn, with an overcast sky, expect rain; but when they fly very high, singing as they rise, expect a fine day. ****
****

If the skylark hovers and glides during its descent, the weather will remain fine, but if it drops straight to ground it will rain. ***

Sparrow

The songs but mainly the flying antics of the Lark dominate the sayings. In the second saw Skylarks only gather in flocks to feed and migrate. The third saying is a sharp and accurate record of the bird. It can sustain its warble up to five minutes most frequently when flying high, almost out of sight. It's the only English bird to sing while ascending and descending vertically.

Sparrow

The chirping of the sparowe in the morning signifyeth rayne.   *

STARLING

*If the hedge sparrow is heard,
before the grape-vine is putting
forth its buds, it is said that
a good crop is in store.*   ✱

Sparrows chirping excessively as a sign of forthcoming rain (there are many similar bird weather saws) may have some deep hidden significance but on the face of it possess little truth.

STARLING

*If starlings and crows congregate
together in large numbers, expect
rain.*   ✱

Starlings roost or sleep at night in flocks numbering thousands. Who hasn't seen and heard the deafening mass blackening the sky as they follow their familiar flight path in the countryside to some safe wood, to return along the same route the following morning. It is such a daily routine, weather forecasting can hardly play any part.

SWALLOW

*In England swallows flying low
foretell rain.*   ✱✱✱

Swallow

*When swallows fleet, soar high,
and sport in air,
He told us that the welkin would
be clear.* ****

*If swallows touch the water as
they fly, rain approaches.* *

*If there are many more swifts
than swallows in the spring,
expect a hot and dry summer.* *

*Low o'er the grass the swallow
wings; 'twill surely rain.* *

*If swallows fly high the weather
will be fine.* ****

*Swallows high,
Staying dry.
Swallows low,
Wet 'twill blow.* ****
*

    The majority of the Swallow weather lore are confined to the bird's flight - high flying predicts good weather, low soaring rain. The Swallow is a migrant remaining in the country from late March to October returning to South Africa for our winter. The saying "one Swallow does not make a summer" (to be found in the summer season section) is true because at the end of March and during April they arrive in ones and twos, only coming in force from mid to late April. Presumably when

Swallows fly low they are avoiding the strong winds aloft (which often bring rain) and when they decide to venture up to high levels the wind is light (usually a sign of settled conditions). But it must be emphasized the evidence points to the Swallow experiencing only *present* weather conditions.

SWAN

> *If the swan flies against the wind, it is a certain indication of a hurricane within twenty-four hours, generally within twelve.*   *

> *The swan is said to build its nest high before floods come up but lower when there will not be unusual rain.*   *

> *Swans are hatched in thunderstorms.*   *

> *There is no doubt that swans have an instinctive prescience of floods, for it is a well-known fact that before heavy rains the birds whose home is on the banks of the Thames raise their nests so as to save their eggs from being chilled by the water.*   *

The maxim from the Thames Valley about the Swan or Moorhen building her nest high in the reeds well above water level in anticipation of wet weather to come is a pure myth. The same applies to the low built nest and follow up of fine weather. The third intriguing Hampshire adage is difficult in finding a suitable explanation, unless the hatching time, which is May or June, vaguely corresponds to the most thundery month of July.

SWIFT

> *When there are many more swifts than swallows in the spring, expect a hot and dry summer.*   *

Swift

When swifts and swallows fly high, eating insects, the day will be fine; although sometimes this occurs during thundery weather. ✱✱✱

This late migrant (arriving from late April) virtually remains flying all the time. The countryman also called it the "Devil Bird" because it flew around houses screaming during late spring and early summer evenings. With flying insects the general rule is that any good breeze or strong wind will allow them to rise to reasonable heights. They will manoeuvre near the ground in calm or gentle conditions (often associated with temperature inversions - a shallow layer above the ground where temperature increases with height). The Swift therefore will feed on flying insects depending on wind profile - often a good strength foretells rain, calm denotes settled weather (these are in opposition to the second maxim and many other sayings).

Thrush

The missel thrush or the storm cock sings particularly loud and long before rain. ✱✱

When the thrush sings at sunset, a fair day will follow. ✱✱

When this bird perches itself

Thrush

upon the topmost bough of a tree and remains there for some time, singing loudly, expect rain.   *

Again most of the lore is concerned with the famous Thrush voice. In the first and third adages the Missel Thrush (named after its fondness of mistletoe berries) is called the Storm Cock because it sits in the topmost tree branches singing its loud harsh "churr" quickly followed by a sharp "click" through all kinds of weather even raging January storms. So instead of presaging rain it remains oblivious in song to all severe weathers.

The second maxim probably refers to the Song Thrush, aptly named, having a much more wholesome song than the Missel Thrush. He begins vocalizing in January (unless severe weather prevents it) for the whole year except for a break July to September.

Titmouse

The titmouse fortells cold, if crying, 'Pincher'.   *

The saw-like note of the great titmouse fortells rain.   *

TURKEY

The Great Titmouse, better known today as the Great Tit, has a call in the spring like "tea-cher, tea-cher" or "pincher, pincher". His other song sounds like the sharpening of a saw.

TURKEY

Turkeys perched in trees and refusing to descend indicate snow.

Waxwing

Turkeys were introduced to England in 1521 by Turkish traders (hence the name) from North America.

Waxwing

*The arrival of the waxwing from
Scandinavia means a severe winter.* ✱✱

This is one of the "finds" of weather lore. For centuries the erratic arrival of large numbers of Waxwings from Scandinavia in September to our East Coast was the excuse for countrymen to call the forthcoming season a "Waxwing Winter". The reason for the huge flocks is that Waxwings eat mainly berries, especially the rowanberry. A failure of the latter in Northern Europe leads to the mass migration of Waxwings to this country. In 1679 they arrived here and also for four consecutive years 1956-9. Unfortunately severe winters did not follow. The reason for poor Scandinavian rowanberry harvests lies with poor weather in seasons *prior* to the sad harvest.

Woodcock

*Cuckoo oats and woodcock hay
Make a farmer run away.*

Woodpecker

The saying refers to the migrating arrival date of the Cuckoo (second to third week in April) and the Woodcock (October to November) from across the North Sea. By these dates the farmer should have sowed his spring oat seed and gathered the after crop of summer hay.

Woodpecker

The green woodpecker's frequent calling is a sign of coming rain.   ***

When woodpeckers are much heard, rain will follow.   ***

In Shropshire the green woodpecker is called 'storm-cock'   ***

The country people doe divine of raine by their cry.   ***

In Shropshire the call of the heigh-ho forbodes rain.   ***

When the woodpecker leaves, a hard winter is expected.   *

When woodpeckers peck low on the trees, expect warm weather.   *

The yaffel, or green woodpecker, cries at the approach of rain, and is described as 'laughing in the sun, because the rain is coming.'   ***

The bird is famouse for its cry of "ha-ha-ha" or "hellew-hellew-hellew" which can at times sound like laughter, so country people nicknamed him the Yaffle. The third and fifth saws are from Shropshire and the reason why the Green Woodpecker is also known as the Rain or Storm Bird is probably because his call can be more clearly heard in strong winds, which often precede rain. The origin may go back further. In Continental bird lore it is said that the Green Woodpecker refused to hollow out rivers and pools at the time of the Creation so was punished by God to drink only rain water.

ANIMALS

When animals seek sheltered places instead of spreading over their usual range, an unfavourable change is probable. ***

If animals crowd together, rain will follow. ***

When animals between sunrise and eight to nine o'clock in the morning assemble in bunches or in one corner of a field, expect a very unsettled day. ***
If after this time they are spread out all over the field, expect a fair day. ***

The last saw comes from West Oxfordshire. An extensive observational programme has been carried out by the author in Yorkshire in the summer of 1980. It mainly covered cows and sheep. The figures and close studies showed that these animals *do* adjust their behaviour pattern to different types of weather *after* the change has taken place and not *before*. For example cows did huddle or crowd together during gale force winds and moderate or heavy rain, but also in fine settled conditions.

Bat

Ass and Donkey

> *If asses having their ears downward and forward, and rub against walls, rain is approaching.* ✱
>
> *If asses bray more frequently than usual, it foreshows rain.* ✱
>
> *Hark! I hear the asses bray;
> We shall have some rain today.* ✱
>
> *It is time to stack your hay and corn
> When the old donkey blows his horn.*

Rutland provided the third saw. The pattern of fanciful but untrue weather prophesies continues.

Bat

> *If bats abound and are vivacious, fine weather may be expected.* ✱✱✱

Cat

> *It will rain if bats cry much or fly into the house.* ✱✱

> *If bats fly abroad after sunset, fair weather.* ✱✱✱

> *When bats appear very early in the evening, expect fair weather; but when they utter plaintive cries, rain may be expected.* ✱✱✱ ✱✱

The favourite food of the Common Bat is the moth which when frequent at night usually signifies fine conditions. Since the bat is a nocturnal creature hunting at night, it uses its very highly developed ultrasonic system. A high-pitched squeak is given which rapidly bounces off objects including the moth and is received instantaneously by the bat. The method helps him to determine the size, speed and distance of his prey. The system is also used for navigation. So excess numbers and bat cries point to abundant moths which of course in turn refers to settled weather conditions.

Bull

> *If bulls lick their hoofs or kick about, expect much rain.* ✱

> *If the bull lead the van in going to pasture, rain must be expected; but if he is careless, and allows the cows to precede him, the weather is uncertain.* ✱

In the second saw the "van" is a cow herd. Sometimes bulls lead or hang behind - they are unpredictable beasts. Both sayings have little to offer.

Cat

> *The cardinal point to which a cat turns and washes her face after a rain, shows the direction from which the wind will blow.* ✱

Cat

> When a cat sneezes, it is a
> a sign of rain. *

> When the cat lies on its brain,
> Then it is going to rain. *

> An old woman promised a fine
> day on the morrow because the
> cat's skin looked bright. *

> When the cat scratches the
> table legs, a change is coming. *

> While rain depends, the pensive
> cat gives o'er
> Her frolics, and pursues her
> tail no more. *

> When cats wipe their jaws with
> their feet, it is a sign of
> rain, and especially when they
> put their paws over their ears
> in wiping. *

> If the cat washes her face
> o'er the ear,
> Tis a sign of weather'll be
> fine and clear. *

The third adage hails from Kent and last from Northern England. Unfortunately all of these well-known habits of the feline bear absolutely no relationship to forthcoming weather. In fact the last two saws have opposite meanings.

Cockle

> Cockles, it is said, have more
> gravel sticking to their shells
> before a tempest. *

Again here is further falsity.

Cow

> When cows fail their milk,
> expect storm and cold weather. ***

Cow

When cows bellow in the evening, expect snow that night. If they stop and shake their feet, or refuse to go to pasture in the morning, or when they low and gaze at the sky, or lick their forefeet, or lie on the right side, or rub themselves against posts, or lie down early in the day, it indicates rain to come. ✻✻

Cows like any other animal are sensitive to cold, gales, wet and snow. They will avoid such hindrances by sheltering, huddling and generally shunning such horrid weather. A close Yorkshire study of cows by the author (1980) showed that although they did react to weather type there was no indication that they could forecast it even as little as one to two hours ahead. The above maxim covers most of the ridiculous relationships between a cow's antics and subsequent weather. The first line unfortunately excludes milk and thunderstorms but see in Thunderstorm chapter.

When cattle lie down in light rain, it will soon pass. ✻✻

Cows and sheep lie down before rain to keep a dry place to lie on. ✻✻✻

Cow

Wiltshire provides the first saw. The very famous theme of cows lying down indicating rain to follow because they are keeping a dry patch is partly true. Cows stand to eat grass and sit to chew the cud. They will sit in any type of weather although very rarely in heavy rain or very wet grass. The Yorkshire test shows variable results with the cow more prone to lie down in dry overcast conditions (68 percent) and sheep in moderate or heavy rain (44 percent).

Cows lying down in:-

Moderate or heavy rain	99/261	(38)
Slight rain	39/165	(24)
Dry overcast weather	153/234	(65)
Partly cloudy weather with sunny intervals	0/99	(0)
A clear sky	81/225	(36)

Sheep lying down in:-

Moderate or heavy rain	72/165	(44)
Slight rain	54/237	(23)
Dry overcast weather	6/405	(1)
A clear sky	27/414	(7)

When cattle remain on hilltops, fine weather to come. ✽✽

When cows sniff the air and walk down hill towards the farmyard, then rain or storm will follow. ✽✽

Derbyshire provides the first maxim. Again cows feed on high or low ground depending on the *current* weather conditions.

When cows huddle in the corner of a field and stand with their tails to the wind, rain is expected. ✽✽✽

This well-known behaviour pattern of the cow, especially the tail against a cold or wet gale force wind (to protect her sensitive head), are conditions of present weather. Cows seem to huddle a lot but less so in dry sunny weather. The Yorkshire test defined "huddled" as two cows within a maximum range of three body lengths of each other. Results with cows near hedges produced sporadic hopeless figures. In fact the availability of grass seems to be the obvious reason.

> Cows huddled in:-
> Moderate or heavy rain 121/261 (46)
> Slight rain 84/165 (51)
> Dry overcast weather 112/234 (48)
> Partly cloudy weather with sunny intervals 30/99 (30)
> A clear sky 87/225 (39)
> Cows near a hedge in:-
> Moderate or heavy rain 90/261 (34)
> Slight rain 51/165 (31)
> Dry overcast weather 36/234 (15)
> Partly cloudy weather with sunny intervals 48/99 (48)
> A clear sky 12/225 (5)

> *He taught us erst the heifer's
> tail to view;
> When struck aloft that showers
> would straight ensue.*   *

> *When a cow tries to scratch its
> ear,
> It means a shower is very near.*   *

> *When cows stampede with their
> tails in the air it tells of
> forthcoming rain and thunder.*   ***

The number of adages concerned with the cow's tail and ensuing weather probably stems from the warble fly. This horrible little creature lays its eggs in the cow's hide during warm humid weather, which can sometimes precede thunderstorms or heavy showers.

Dog

> *Dogs making holes in the ground,
> howling when anyone goes out,
> eating grass in the morning, or
> refusing meat, are said to
> indicate coming rain.*   *

> *When dogs eat grass, it will be
> rainy.*   *

> *If spaniels sleep more than
> usual, it foretells wet weather.*   *

Dog

If dogs roll on the ground and scratch, or become drowsy and stupid, it is a sign of rain. *

If dogs do much barking in the night the weather is about to change. *

One of the most popular dog weathers saws is the eating of grass to be followed by rain. Dogs frequently eat long grass mainly for medicinal purposes. They can hear sounds beyond the human receiving range. So in thundery conditions the high pitch of static and certain thunder tones can be detected about one to two hours before a thunderstorm is imminent. The other dog activities described above are due to natural and obvious causes.

Fish

When the wind is in the east, then the fishes do bite the least;
When the wind is in the west, then the fishes do bite the best;
When the wind is in the north, then the fishes do come forth
When the wind is in the south, It blows the bait into the fish's mouth. ****

Fish

If, during damp weather, fish bite readily and swim near the surface, an improvement is likely, or, if it remains cloudy, it will be quiet rather that windy. **

Fishes rise more than usual at the approach of a storm. In some parts of England, they are said not to bite so well before rain. **

When fish bite readily and swim near the surface, rain may be expected: they become inactive just before thunder showers. **

*Fish bite the least
With wind in the east.* ****

Fish can forecast cold weather for they keep to the cooler, lower water and are reluctant to take hook. **

Supposedly there is a relationship between the biting rate of the freshwater fish and the subsequent weather. Again, fish certainly react to water temperature change but there is such a time lag between say the start of a cold easterly wind and the cooling of the river water by 0.1°C that it is often hours before the fish's biting rate is reduced. If conditions are normal then the biting is also normal but a prolonged South or East wind will eventually increase or decrease it. Raindrops on a water surface reoxygenate the water resulting in the fish becoming more active increasing the biting rate.

> When trout refuse bait or fly,
> There ever is a storm a - nigh. *
>
> If eels are very lively, it
> is a sign of rain. *
>
> When pike lie on the bed of a
> stream quietly, expect rain or
> wind. *

Good fish weather lore but contains little truth.

Fox

> When foxes bark and utter shrill
> cries expect a violent tempest
> of wind and rain within three
> days. *

An interesting but untrustworthy maxim.

Goat

> The goat will utter her
> peculiar cry before rain. *
>
> If goats and sheep quit their
> pasture with reluctance, it
> will rain the next day. **
>
> Flocks of goats graze down the
> mountains before the approach
> of a storm, and upwards before
> fair weather. ***
>
> Should you notice a goat graze
> with his head to the wind,

Hedgehog

expect a fine day; but if he crops with tail to the wind, look out for rain during the day.   *

The reader will notice the same pattern of weather saws for goats, sheep and cows - presumably for all domestic grazing animals. The same invalid relationship equally applies here.

Hare

When hares move from low to high ground, very heavy rain and floods are expected.   *

Another high to low ground for bad weather theory.

Hedgehog

Observe which way the hedgehog builds her nest,
To front the north or south, or east or west;
For if tis true that common people say,
The wind will blow the quite contrary way.   **

The hedgehog commonly has two holes or vents in his den or cave, the one towards the south and the other towards the north; and look which one of them he stops - thence will great storms and winds follow.   **

Similar maxims can be found in the Mice and Mole sections. Again it is dubious whether such operations are related to warm and cold weather.

Horse

If horses stretch out their necks and sniff the air, rain will ensue.   *

Leech

> *Horses sweating in the stable is a sign of rain.*   *

> *If they start more than ordinary and are restless and uneasy, or if they assemble in the corner of a field with their heads to leeward, expect rain.*   **

> *If young horses do rub their backs against the ground, it is a sign of great drops of rain to follow.*   *

> *Horses and mules, if very lively without apparent cause, indicate cold.*   **

> *When horses lie on their heads upon the ground, it is a sign of rain.*   *

All six sayings have no truth in their weather connections. As in the Cat section, the various horse's actions are due to natural causes or health reasons.

Leech

> *A leech confined in a bottle of water is always agitated when a change of weather is about to take place. Before high winds it moves about with much celerity. Previous to slight rain or snow it creeps to the top of the bottle, but soon sinks; but if the rain or wind is likely to be of long duration, the leech remains a longer time at the surface. If thunder approaches, the leech starts about in an agitated and convulsive manner.*   **

Leech

The Medicinal Leech *(Hirudo Medicinalis)* used by old-style apothecaries for sucking human blood was often agile when placed in water. This observation inspired a certain Dr George Merryweather (a most appropriate name), a general practitioner of Whitby, North Yorkshire, to conceive an apparatus for forecasting tempests. He described the invention seen in the figure as "an atmospheric Electromagnetic Telegraph, conducted by Animal Instinct. The Tempest Prognosticator - two words expressive enough to all foreigners to understand." The illustration is from his original machine exhibited at London's Great Exhibition of 1851 expecting that "our Whitby pigmy temples" would be distributed all over England.

MOUSE

The machine (a copy is on view in the Whitby museum) consisted of 12-pint bottles of clear glass distributed around the base of a circular wooden stand. At the top was a bell surrounded by 12 hammers. Each bottle with a metal tube in its neck had a piece of whale bone and wire attached to a small chain which in turn was connected to the upper hammers. Then "into each bottle was poured rainwater to the height of an inch and a half, and a leech was placed into every bottle, - when influenced by the electromagnetic state of the atmosphere a number of the leeches ascended into the tubes; in doing so they dislodged the whalebone and caused the bell to ring." Dr Merryweather was so convinced of the leech's prognostic powers that he besought the Government to establish leech-warning stations, which needless to say were turned down.

MOUSE

If mice run about more than usual, wet weather may be expected. **

When the field mouse makes its burrow with the opening to the south, it expects a severe winter; when to the north, it apprehends much rain. *

The first saw is similar to the Rat saying. Wiltshire comes up with the last adage and is identical in meaning to one of the Hedgehog maxims. A Field Mouse to purposely build his home entrance facing south for warm weather or north for cold seems highly unlikely. The convenience of food and lie of the ground are more likely factors.

MOLE

Moles plying their works, in undermining the earth, foreshows rain; but if they do forsake their trenches and creep above ground in summertime, it is a sign of hot weather; but if all of a sudden they do foresake the valleys and low grounds, it

MOLE

foreshows a flood near at hand; but their coming into meadows presages fair weather, and for certain no floods. *

Previous to the setting in of winter the mole prepares a sort of basin, forming it in a bed of clay, which will hold about a quart. In this basin a great quantity of worms is deposited; and, in order to prevent their escape, they a partly mutilated, but not so much as to kill them. On these worms the moles feed in the winter months. When these basins are few in number, the following winter will be mild. **

If moles throw up their earth more than usual, rain is indicated. *

When the mole throws up fresh earth during a frost, it will thaw in less than forty-eight hours. *

When moles dig holes as usual but build no hills on the surface, a long dry spell is expected. *

It is almost tempting to believe some of these weather saws, they appear to include undeniable facts. Unfortunately there is little truth in the mole's prowess as a weather forecaster. This likeable "gentleman in velvet" is a loner with a great appetite for earthworms. His nest chamber or "fortress" is joined by numerous escape and feed tunnels. The key to the meaning of the saying is the availability of the earthworm. The adult mole is constantly on the move, capable of devouring 50 or 60 worms or grubs each day. If he leaves off hunting for 10 hours death is certain. So if previous seasons have produced an excess or deficite of worms appropriate methods have to be employed by the mole. The second saw is perfectly true - the mole always stores worms for winter. In fact *during* a very cold winter,

Pig

since he does not hibernate, he burrows deeper into the ground, as do other grubs and worms, thus the same feeding pattern continues but at a lower depth.

Pig

> *Hogs crying and running unquietly up and down with hay or litter in their mouths foreshadows a storm to be near at hand.* ✱

> *When pigs carry straw to their sties, bad weather may be expected.* ✱

> *When pigs carry sticks, The clouds will play tricks; When they lie in the mud, No fears of a flood.* ✱

> *Hogs rubbing themselves in winter indicate a thaw.* ✱

The usual set of animal quirks related to weather. All are false being caused by medical, hunger or other obvious reasons.

> *Swine are so terrified and disturbed when the wind is getting up, that countrymen say that this animal alone "sees the wind", and that it must be frightful to look at.* ✱

This Lord Bacon pig (it had to happen!) weather maxim renders further investigation. There is obviously little truth in the adage but it is interesting to wonder how the relationship between pigs and winds evolved. Is the phrase "pigs might fly" connected?

Rabbit

> *When rabbits are out at strange times of day rain is expected.* ✱

Sheep

No meteorological connections occur here.

Rat

*If rats are more restless than
usual, rain is at hand.* ✱

Although rats are experts of conditioning, the "more restless" habit is really old hat.

Sheep

*If old sheep turn their backs
towards the wind, and remain so
for some time, wet and windy
weather is coming.* ✱

*When sheep turn their backs to
the wind, it is a sign of rain.* ✱

SHEEP

Sheep act similarly to cows in that they are susceptible to adverse weather conditions. It was closely observed by the author (in Yorkshire 1980) that sheep reacted only to *present* weather types.

> *All shepherds agree in saying that before a storm comes sheep become frisky, leap and butt or "box" each other.* *
>
> *If sheep gambol and fight, or retire to shelter, it presages a change in the weather.* *

Again excess or lack of sheep activity seemed to occur *during* a particular weather condition.

> *Old sheep are said to eat more greedily before a storm, and sparingly before a thaw. When they leave the high grounds, and bleat much in the evening and during the night, severe weather is expected. In winter, when they feed down the hill, a snow storm is looked for; when they feed up the burn, wet weather is near.* ***
>
> *If sheep feed uphill in the morning, a sign of fine weather.* ***
>
> *When a moorland shepherd meets his sheep on a winter's night coming down from the hill-tops (where they prefer to sleep) he knows that a storm is brewing.* ***
>
> *When sheep begin to go up the mountains, shepherds say it will be a fine day.* ***

Derbyshire provides the second adage. Sheep do feed on hills or in valleys when warm or cold weather prevails. It was observed that at least 12-24 hours of the appropriate weather had

Sheep

to occur before sheep took up their relevant residence. Not forgetting that areas of new grass would also influence their move.

> *When sheep do huddle by tree and bush,*
> *Bad weather is coming with wind and slush.* ***

Sheep huddle together, more in wet weather than dry. Their sheltering against fences or walls in foul weather is a fallacy.

Sheep next to hedge in:-

Moderate or heavy rain	21/165	(13)
Slight rain	16/237	(7)
Dry overcast weather	21/405	(5)
A clear sky	81/414	(20)

Sheep huddling in:-

Moderate or heavy rain	57/165	(35)
Slight rain	78/237	(33)
Dry overcast weather	102/405	(25)
A clear sky	54/414	(13)

> *In a long cold spell, pregnant sheep will hang on to their lambs, with rain and higher temperatures they all lamb at once.*

Lambing is in full swing in February. On the whole ewes drop their offspring after the normal 145-150-day gestation period. February can have cold snowy or warm dry days.

Squirrel

> *When squirrels lay in a large supply of nuts, expect a cold winter; but:* **
> *When he eats them on the tree, Weather as warm as warm can be.* **

This adage is like the "red berries, severe winter" theme. Abundant nuts due to a previous good weather winter, spring and summer are the reasons for the squirrel's avarice.

WORM

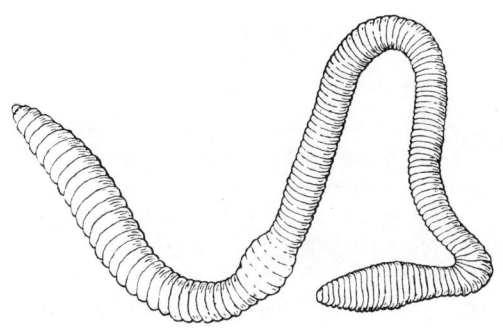

If many earthworms appear, it presages rain. ✸✸

What reader has not seen earthworms appear at night under a heavy dew on the lawn and when digging to find them for fishing bait. They are always found in moist soil. The earthworm experiences 75-90 percent of its body weight made up of water so consequently has to keep to wet earth. But the main reason for the night appearance of many earthworms is temperature and light. They are most active when the soil temperature ranges 2-10.5°C with rain to have fallen within the previous four days. It also possesses a diffuse light sense which attracts it to *dim* light. All these factors account for the above saw which contains no forecast value.

When the common garden worm forms many "casts", rain or frost will follow according to the season of the year. Where they appear in the daytime, expect rain; but when early in the evening, it indicates a mild night with heavy dew and two days fine weather. ✸✸

Worms descend to a great depth before either a long drought or

Frog

> *a severe frost.* ✱✱

The earthworm descends low into the ground because of *present* soil conditions. That is it becomes too dry with near-surface temperature falling low.

REPTILES

> *Almost any of the reptiles which pass the winter in a semi-dormant condition show signs by their attitude when any marked weather change ensues.*

This is perfectly true. Semi-dormant reptiles on encountering long periods of warm weather in winter or early spring will normally react as if official spring had arrived.

Frog

> *Croaking frogs in spring*
> *We'll be three times frozen in.* ✱

Male frogs croak at night in March to attract females. So chances are they could be frozen three or more times. All frogs make noises which mainly relate to social intercourse.

> *The louder the frog, the more the rain.* ✱

> *If frogs make a noise in the time of cold rain, warm dry weather will follow.*

Noise often travels quicker in stable windy conditions, often to be experienced before rain, so a male frog's croak would carry far (see Sound chapter). The second adage seems ludicrous.

> *Yellow frogs are accounted a good sign in a hay field, probably as indicating fine weather.* ✱

SNAKE

> *If frogs, instead of yellow,*
> *appear russet green, it will*
> *presently rain.* *

  The Common male Frog is olive grey or brown and female a light buff to reddish olive, but both can to some extent vary their shades according to the colour of the background. So the reason is due to camouflage not meteorology.

> *Great quantities of frogs,*
> *small and great, appearing at*
> *unusual times and in unusual*
> *places, presage great dearth*
> *of corn or great sickness to*
> *follow: where they appear.* **

  Female frogs produce thousands of tadpoles but as easy prey to other animals, birds and fish, only a steady number survive as frogs around June (three months of evolution from spawn to frog). So a great quantity shows some upset in the natural sequence.

> *Tree-frogs piping during rain*
> *indicate a continuance.* *

> *The green tree-frog becomes*
> *very unquiet before rain.* *

> *Tree-frogs crawl up to the*
> *branches of trees before a*
> *change of weather.* *

  The last saw is interesting. In olden times, especially in Germany, the Common or Green Tree Frog was kept as an animal barometer in tall glass cylinders with tiny ladders inside and water at the bottom. When the tree frog sat on the top rung it was a sign of "set fair" weather - to return to the water signified an approaching thunderstorm. Like the leech the tree frog unfortunately does not react to atmospheric pressure.

SNAKE

> *Snakes are out before rain,*
> *and are therefore more easily*
> *killed.* *

Snake

When snakes are hunting food, rain may be expected; after a rain they cannot be found. *

Snake trails may be seen before houses before rain. *

Rain is foretold by the appearance and activity of snakes. *

If snails and slugs come out abundantly, it is a sign of rain. *

The predominant theme of snakes and rain may be connected with the three English snake's great fondness of water and swimming. Certainly the Viper, Grass and rarer Smooth Snake will bask or rest in warm sunny weather, so it is quite possible the countryman has related the snake's active feeding time (May to October - they hibernate in winter) to rain. Unfortunately snakes are bad weather prophets.

Toad

When the toad is of a browner colour than usual, expect rain. *

If toads come out of their holes in great numbers, rain will fall soon. **

Both similar to saws in the Frog section.

Tortoise

Ant

> *Tortoises creep deep into the ground, so as to completely conceal themselves from view, when a severe winter is to follow.* *

This theme occurs in many animal weather sayings. The tortoise hibernates deep into the ground through *present* cold weather conditions.

INSECTS

Ant

> *Ants withdraw into their nests and busy themselves with their eggs before a storm.* ***

> *If ants are more than ordinarily active, or if they remove their eggs from small hills, it will surely rain.* ***

The world of the ant is similar to the bee. A very highly developed social order and purpose has formulated. Before the reader tries to infer ants as invokers of sun or rain let us quickly crush this hope by saying that there is little evidence to justify such a thought. Having stated this one still has to marvel at their advanced senses and discipline. The saws are true in that worker ants frequently change the position of their eggs or larvae around in the nest chambers according to change in temperature and humidity of *present* conditions.

> *Ants sometimes get down fifteen inches from the surface before very hot weather.* **

> *If ants their walls do frequent build,*
> *Rain will from the clouds be spilled.* **

Honey Bee

> *When ants are situated in low
> ground, their migration may be
> taken as an indication of
> approaching heavy rain.* **

> *In the beginning of July the
> ants are enlarging and building
> up their piles, an early and
> cold winter will follow.* *

> *An open ant hole indicates
> clear weather, a closed one,
> an approaching storm.* *

With their unique language of odours, especially with regard to food smell and alarm scents, the observations in the sayings are probably correct but only regarding ant activity.

> *Expect stormy weather when ants
> travel in lines, and fair
> weather when they scatter.* ***

Another marvellous countryman's observation is of ant movement. In 1933 T.C.Schneirla found with use of a mirror that a homing ant's path is partly guided by the direction of the sun. It seems that the ant also compensates for gravity. Cloudy conditions would presumably see the ant following a meandering course.

Honey Bee

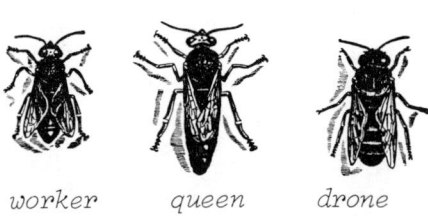

worker   queen   drone

> *Bees early at work will not go
> on all day.*

Honey bees have possibly the most highly developed social laws and senses in the insect world. The worker bee (the one who performs the gathering and storing of flower nectar and pollen) is always more active in warm sunny but calm or light breezy days. It hates wet stormy or cold weather. So, as the

Honey Bee

saw suggests, an early warm sunny start will allow flowers to open allowing the worker bee to go about his task. His labour rate is so fast, an early ending becomes apparent by late afternoon.

>*Bees will not swarm
>Before a near storm.* ✱✱✱✱✱

>*When the bees crowd out their hive,
>The weather makes it good to be alive.* ✱✱

>*When the bees crowd into their hive again
>It is a sign of thunder and of rain.* ✱✱

The first saying is absolutely true. The first swarm with the old queen takes place in quiet placid sunny weather. Swarms *do* occur in rain showers and storms but only with very young queens. The second and third saws may apply to these differing swarms.

>*When bees to distance wing their flight,
>Days are warm and skies are bright;* ✱✱✱✱
>*But when their flight ends near their home,
>Stormy weather is sure to come.* ✱✱✱✱

>*If bees stay at home,
>Rain will soon come;* ✱✱✱✱
>*If they fly away,
>Fine will be the day.* ✱✱✱✱

>*A bee was never caught
>in a shower.* ✱✱✱

Foraging of nectar and pollen by the worker bee is perfect over long distances in quiet sunny weather. Rain or showers have a hostile effect on them by drastically cutting down their search radius. Infact they possess a biological clock which gives them an instant indication of the sun's position even

Beetle

on partly cloudy days. Their social contact is so advanced that a worker returning from a new nectar source will perform the "bee dance" in the hive by waggling its body into a rough figure of eight. The angle of the diagonal combined with the sun's position instantly communicates the distance and direction of the nectar to the other bees.

> *Whenever the bees get about in February, I have always noticed that we are certain to get wind and rain next day.* **

When warm February weather occurs, worker bees become restless. Whether the settled conditions continue or not is unrelated to the bees.

> *A swarm of bees in May is worth a load of hay,* *****
> *A swarm of bees in June is worth a silver spoon,* ****
> *A swarm of bees in July is not worth a fly.* ***

Refer to the May chapter for the meaning of this saw.

Beetle

> *The clock beetle, which flies about in the summer evenings in a circular direction, with a loud, buzzing noise, is said to foretell a fine day.* ***

> *If the clock beetle flies in a circle and buzzes, it is a sign of fine weather.* ***

> *A certain long-bodied beetle is called in Bedfordshire the "rain beetle", on account of always appearing before rain.* ***

192

BUTTERFLY

Bedfordshire provides this adage. Apparently the Rain Beetle is any of several black hairy beetles that belong to the genus *Pleocoma*, closely related to the Scarab Beetle.

> *When little black insects appear
> on the snow, expect a thaw.* ✱✱✱

Presumably the start of a mild spell is the cause for a sudden appearance of black insects.

BUTTERFLY

> *The early appearance of
> butterflies is said to
> indicate fine weather.* ✱✱✱

Abundance of butterflies of course means a previous excellent breeding season when all conditions were perfect. Also butterflies are chiefly seen in warm sunny weather.

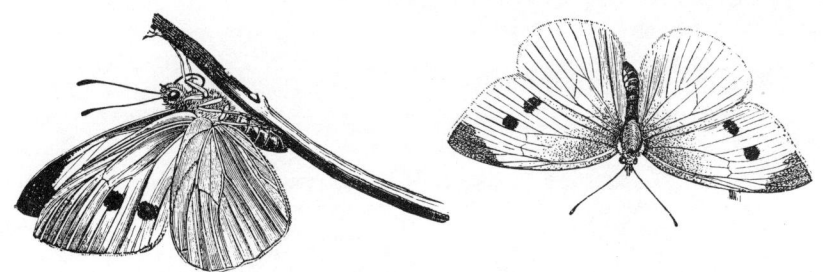

> *When the white butterfly flies
> from the south-west, expect rain.*

A South-Westerly is notorious for rain and changeable weather. The insertion of the White Butterfly in the adage just specifies the time of year - summer.

CRICKET

> *Before rain the beetles and
> crickets are more troublesome
> than usual.* ✱✱

Fly

> *When crickets chirp unusually,
> wet is expected.* **

Classical response to forthcoming rain - all false.

Firefly

> *Fireflies in great numbers
> indicate fair weather.* **

This saying has the usual theme where excess numbers of insects indicate good weather - all incorrect.

Flea

> *When fleas do very many grow
> Then twill surely rain or snow.* **

> *When eager bites the thirsty
> flea
> Clouds and rain you sure shall
> see.* *

The second saw is like the first fly maxim. No reliability can be placed here.

Fly

> *If flies' stings are more
> troublesome than usual,
> change approaches.* **

Fly

> *When harvest flies hum,*
> *Warm weather to come.* **

The fly sayings are all related to *actual* weather conditions. They are separated into their specific groups.

> *House flies coming into the house*
> *in great numbers indicate rain.* **

> *If flies in the spring or*
> *summer grow busier or blinder*
> *than at other times, or are*
> *seen to shroud themselves in*
> *warm places, expect either*
> *hail, cold storms of rain,*
> *or much wet weather.* **

The usual activity theme.

> *A fly on your nose, you slap, and*
> *and it goes;*
> *If it comes back again, it will*
> *bring a good rain.* *

> *If flies cling much to the*
> *ceilings, or disappear,*
> *rain may be expected.* *

Silly but likeable saws.

> *If in autumn the flies repair*
> *unto their winter quarters,*
> *it presages frosty mornings,*
> *cold storms, and the approach*
> *of winter. Storms or small*
> *flies swarming together and*
> *sporting in the sunbeams give*
> *omen of fair weather.* **

The fly becomes a sensational weather prophet.

Glow Worm

Gnat

*When the glow-worm lights her
lamp,
The air is always damp.* ✱✱

*If glow-worms shine much, it
will rain.* ✱✱

*When they shine more brightly
than usual, they indicate rain
within forty-eight hours, more
especially when they remain
luminous a short time after
midnight.* ✱✱

No forecast of rain applies here. The wingless female glow-worm (*Lampyris noctiluca*), which is a beetle, emits small areas of intermittent green light on her thorax and abdomen. The larvae also transmit this nightime luminescence. The glow is only connected with mating.

Gnat

*If little flies or gnats be
seen to hover together about
the beams of the sun before
it set, and fly together,
making, as it were, the form
of a pillar, it is a sure
token of fair weather.* ✱✱

*If gnats play up and down, it
is a sign of heat, but if in
the shade, it presages mild
showers. If they collect in
the evening before sunset,
and form a vortex or column,
fine weather will follow;
while if they sting much, it
is held to be an unfailing
indication of rain.* ✱✱

*If gnats fly in compact bodies
in the beams of the setting
sun, expect fine weather.* ✱✱

Hundreds of male gnats or midges forming a pillar or mass above the ground on a summer's evening usually occurs in Sept-

Snail

ember. They are waiting for a female easily recognised by her flight tone of 300 beats per second which they receive on an antenna. Although the mass flight takes place on a warm evening the maxim's meaning is of a sexual not a forecasting nature.

> *Many gnats in spring indicate*
> *that the autumn will be warm.*   ****

Abundant gnats in spring indicate a warm season. Warm or very warm springs were tested for similar autumns resulting in a low figure of 49 percent.   55/112   (49)

> *Gnats in October are a sign of*
> *long fair weather.*   **

Gnats in October are a sign of unusual warm weather which may or may not last.

> *If gnats fly in large numbers,*
> *the weather will be fine.*   **

> *If gnats bite sharper than usual,*
> *expect rain.*   **

Familiar themes covered by most insect weather lore.

Hornet

> *Hornets building nests high*
> *before warm summers, and low*
> *before cold and early winters.*   *

Akin to rook weather lore with similar conclusions.

Snail

> *When black snails cross your*
> *path,*
> *Black cloud much moisture hath.*   *

> *Black snails indicate black*
> *clouds with much moisture.*   *

Spider

Because most slugs and snails like moist areas it probably represents the main reason for their pseudo reputation as rain prophets.

Spider

Spiders work hard and spin their webs a little before wind, as if desiring to anticipate it, for they cannot spin when the wind begins to blow. *

Before rain or wind spiders fix their frame-lines unusually short. If they make them very long, the weather will usually be fine for fourteen days. *

If spiders break off and remove their webs, the weather will be wet. *

If spiders make new webs, and ants build near hills, the weather will be clear. *

When the spider cleans its web, fair weather is indicated. *

If spiders in spinning their webs make the terminating filaments long, we may, in proportion to their length, expect rain. *

When spiders' webs in air do fly,

SPIDER

The spell will soon be very dry. ✳✳

If spiders undo their webs, tempests follow. ✳

If the garden spiders break and destroy their webs and creep away, expect continued rain. ✳

The majority of spider weather lore are concerned with its web. All kinds of future weather has been attributed to this creature. Unfortunately no such prophetic power exists. Like so many instances in animal saws they react to *present* weather conditions. Of the several hundred kinds of spiders in this country no two spin their web in the same way.

Spiders' webs scattered thickly over a field covered with dew glistening in the morning sun indicate rain. ✳✳✳

When you see a gossamer flying, Be sure the air is drying. ✳✳✳

The gossamer or fine thread found on calm autumn mornings in dewy fields is also dealt with in the November chapter. Gossamer is initiated by hundreds of tiny baby spiders just out of the cocoon. On a quiet warm autumn evening they stand on the ends of plants and grass and pour out a stream of silk which is gently caught by any breeze leaving the fields covered in fine gossamer. Such fine mornings may or may not last.

If the spiders are indolent, rain generally soon follows. Their activity during rain is a certain proof of its short duration. If they mend their webs between six and seven pm, it is the sign of a serene night. ✳

If the spider works during rain, it is an indication that the weather will soon be clear. ✳

Spider

*Spiders, when they are seen
crawling on the walls more
than usually, indicate that
rain will probably ensue.
This prognostic seldom fails,
particularly in winter.* ∗∗∗

Spiders do spin webs in slight rain but avoid activity in heavier precipitation or strong winds. Again victims of prevailing weather conditions.

*When, after a long drought, you
observe in hedges some very
densely-woven webs, funnel-shaped,
there will be a change of weather
within three days.* ∗∗

Whichever species of spider spin this type of web they would not have any pre-knowledge of future weather.

Spiders bring an easterly wind.

This maxim from Whitstable, Kent, is intriguing in its strangeness. One cannot possibly think how the easterly wind becomes apparent with a spider's appearance. Even in early November when baby spiders emerge the normal weather pattern is unsettled and mobile. (See November chapter.)

*If spiders fall from their webs
or from the walls, it signifyeth
rain.* ∗

Presumably sudden increase in wind would be the cause for falling spiders.

Wasp

*When wasps build their nests
high on the banks of a stream
you may expect a wet summer;
but if near the level of the
water, a dry summer is said to
be indicated.* ∗

Wasp

Wasps building nests in exposed places indicate a dry season.   *

These two maxims follow the usual run of mill activities in animal and insect weather - both being false.

Woodlice

If wood lice run about in great numbers, expect rain.   **

This theme can be found in many insect weather adages.

Cicada Lava

It is easy to foretell what sort of summer it will be by the position in which the lava of Cicada (Aphrophora Spumaria) is found to lie in the froth or cuckoo spit in which it is enveloped. If the insect lie with its head upwards, it infallibly denotes a dry summer; if downward, a wet one.   *

This beautiful piece of country weather lore seems a shame to discredit. One almost feels one wants to forget the scientific and statistical evidence and believe in such a delightfully written tale. But the position of the larva depends on the weather conditions *at the time*.

MOON

Weather lore related to the moon is both varied and fascinating, except for lunar haloes and colourings (refer to solar and lunar and sky colours chapters), there is no truth in them. Apart from the moon causing a very small measurable tidal movement of the Earth's atmosphere and sea tides (which has negligible effect on the weather), no other meteorological consequence is detectable. One wise sage obviously know this when he originated the famous true weather saw below.

The moon and the weather
May change together,
But change of the moon
Does not change the weather.
If we'd no moon at all,
And that may seem strange,
We still should have weather
That's subject to change. ✶✶✶✶✶✶

Parhelia, or mock suns, and
paraselenae, or mock moons,
very seldon occur, but are
generally followed by fair
weather. ✶✶✶

MOON

> *If two or three moons appear at
> a time, it presages great wind
> and rain and unseasonable
> weather for a long time to
> follow.* ****

The two or three moons refer to the paraselenae or "mock moons". They are moon images very similar to "mock suns" or parahelia. These weak mock moons are seen on either side of the moon at the same elevation (a single one occurs on one side). They are caused by refraction or bending of moonlight as it hits ice crystals (hexagonal) in high Cirrus clouds (see cloud chapter). Mock moons are poorly coloured and very rare because of their weak light intensity. They are therefore mostly seen at time of full moon. The suggestion of observing them 2 to 3 days after full moon in the above saw therefore seems strange.

> *Moonlit nights have the
> hardest frosts.* ***
>
> *Clear moon
> Frost soon.* ****

Moonlit nights (the few days around full moon) are only visible with little or no cloud, which of course is perfect for the lowest temperatures which frequently produce frosts in the winter half year. The saying is untrue in summer.

> *The moon appearing larger at
> sunset, and not dim, but
> luminous, portends fair weather
> for several days.* ***

This is a Bacon maxim. The appearance of a clear moon, whatever phase it has reached, again means the sky is clear or partly cloudy at that time. Sometimes these dry conditions can last a few hours or for days. A cloudy moon would have similar results. The significance of the clear moon at sunset is clever as it is the time of day when unstable cloud disperses inland. The saying has little else to offer.

> *If the full moon rises red,
> expect wind.* ****

Moon

> *If the full moon rises pale,*
> *expect rain.* ****

> *If the moon appears a reddish-*
> *brown through the haze, the*
> *weather will stay fair.* ****

Moon colour saws are similar to those in the Sun chapter.

> *A fog and a small moon*
> *Bring an easterly wind soon.* *

A Cornish saw not unlike a saying in the South wind chapter where "a southerly wind" is substituted here by "a small moon". The poor results there (29 percent) equally apply here.

> *If the moon changes with the*
> *wind in the east, the weather*
> *during that moon will be foul.* *

Moon changes strictly apply to the four phases or quarters (first quarter, full moon, last quarter and new moon), each change lasting about 7 days. But most people remember just the new and full moon. These were tested with an Easterly wind over the period 1959-71 with the weather during the following week where at least 5 days had to be wet.   7/69 (10)

> *Five changes of the moon in one*
> *calendar month indicate cooler*
> *weather.* ***

A lunar cycle is 28 days so some calendar months can include 5 lunar phases. These, for some magical reason, are supposed to bring cooler weather. 38 percent such cases were true.
11/29 (38)

> *If the lunar period has*
> *continued rainy throughout,*
> *good weather will follow for*
> *several days, followed by*
> *another period of rain, and*
> *vice versa.* *

MOON

If the moon be fair throughout and rain at the close, the fair weather will probably return on the fourth or fifth day.   *

If the moon is rainy throughout, it will be clear at the change, and perhaps the rain will return a few days later.   *

In general a rainy period suggests a mobile weather pattern which can either continue or experience a temporary or complete change. The moon takes no part in these natural weather sequencies.

When the moon runs low, expect warm weather.   *

The moon's low orbit has no influence on the weather.

When the moon runs high, expect cool or cold weather.   *

A dry moon is far north and soon seen.   *

The farther the moon is to the south, the greater the drought, the further west the greater the flood, and the farther north-west, the greater the cold.   *

If the new moon is far north, it will be cold for two weeks; but if far south, it will be warm.   *

New moon far in the north, in summer, cool weather, in winter, cold.   *

New moon far in the south indicates dry weather for a month.   *

Moon

The various orbital positions of the moon in relation to an observer on the Earth bears no relationship with weather.

> *If the moon is seen between the scud and broken clouds during a gale, it is expected to cuff away the bad weather.* ∗∗

"Scud" refers to fast-moving clouds, "cuff away" means to strike away. But regardless how colloquial the saying is, there is no moon/weather relationship.

> *Sowe peason and beans in the wane of the moon,*
> *Who soweth them sooner, he soweth too soon.* ∗

This is one of the famous "waxing and waning" pieces of moon farming lore. Of course waxing is the increasing of the moon (new to full) and waning the decreasing (full to new) in the moon's illumination. Waxing was always thought to bring cold weather, so sowing peas and beans would traditionally be a pointless task.

> *The weather that comes in with the moon will stay like it for a month.* ∗

Hopeless results.   0/161 (0)

> *When the moon is visible in the daytime, the days are relatively cool.*

Visible lunar orbits in the daytime only suggest clear or partly cloudy skies.

> *Frost occurring in the dark side of the moon kills fruit buds and blossoms, but frost in the light of the moon will not.* ∗

Moon

Another famous old superstition that frost occurring in the old and new moon is more severe than under a full moon. The latter is supposed to have magical "warming" powers from its extreme moonlight. Nice but fictional.

If the moon appears with the points of the crescent turned up, the month will be dry. If the points are turned down, it will be wet. *

A new moon with sharp horns threatens windy weather. *

If one horn of the moon is sharp and pointed, the other being more blunt, it rather indicates wind; but if both are so, it denotes rain. *

Sharp horns do threaten windy weather. *

People speak of the new moon lying on her back or being ill-made as a prognostic of wet weather. *

New moon on its back indicates wind; standing on its point indicates rain in summer and snow in winter. *

The bonnie moon is on her back;
Mend your shoes and sort your thack. *

If the moon is on its back in the third quarter, it is a sign of rain.

When the moon lies on her back,
Then the south-west wind will crack; *
When she rises up and nods,
Then north-easters dry the sods. *

Moon

When the new moon lies on her back,
She sucks the wet into her lap.   *

When the moon's horns are sharp
and well defined, expect rain
the following day, or, in
winter, frost.   *

The third maxim comes from the ancient pen of Bacon and 10th hails from Ellesmere in Shropshire. Variations of these famous new moon saws are concerned with the rare occurrence of its up-or-down turned points and sharp or blunt '"horns". The major myth childishly relates that rain is held in reserve in the upturned points for wet weather to come. Conversely the down-turned hold no water so dry weather will follow. This explanation is contradicted in the first saw. Again all these maxims are untrue.

If a snow storm begins when the
moon is young, it will cease at
moonrise.   *

At the time of the new or full
moon when the present weather
continues stormy and wet turning
to clear and dry; one forecasts
the fine weather to remain for
the following quarter. If it
lasts it usually continues until
the next full or new moon. If
it lasts this long it will be
probably fine for a total of
four or five weeks.   *

As many days from the first new
moon, so many times will it
thaw during winter.   *

Really one has to wonder at the inventiveness of these sayings.

If mist in the new moon,
rain in the old;   ***
If mist in the old moon,
rain in the new.   ***

Moon

> *Auld moon mist*
> *Ne'er died of thirst.*   ***

The first four days of the new moon and last four days of the old were tested. At least two days from each period had to have its appropriate forecast weather. Again all contained unsatisfactory results.

                 Mists in new moon rain in old   17/38   (45)
                 .. .. old .. .. .. new   12/30   (40)

> *When the new moon comes in at*
> *midnight, or within thirty*
> *minutes before or after, the*
> *following month will be fine.*   **

A novel maxim with a low rating.   3/10   (30)

> *When the change of the moon*
> *occurs in the morning, expect*
> *rain.*   ****

> *Moon changing in morning*
> *indicates warm weather; in*   **
> *the evening, cold weather.*   **

The change of moon was more likely to be a full or new moon. Morning was defined as 0001-1200 local time and evening 1700-2230 with warm or cold weather to follow within two days. One can see that poor results emerge.

                 Morning moon then rain   71/137   (52)
                 Morning moon then warm weather   35/137   (25)
                 Evening .. .. cold ..   14/67   (21)

> *A Friday's moon*
> *Is a month too soon.*   *

A Sussex saying meaning a Friday's full moon is the worst weekday it could happen for severe weather. "A month too soon" means too premature.

> *A Saturday moon,*
> *If it comes once in seven years,*
> *comes once too soon.*

Moon

A Saturday full moon is a bad one not wanting to be seen during a 7-year period.

> *If the moon on a Saturday be
> new or full,
> There always was rain, and
> there always wull.* ****

A Worcestershire maxim which was tested for new or full moons and rain within two days. For some reason the results are good, in fact the best of the whole moon chapter. Compare these figures with the weekday chapter.   29/48 (60)

> *Saturday's change and Sunday's
> full
> Never brought good and never
> brought wull.* *

> *A Saturday's change and a
> Sunday's full moon
> Once in seven years is once
> too soon.* *

> *A Saturday's change and a
> Sunday's full
> Comes too soon whenever it wull.* *

Norfolk originated the first adage and Dorset the third. The general flow is "Saturday change and Sunday's full" and does *not* refer to a Saturday moon "change". It is a weather change from bad to good continuing into Sunday with clear weather when the full moon can be observed. Of the 23 Sunday full moons from 1959-71, 15 were visible, but no major change occurred on the previous Saturday, so a test was not run.

> *If the moon changes on a Sunday,
> there will be a flood before the
> month is out.* **

A Worcestershire saw with new and full moon changes.
          12/41 (29)

MOON

> *The nearer to twelve in the*
> *afternoon, the drier the moon*   ✱✱✱
> *The nearer to twelve in the*
> *forenoon, the wetter the moon.*   ✱✱✱

A Herefordshire maxim. The full moon is the one tested with a dry moon occurring 1200-1800 local time and a wet moon 0600-1200. Only average results emerge.

            Wet 0600-1200 local time   19/43   (44)
            Dry 1200-1800   ..   ..   15/31   (48)

> *A hundred hours after the new*
> *moon regulates the weather*
> *for the month.*   ✱✱

An unusual Huntingdonshire saw. Around 4 days after a new moon the weather (combination of rainfall and temperature categories) was tested against similar conditions for the following month but low ratings evolved.   35/146   (24)

> *The first and second never mind,*
> *The third regard not much;*
> *But as the fourth and fifth you*
> *find,*
> *The rest will be as such.*   ✱

Another Huntingdonshire saying following the usual fictional mould.

> *If the new moon is not visible*
> *before the fourth day, the air*
> *will be unsettled for the whole*
> *month.*   ✱✱✱

Bacon penned this one. A shrewd observation that 4 days of unsettled weather usually continues for some time but not usually for a month. The new moon's appearance is immaterial.

> *To see the old moon in the arms*
> *of the new one is reckoned a*
> *sign of fine weather, and so is*   ✱✱✱
> *the turning up of the horns of*
> *the new moon.*   ✱

Moon

*To see the old moon in the arms
of the new one is a sign of bad
weather to come.* ✸✸

The first comes from Suffolk. Both are famous sayings and are opposed in meaning. "To see the old moon in the arms of the new" calls for a very clear atmosphere usually of polar origin. The forecast of fine weather (45 percent) and wet (30 percent) was still an unsatisfactory result.   9/20 (45)
6/20 (30)

*Two full moons in a calendar
month bring on a flood.* ✸

A Bedfordshire maxim implying torrential rain.   0/6 (0)

*The new moon grows fat on
clouds.* ✸✸✸

A beautiful saw meaning that as a moon gets fuller it eats cloud - hence all full moons have clear skies. However only on 43 percent of occasions this happened.   46/106 (43)

*The weather is generally clearer
at the full than at other ages of
the moon; but in winter the
frost then is sometimes more
intense.* ✸✸✸

A Bacon adage with the full moon clear on 43 percent (see previous saw) of occasions and 38 percent under a new moon.
New moon clear   38/100 (38)

*Near full moon, a misty sunrise
Bodes fair weather and cloudless
skies.* ✸✸✸

Similar sayings in the weekday and fog/mist chapters explain this adage. The appearance of a full moon is superfluous.

The full moon brings fine weather. ✸✸✸

Moon

Tested on the weather remaining fine for at least three days after the full moon.   54/158 (34)

If the moon is distinct, neither too sharp in outline nor, on the other hand, "watery" and blurred, the weather will stay fair for the time being.   **

This is not altogether correct. A clear moon, whatever its phase, really denotes clear polar air which is frequently showery by day.

STARS

The obscuring of the smaller stars in a clear night is a sign of rain. ****

When the stars begin to huddle, The earth will soon become a puddle. ****

These two adages are similar. For the stars to "huddle" or be in a confused mass, *Cirrus* cloud is present. The night sky then contains areas of dim stars and clear ones not affected by the *Cirrus*. The saws are true and the percentage figures given in the Cirrus/Cloud Chapter for rain to follow *Cirrus* within one, two or three days apply here.

Excessive twinkling of the stars indicates heavy dews, rain, and snow, and stormy weather in the near future. ***

When the stars flicker in a dark background, rain or snow follows soon. ****

When the sky seems very full of stars expect rain, or, in winter, frost. ****

Excessive star twinkling refers to excellent visibility which means an airstream with a polar origin is imminent. These airstreams are usually blowing in a N.W. to N.E. direction. Any of the weather forecast in the saws could occur but an emphasis on cold temperatures must be an obvious choice.

A star dogging the moon foretells bad weather. *

If a big star is dogging the moon, wild weather may be expected. *

STARS

> *One star ahead of the moon,*
> *towing her, and another astern,*
> *using her, is a sure sign of a*
> *storm.*   *

The third maxim comes from Lancashire. There is absolutely no truth here.

> *Moon in a circle indicates storm,*   *****
> *and number of stars in the circle*
> *indicates the number of days*
> *before a storm.*

The first part is explained in the Moon/Sun Halo Chapter, but the remainder is complete rubbish.

> *Comets are said to bring bad*
> *weather.*   *

> *If many meteors in summer,*
> *expect thunder.*   **

> *After an unusual fall of*
> *meteors, dry weather is*
> *expected.*   ***

A meteor was always regarded as a "shooting star". When appearing in numbers they are known as "meteor showers". Of course they are fragments of solid material entering the Earth's atmosphere at tremendous speeds with blazing trails. There are about 14 periods when these showers reach a maximum frequency. They are 3-4 January, 21 April, 4-6 and 4-23 May, 1-16 June, 26 June-5 July, 28 July, 5-14 Aug, 10 and 20-23 Oct, 3-10 and 16-17 Nov, 12-13 and 22 Dec. The average weather pattern (to be found at the beginning of each month in the Month's Chapter) *after* these dates produced 6 wet, 6 dry and 2 average weather periods. So little reliability can be placed in these maxims.

> *When the water looks black, the*
> *Cornwall folk say the thunder*
> *planet is about and a storm is*
> *coming.*   *

> *It rains by planets.*   *

STARS

Cornwall provides the first saying. The thunder planet remains a mystery.

> *When the Great Bear is on this side of the North Pole, the summer is dry; if he gets on the other side, the summer is wet, especially if he be then in conjunction with Venus and Jupiter.*

Another astronomical-cum-weather adage with hardly any truth.

WIND

Before the middle of the 19th century, when weather charts and the understanding of depression movement evolved, the most useful and regularly used weather lore was related to surface wind direction. Each quadrant, whether south-west or east, had its own individual weather being of paramount importance to the practical lives of farmers, shepherds and all countryfolk.

Wind roaring in chimney, rain to come. ****

A brisk wind generally precedes rain. ****

It is often true that gales or a gradual increase in wind strength often precede rain.

The whispering grove tells of a storm to come. ****

This is mainly associated with showers where gusts of wind and cold downdraughts often occur ahead of a heavy shower or thunderstorm.

Wind storms usually subside about sunset, but if they do not, they will go on for another day. *****

The smaller and lighter winds generally rise in the morning and fall at sunset. *****

These two are wonderful pieces of weather observation. In a gentle airstream the wind will normally increase after sunrise and dramatically decrease around sunset as long as the day is not overcast and air temperature is allowed to rise and fall normally. As the sun rises the temperature profile in the first few hundred feet above the ground (lapse rate) changes

WIND

becoming steeper and therefore unstable. This allows the air to become turbulent with the nett result of strengthening the wind. After the maximum day temperature is reached (around 2-3 pm) it begins to decrease. Its greatest fall is just after sunset, allowing a sudden decrease in the wind speed. If the day has persistent low-cloud cover keeping air temperature steady, or if a strengthening airstream occurs caused by the passage of a depression or trough, wind strength will not follow the normal day and night time pattern. Therefore a strong wind at night often remains another day.

> *When after a rough and stormy day there is a lull at the going down of the sun, old men say: 'Us shall have better weather now, for the wind's gone to sleep with the sun.'* ****

The above saying is from Devon.

> *A storm will go three miles out of its way to come by Habberley to Churton.* ***

> *There'll be some rain, for the wind has got to Habberley Hole.* ****

The first of these Shropshire weather saws relates to the effect of topography on weather. Churton or Church Pulverbatch (Shropshire) lies two miles east of Habberley village which is situated amongst steep hills up to 1,500 feet above sea level. More important is the narrow gorge lying between the villages. This 'funnels' or magnifies the strength of a westerly wind or storm. This is very similar to a wide flowing river increasing its current on entering a narrow channel. The second adage applies to Shrewsbury town lying about 9 miles north-east of Habberly Hole (a long deep ravine). Shrewsbury would receive a wet south-westerly, strengthened by the 'funnelling effect' of Habberly Hole.

> *We shall have rain, for the wind is in Bodjham Hole.* ****

WIND

> *Sure to rain, the wind's in Flammer's Hole.* ****

Bodjham Hole near Ashford Vale in East Kent and Flammer's Hole on the Chilterns above Dunstable, Bedfordshire, continue the topographical story.

> *If rain falls before the wind commences, the wind will last longer than the rain. But if the wind blows first, and is afterwards laid by rain, it does not often rise again, and if it does, it is followed by fresh rain.* ****

This old maxim, mentioned by Bacon, looks long and complicated, but is full of sense and observation.

> *Always a calm before a storm.* ***

> *After a storm comes a calm.* ***

The top phrase is a most famous saying equally applied to weather and human behaviour. Unfortunately, if taken literally, it is not always true. Obviously wind speed will increase and decrease but the only cases for a calm before a storm and vice-versa occur with heavy showers and passages of quiet ridges of high pressure and vigorous depressions.

> *When the wind backs and the weather glass falls,*
> *Then be on your guard against gales and squalls.* ***

Another half-true weather saw. When depressions or troughs cross the British Isles, the wind usually backs (a change from one direction to another in anticlockwise fashion - such as north to west. Veering has the opposite meaning.) before their arrival bringing rain with gales. Backing occurs around sunset with a pressure fall on most days but is not connected with ensuing rain.

WIND

> *The wind is said to go
> "withershins", or contrary to
> the course of the sun.*

> *Winds that change against the sun
> Are always sure to backward run.* ****

> *When the wind veers against the sun,
> Trust it not, for back 'twill run.* ****

> *The veering of the wind with
> the sun prognosticates drier
> or better weather; the backing
> of the wind against the sun,
> indicates rain, or more wind,
> or both together.* ****

> *A veering wind, fair weather.* ****
> *A backing wind, foul weather.* ****

"Withershins" or "widdershins' mean a backing in the wind from west to east against the apparent course of the sun in these northern latitudes. It is always a good rule that when a strong wind backs rain is sure to follow.

> *It is a sign of continued fine
> weather when the wind changes
> during the day so as to follow
> the sun.* **

This seems correct at first glance but it is rare for the wind to veer from east to west during daylight.

> *If the wind follows the sun's
> course, expect fair weather.* ****

This is subtly different from the previous saying beginning with poor weather and ending with settled conditions.

WIND

> *In the northern hemisphere a
> person with his back to the
> wind has lower pressure on his
> left hand side than on his
> right - the converse is true
> in the southern hemisphere.* *****

A man called Buys Ballot of Utrecht originated this correct law in 1857. Imagine a depression or low, i.e. a circle of winds blowing in an anticlockwise direction (in the northern hemisphere). Now if the centre was situated in the Midlands, southern England would experience a westerly wind - so with one's back to it, the left-hand side would point north towards the lower pressure (the depression centre).

> *A sudden storm lasts not three
> hours.* ****

> *The sharper the blast
> The sooner 'tis past.* ****

Sudden storms or winds usually pass with a quick passage, but if wind increases gradually, it generally lasts longer.

> *Winds changing from foul to
> fair during the night are not
> permanent.* ***

> *A blustering night can lead to
> a fair day.* ***

The effect of nightime is unimportant in these two saws. Foul to fair changes can equally be permanent or temporary. The controlling factors of the true meaning lie elsewhere.

> *The wind never blows steadily,
> whether it be a winter's storm
> or a mild summer's breeze, but
> always in what the old
> wind-millers used to call
> plervets.* *****

The wind trace shows a continual reading. It is typical of

Wind

a breeze with the characteristic high and low gust range. The speed is never steady, but fluctuates within a few knots in as many seconds. The direction reacts similarly but is even more sensitive, often ranging over 60 degrees in one second.

> *Wind east or west*
> *Is a sign of a blast;*
> *Wind north or south*
> *Is a sign of drought.*

    ****

    ***

> *North wind cold,*
> *East wind dry*
> *South wind warm and often wet,*
> *West wind generally rainy.*

    ****

> *The south wind always brings wet weather,*
> *The north wind wet and cold together;*
> *The west wind always brings us rain,*
> *The east wind blows it back again.*

    ****

> *North winds send hail, south winds bring rain,*
> *East winds we bewail, west winds blow amain;*
> *North-east is too cold, south-west not too warm,*
> *North-west is too bold, south-west does no harm.*
> *The north is a noyer to grass of all suites,*
> *The east is destroyer to herb and all fruits;*
> *The south, with his showers, refresheth the corn,*
> *The west to all flowers may not be foreborne.*
> *The west, as a father, all goodness doth bring;*
> *The east, a forbearer, no manner of thing;*

WIND

> *The south, as unkind, draweth*
> *sickness too near;*
> *The north, as a friend,*
> *marketh all again clear.* ****

Easy-to-remember rhymes for the countryman, providing the basic weather characteristics for different wind directions. Bacon penned the second saying and the third originates in Plymouth.

> *No weather is ill*
> *If the wind be still.* ***

In calm situations rain is rare, but frost and fog are common. It all depends on the type of weather the countryman or farmer requires.

> *All winds bring rain.* **
>
> *Every wind has its weather.* *****

The last saying is a just reminder that every airstream possesses its own weather. A regular wind direction has subtle differences in cloud cover, precipitation and visibility.

> *The wind that will blow out a*
> *candle will help to kindle a*
> *fire.*
>
> *A little wind kindles, much*
> *puts out the fire.*

A light gentle wind is needed to blow out a candle and to constantly generate flames in a fire. A strong and erratic wind will extinguish any blaze.

> *When the wind goes down hill it*
> *will be a duck's frost afore*
> *morning.* ***

Wind

Wind that "goes down hill" occurs on clear evenings and nights. It is a cold dry breeze, known as a katabatic wind and possesses denser air than its surroundings and often blows down the slope of a valley sometimes causing frost hollows. It is also known as the "drainage wind" and "mountain breeze". It certainly foretells cool conditions in summer and winter frosts.

> *It's an ill wind that blows nobody good.*

Although bad weather and a wretched wind cause havoc with most people, there are always some that benefit.

> *Sudden gusts never come in a clear sky, but only when it is cloudy and with rain.*   *

This is incorrect. On a hot day with light breezes of say 8 knots, sudden gusts of 12 to 18 knots frequently blow. They are helped by the instability caused by uneven distribution of high temperatures across fields, woods and hills.

> *Unsteadiness of wind shows changing weather.*   *

This is untrue. Wind, by its nature, constantly changes in speed and direction, which can be applied to a dry, wet or changeable weather type.

> *A frequent change of wind, with agitation in the clouds, denotes a storm.*

The maxim is too vague. With so many different cloud types and consequent weather the saying needs to be clearer and more specific.

North Wind

North Wind

The north wind is cold in autumn, winter and spring; sometimes intensely cold in southern districts. Snow and sleet are common in winter with late-spring and early-autumn snow in northern districts on high ground. Also northerlies are connected with late-spring frosts. The onset of a north-type airstream is often accompanied by high winds.

> *A northern air*
> *Brings weather fair.*   ***

Mostly true, although wintry showers, especially over the Pennines and north-facing hills, can be a nasty feature.

> *The north wind, if it should*
> *rise by night (which is unusual),*
> *hardly ever lasts beyond three*
> *days.*   ***

Bacon wrote this saying. It is hinting that the northerly wind, by freshening at night, is strictly connected with a polar depression moving from Arctic regions into the North sea. In some cases the northerly, as a permanent feature, continues beyond three days.

> *The north wind is best for*
> *sowing of seeds.*   ****

The best conditions required for sowing winter and spring cereal seed are a dryish topsoil; certainly not wet or too moist. A cool dry northerly provides the ideal conditions. However I am sure the farm-labourer hand-scattering the seed would have wished for warmer working weather.

> *All bad things come out of the*
> *north. A bleak, bad wind, and a*
> *biting frost, and a scolding wife*
> *come out of the north.*   ****

This is more typical of the north wind in the winter half-year.

NORTH WIND

> *A north wind is a broom for the*
> *Channel.*   ****

The English Channel is referred to in this Cornish weather saw which must mean that as a cold northerly burst sweeps across the water it brings dry clear conditions.

> *Whenever the wind first blows*
> *from the north, after having*
> *been for some days in another*
> *direction, a fine day or two*
> *will be almost sure to follow.*   ***

Not always true - the northerly can possess rain or snow.

> *The north wind doth blow,*
> *And we shall have snow.*   ***

This saying is only true when applied to the period from about October to April, otherwise rain showers are the usual precipitation.

> *In a north wind it seldom*
> *thunders.*   ****

If the northerly wind has a well-established airstream, then thunder is rare. Any wind direction can occur in the vicinity of a thunderstorm.

> *Cream makes most freely with a*
> *north wind.*   *****

Until the middle of the 19th century cream was raised by leaving cow milk in shallow pans for a day or two. The lighter cream, or fattier part of the milk, mainly rose to the top. A fall in temperature speeded up the process. So in a cold northerly cream would certainly make "most freely". In fact icy water was introduced in the 1870's to further accelerate cream raising.

North Wind

> *If there be within four, five or six days two or three changes of wind from the north, through east without much rain and wind, and thence again through the west to the north with rain or wind, expect continual showery weather.* ✳✳✳✳

These complicated sets of wind changes seem to indicate minor wind disturbances finally followed by a very cold showery blast from the polar regions.

> *If the north-west or north wind blows with rain or snow during three or four days in the winter, and then the wind passes to the south through the west, expect continued rain.* ✳✳✳✳✳

Another true maxim. The destruction of a three or four-day northerly is frequently caused by the eastward movement of a depression across the United Kingdom. This would back the wind from north to south through west bringing rain.

> *But the north wind often both rises and falls without any change in the weather.* ✳✳✳✳

Bacon observed this characteristic in the northerly wind which can be applied at times to any direction, especially during the daytime.

> *Northerly winds bring showers rather than continuous rains or snow.* ✳✳✳✳✳

Perfectly correct - a very cold unstable airstream produces showers instead of general continuous rain.

North-East Wind

North-East Wind

The north-east wind is cold or very cold often with snow or sleet in winter and hail showers or rain and drizzle in summer.

> *The wind from the north-east*
> *Neither good for man or beast.* ****

> *North-east is bad for man and*
> *beast.* ****

This direction, especially with rain or sleet, has a biting damp cold that seems to penetrate everything in its path.

> *If the wind is north-east three*
> *days without rain,*
> *Eight days will pass before*
> *south wind again.* ******

This is one of the famous 26 weather rules of the Shepherd of Banbury (Oxfordshire), first printed in 1744. He was a most observant shepherd who was familiar with the persistence of north-easterlies. A test produced an excellent result of 81 percent. 13/16 (81)

> *North-east wind brings a long*
> *storm.* *****

> *If the wind is from the*
> *north-east, its storm will*
> *be a hard one.* *****

A well-established north-easterly wind produces very good results when lasting for two days or more. The figures are not so good for the sequence to last at least three or four days respectively with 44 and 28 percent. Long-term north-easterlies are a feature of the permanent Scandinavian anticyclone; short-term ones are related to fast-moving depressions rushing east up the English Channel or across Northern France into the Continent. 91/137 (66)
60/137 (44)
39/137 (28)

East Wind

*In summer, if the wind holds
off a day or more in the
north-east, a severe storm
is coming.* ✶✶

Poor results of 21 percent occur for a severe storm to follow summer north-easterlies. 9/43 (21)

East Wind

The east wind is cold in autumn, winter and spring, sometimes intensely cold in southern and exposed areas elsewhere. Occasionally snow occurs in the south and snow or sleet showers in east and north-east England but fine weather can happen in the north-west. Also it is warm in summer, sometimes thundery but fairly dry except in the east and south.

*When the wind is in the east,
It is neither good for man or
beast.* ✶✶✶✶

*A right easterly wind
Is very unkind.* ✶✶✶✶

The coldest and most biting weather arises in an east or north-east wind.

*A dry east wind raises the
spring.* ✶✶✶✶

This Cornish saying is hinting that dry clear easterlies in early spring, mainly through their sunshine and soil drying properties, will bring on the season.

*When the rain is from the east,
It is for four-and-twenty hours
at least.* ✶✶✶✶✶

Rain in an easterly is more frequent in the warmer months of April to September. The remaining year usually experiences sleet or snow. Very good results occur. 53/79 (67)

East Wind

> *Wet weather with an east wind*
> *continues longer than with a*
> *west, and generally lasts a*
> *whole day.* *****

Bacon came up with a winner with this maxim. The summers of 1861-1971 with wet cyclonic westerlies lasted on average 2.7 days; wet easterlies 3.5 days.

> *An easterly wind's rain*
> *Makes fools fain.* ****

A cold easterly rain is raw and of little use to any countryman, and would certainly make a fool fain or glad.

> *If an east wind blows against*
> *a dark, heavy sky from the*
> *north-west, the wind decreasing*
> *in force as the clouds approach,*
> *expect thunder and lightning.* ****

This refers to summertime when thunderstorms are sometimes associated with warm easterlies.

> *The east and north winds, when*
> *they have once begun, are more*
> *continuous; the south and west*
> *winds are more variable.* ***

Annually the two persistant wind quadrants are west and east with average lengths of 3.6 and 2.4 days. The north and south quadrants experience a temporary nature with means of 1.8 and 1.9 days.

> *The eastern winds make our fresh*
> *waters much clearer than the*
> *west.* ***

This is very similar to the Cornish saying in the north wind section. Inland fresh water areas receive the benefit of fresh clear cold easterlies.

South Wind

> *The eastern wind is drier, more biting and deadly, and if blowing much in the spring, injureth fruits by breeding worms.* ***

There are many occasions when an easterly is moist with wintry precipitation.

> *There are a hundred days of easterly wind in the first half of the year.* *

This West Country saying is totally false. When an easterly is tested as the predominant daily wind, disastrous results follow. The best year was 1963 with 43 days from January to May. 0/111 (0)

> *An east wind is a 'lazy wind', that is, it won't blow round you, but it blows straight through you.* ****

The "lazy wind" also applies to the north and north-east wind. Often the strength and direction of an easterly wind remain fairly constant during the night and day, hence the straight character of the wind.

> *An east wind, like an old man, lies down in the sun.* *

This is untrue; the strength is fairly constant. It is opposite in character to the north-west wind which decreases around sunset.

South Wind

The south airstream is warm and thundery in spring and summer and mild in autumn. In winter it is mild or cold depending whether it has maritime or continental origin.

South Wind

> *The weather usually clears at*
> *noon when a southerly wind is*
> *blowing.* **

A most unsatisfactory rule. The time of day makes little difference in determining when wet weather changes to dry. If by weather fog is included then on spring and autumn mornings the time of day is important. Usually these fogs will clear before or around midday.

> *If the wind continues any*
> *considerable time in the south,*
> *it is an infallible sign of*
> *rain.* ****

> *When the leaves curl with the*
> *wind from the south, it indicates*
> *rain.* ****

The definition of "any considerable time" was taken as three days or more with rain to follow within one. The result of 53 percent is only fair - similar results can be applied for a dry day to follow. Not all southerlies are eroded by depressions or summer thunderstorms producing rain. Often the Continental anticyclone will persist leaving a dry south airstream for a number of days. 26/49 (53)

> *A southerly wind with a fog*
> *Brings an east wind in snog.* **

> *An out (southerly) wind and a*
> *fog*
> *Bring an east wind home snug.* **

These Cornish sayings include the dialect words "snog" and "snug" which mean with certainty. A test looked into southerlies remaining for two days or more followed by an easterly within seven. Poor results occurred. 29/99 (29)

> *A southerly wind and a cloudy*
> *sky*
> *Proclaim it a hunting morning.* *****

South Wind

The fox-hunting season used to occur from November to April. Also related is the hunter's moon, which is the next full moon after the harvest moon (nearest full moon to the autumn equinox around 21st September). Now the strongest fox scent for hounds occurs in mild, moist conditions, so a cloudy south wind would provide such a morning.

> *When the south wind either rises or falls, there is generally a change of weather, from fair to cloudy, or from hot to cold, or vice versa.* ***

This old Bacon fable is partly true. It is similar in character and result to the second saw in this section.

> *The south wind, when gentle, is not a great collector of clouds; but it is often clear, especially if it be of short continuance. But if it lasts or becomes violent, it makes the sky become cloudy and brings on rain, which comes on rather when the wind ceases or begins to die away, than when it commences or is at its height.* *****

> *The southern wind
> Doth play the trumpet to his purposes,
> And by his hollow whistling in the leaves
> Foretells a tempest and a blustering day.* *****

The first Bacon and second Shakespeare (from *Henry IV*) sayings vary in literal style but possess the same meaning. The first part was tested with southerly winds lasting less than four dry days which produced an outstanding 79 percent result. Part two was defined as a southerly lasting three days or more and rain within one. Again the results were very good.

South Wind

30/38 (79)
80/111 (72)

The south wind warms the aged. ✳✳✳✳✳

*When the wind is in the south
It blows the bait in the fishes'
mouth.* ✳✳✳✳✳

The southerly wind is mostly warm or mild, hence the good 70 percent result. The meaning of the second saw probably refers to the gradual heating of fresh water rivers, especially in a continual southerly. This warmer water stimulates fish to become more active and hungry. 166/237 (70)

*If, when the south wind is
blowing, any piece of glued
furniture makes a noise, it
indicates a change to the
north.* ✳✳

Furniture will "creak" or "make a noise" with warm temperatures and high humidity which is typical of a southerly. The test gave poor results confining itself to any change to northerly within four days. 14/85 (16)

*When the wind's in the south,
The rain's in its mouth.* ✳✳✳✳✳

Another very true adage with 70 percent correct results. All southerlies were tested when lasting for at least one day followed by rain within 24 hours. 165/235 (70)

*A southerly wind with showers
of rain
Will bring the wind from the
west again.* ✳✳

Poor figures are achieved (25 percent correct) with showers and a southerly wind veering to the west within two days.
21/85 (25)

South Wind

*Fair weather for a week, with a
southern wind, is like to
produce a great drought, if there
has been much rain out of the
south before. The wind usually
turns from north to south, with
a quiet wind without rain, but
returns to the north, with a
strong wind and rain; the
strongest winds are when it turns
from south to north-by-west.
Also when the north wind first
clears the air (which is usually
once a week) look out for squalls.*

****

****

****

*****

This is the famous Shepherd of Banbury's 17th saying. The first section produced only a few number of occasions - too small to record. The second part concerned with a northerly breaking down into a light southerly is frequently correct especially when high pressure cells form or drift across Central England into Europe. When tested a return of 59 percent was recorded. Wind returning to the north with rain within two days gave 53 percent. The more impressive 64 percent was valid for the notable strength of the northerly occurring when a deep depression travels eastward slowing down as it enters the North Sea.

13/22 (59)
31/58 (53)
37/58 (64)

*If the wind in daytime shifts
from north to south-west or
south, rain is pretty sure to
follow, if, on the other hand,
it shifts from south to
south-west or north, the
weather will probably clear up.*

******

***

A Devon saying covering the general rule relating wet and dry weather to be expected after a backing or veering of wind - in this case north to south-west and south-west to North. The daytime is not really significant, the weather change is effective throughout the 24 hours. The tests included cases where wet or drier conditions occurred within two days of wind change. A remarkable 100 percent resulted in the backing and rain figures.

34/34 (100)
27/58 (47)

South-West Wind

*The north wind is best for
sowing seed, the south for
grafting.*

A cool northerly leaves topsoil dry enough for seed sowing. The southerly may be warm for grafting or farm labouring, but it is often humid leading to unpleasant sweaty conditions.

*The south wind, during the
winter months, will bring mild,
cloudy weather, with drizzle.* *********

Another correct adage tested from January to February 1861-1971 for wet weather and mild conditions.   65/89   (73)

South-West Wind

The south-west wind is mild, humid with prolonged rain. This changeable airstream is the prevailing wind over England closely followed by the east or north-east direction.

*A south-west blow on ye,
And bluster ye all over.* ********

Taken from Shakespeare's *Tempest*, he conjures up two of the characteristics of a south-westerly - its strength and mildness.

*Three south-westers, then one
heavy rain.* *****

Ambiguous weather lore - does it mean three consecutive or separate south-westerly days? The latter was researched showing poor results. Heavy rain can occur under any south-west airstream - a gradual accumulation of separate south-westerlies resulting in heavy rain is a myth.   9/66 (14)

*In fall and winter, if the wind
holds a day or more in the*

South-West Wind

> *south-west, a severe storm is*
> *coming.* ★★

A severe storm was tested to fall within two days after the south-westerly was established. Poor results.

45/214 (21)

> *When the wind shifts around to*
> *the south and south-west,*
> *expect warm weather.* ★★★★★★

Predictable statement with expected excellent results of 92 percent. The exception occurs with a depression centred over Northern Britain in the spring and winter. Then the south-westerly has polar oceanic origin.

61/66 (92)

> *When after a stiff breeze there*
> *ensues a dead calm and drizzling*
> *rain, with a fall in the*
> *barometer, expect a gale from*
> *the south-west.* ★★★

This only occurs when a stiff north or north-west blast is replaced by a ridge of high pressure ahead of a depression in the Atlantic. The wind will become calm after the northerly with clear conditions. Sometimes drizzle falling in the ridge well ahead of the depression from a warm front can be experienced. As the depression moves east it brings south-westerly gales and falling pressure, so the saying's weather sequence is fulfilled. It is more often incorrect when a south-west airstream occurs following the passage of a cold front. A wave can form on the front bringing drizzle and falling pressure but is often followed by a veer to north-west winds.

> *If the wind is from the*
> *north-west or south-west,*
> *the storm will be short.* ★★★
> *If from the south-west a*
> *warm one.*

The length of rain storms in a south-westerly can last from a few to many hours. The north-west airstream is usually renouned for short-lived showers.

West Wind

West Wind

The west wind is generally unsettled with changeable weather, usually with most rain falling in North, North-West and South-West England. It is cool in summer and mild in winter with frequent gales.

> *When the wind is in the west,*
> *The weather is always best.*   ****

> *The wind in the west*
> *Suits everyone best.*   ****

> *When wind is west*
> *Health is best.*   ***

The changeable westerly has such a varied menu it pleases nearly everyone.

> *When the rain comes from the west,*
> *it will be not more than a few*
> *hours before the weather improves,*
> *and becomes brighter, but showers*
> *are likely to follow.*   ****

This is perfectly true. A trough with rain in a westerly airstream lasts around four hours bringing cooler showery type weather in its wake.

> *The west wind is a gentleman,*
> *and goes to bed.*   *****

The westerly, like the north-westerly, is drastically reduced in strength under clear skies around dusk and hence "goes to bed".

> *Wind west, rain's next.*   *****

North-West Wind

> *A western wind carrieth water*
> *in his hand.*   *****

Both maxims are very true, especially the first one from Devon. Strong westerlies are associated with mobile Atlantic depressions and showery troughs. Lighter westerlies can belong to this hybrid and are also connected with settled dry weather from high pressure centres over France and Biscay.

North-West Wind

The north-west wind has cool, changeable weather, particularly in North and East England, sometimes accompanied with fresh or gale force winds.

> *Do business with men when the*
> *wind is in the north-west.*   *****

> *When the wind is in the*
> *north-west,*
> *The weather will be at*
> *its best.*   ****

> *North-west is far the best.*   ****

The first is a lovely Yorkshire saying meaning that its cool fine weather sometimes occurring in a north-westerly can improve temper. A man in good spirits is always easier to do business with.

> *In summer, if the wind changes*
> *to the north-west, expect*
> *cooler weather.*

This is just a statement of fact. A north-west airstream brings cool temperatures the year round.

> *An honest man and a north-west*
> *wind generally go to sleep*
> *together.*   *****

North-West Wind

Another lovely country adage beautifully phrased. The north-west wind, in a clear evening, will abate in strength quite dramatically around sunset. The reason is the rapid drop in temperature and change of vertical temperature profile or lapse rate.

> *A nor'wester is not long in debt to a sou'wester.* ********

The set of four figures give the general picture for south-westerlies to follow north-westerlies. To occur within one or two days 47 and 57 percent chances arose. Better figures of 66 and 71 percent followed when applied to the wind backing within 3 and 4 days.

111/236 (47)
134/236 (57)
155/236 (66)
167/236 (71)

> *North-west wind brings a short storm.* *******

> *If the wind is from the north-west or south-west, the storm will be short. If from the north-west a cold one.* *******

Showers are usually short and gusty but prolonged rain and winds can occur especially in warm sector conditions.

> *If in unsettled weather the wind veers from south-west to west or north-west at sunset, expect finer weather for a day or two.* ********

This is usually true. It implies that a veering wind, often associated with cold fronts and troughs, brings short settled periods. Sometimes the time of day is important - if the veer to north-west occurs in the morning, showers could form as temperatures rose. If the veer happens at sunset then low temperatures would allow a clear night. Also a situation can present itself with a cold front wave forming returning wet

North-West Wind

weather for a few hours after a temporary veer from south-west to north-west.

> *A north-westerly gale*
> *Brings showers of hail.*   ✲✲✲

> *With the rain from the*
> *north-west, expect showers*
> *of hail.*   ✲✲✲

Hail showers can occur in a north-west airstream but it's the colder more unstable northerly where they often originate.

RAIN

Some rain, some rest;
Fine weather isn't always
the best.

To a farmer fine weather is welcome but a long sequence of slight rain then sun and so on is more appreciated.

No one so surely pays his debt
As wet to dry and dry to wet. *

Be it dry or be it wet
The weather'll always
pay its debt. *

Wiltshire provides the first saw. Many countrymen believe that there is a true balance between wet and dry weather. For example that a summer drought will be followed by an autumn deluge and vice-versa. A test was carried out over the period 1727-1971 where monthly wet and dry totals were totalled over

Rain

each calendar year. The author thought a 12-month period would be long enough to test the theory of equal dry and wet spells. So when equal annual monthly totals occurred a correct mark was allotted. Unfortunately mother nature does not work in these mysterious ways hence the very low rating of 11 percent.

27/245   (11)

> *Rain, rain pouring*
> *Sets the bulls a-roaring.*   *

This Suffolk saying contains poor observation - bulls roar for many different reasons. (See cow/bull section of the Animal chapter.)

> *Rain from the east,*
> *Two days at least.*   *****

> *Rain from the east,*
> *Will last three days at least.*   ***

Similar adages and test figures can be found in the Wind chapter under the easterly section.

> *Rain from the south prevents*
> *the drought;*
> *But rain from the west is always*
> *best.*

> *Rain with south or south-west*
> *thunder brings squalls on*
> *successive days.*   *

> *If it rains at midnight with a*
> *southerly wind, it will*
> *generally last about twelve*
> *hours.*   ****

Again other saws akin to the previous ones which can be compared with those in the various direction sections of the Wind chapter are interesting weather lore.

> *The faster the rain, the quicker*
> *the holdup.*

Rain

This maxim hails from Norfolk stating the obvious that heavy rain will fill dykes or flood ground quickly and consequently hold up many jobs on the land.

Rain long foretold, long last;
Short notice, soon past. ****

Small showers last long, but
sudden storms are short. ****

If it rains well
it will shine well. ***

The second adage appears in Shakespeare's *Richard II*. All three are very true. Sudden rain or showers frequently pass through under an hour but the gradual expectation of slight rain continues much longer.

Rain at seven, fine at eleven, ****
Rain at eight, not fine till eight. **

Next follows one of the most famous of all English weather lore. Of course seven is included to rhyme with eleven. The reader must remember that rain does not fall conveniently at any *special* time, it is not geared to any clock, it falls at any moment of the 24-hour day. Test figures over 317 days in 1978-79 (in mainly spring, summer and autumn to avoid winter sleet and snow in Oxfordshire) showed that rain occurred least at 0300 local time with 30 occasions (9.8 percent) and most at 0700 with 47 occasions (15.3 percent) - so little hourly variation. The test also showed that by measuring the duration of rain, drizzle and showers the average length of rainfall was 2.5 hours. Rain at 0700 and fine before 1100 produced a good result of 57 percent - remember that frontal rain could cease say at 0930 followed by immediate showers. The *prolonged* rain period from 0800 till 1800 would therefore seem unlikely and in fact produces only 13 percent.   27/47   (57)
                                                                            5/40   (13)

Rain before seven
Lift before eleven. *****

Rain

Fine before seven
Fine before eleven.   *****

These maxims are the ones most people remember. Notice there is a subtle difference between these and the previous saws. It's rain *before* 0700 and fine before 1100 that's tested here. A better result of 69 percent is achieved.   27/39 (69)

If rain begins at early morning light,
Twill end ere day at noon is bright.   ******

Rain was investigated to begin around dawn. "Ere" means before so a dry 1200 (noon) was searched for. The final figure was excellent with 87 percent, but remember only March to August with sunrises varying from 0400 to 0700 were checked. The winter figures would shorten the time period between sunrise and noon and presumably offer a lower percentage.
                                                        40/46 (87)

For a morning rain leave not your journey.   ***

Testing was limited to any rain from sunrise to 1200 followed by no rain 1200 to sunset. Not a very encouraging result. The figures vary so much between this saw and the previous one because often a shower or occasional slight rain would occur during the afternoon even though there was a dry noon.
                                                        37/87 (43)

If it rains before daylight it will hold up before eight o'clock. If it rains about ****
noon it will continue throughout the afternoon. If it rains *
before nine p.m. it will rain the next day. *****

If the rain ceases after mid-day it will rain the next day. If ****
the rain ceases before mid-day it will be clear next day. ***

If it rains before five p.m. it will rain throughout the

Rain

> *night. If it rains between*   ***
> *eight o'clock and nine o'clock*
> *in the morning it will continue*
> *until mid-day if it has not*   **
> *ceased by then it will carry on*
> *until the evening.*   ***

This long and specific piece of weather lore was tested for eight of its prophesies. The middle section concerned with wind directions was left (these are dealt with in the Wind chapter). The eight results varied from 14 to 76 percent depending on the time involved with each rain prognostication.

```
Rain before daylight will cease before 0800    23/38  (61)
 "     "    noon       "   continue through-
                       out afternoon (till 1700)  6/43  (14)
 "  after 2100 clearing overnight will rain
                                again next day  68/89  (76)
 "  ceases after 1200 then rain    "    "       24/39  (62)
 "    "      "    "   before "     "    clear   "  "    9/26  (35)
 "  before 1700 then rain throughout night     14/36  (39)
 "    "    0800-0900 then rain till 1200       14/52  (27)
 "    "     "    "    "    "    "    evening    5/14  (36)
```

> *Night rains*
> *Makes drowned fens.*   ****

This East Anglian maxim is possibly hinting that no evaporation occurs at night so more rain affects the earth.

> *Rain a short time before*
> *sunrise will be followed at*
> *least by a fine afternoon;*   ****
> *but rain soon after sunrise*
> *generally by a wet day.*   **

The first part of this adage was tested by noting rain during the hour before sunrise followed by a fine afternoon (1200-1700 hour). Only a 54 percent correct result emerged. Rain during the hour after sunrise with a wet afternoon produced only 28 percent.
    20/37 (54)
    11/39 (28)

> *A hasty shower of rain falling*
> *when the wind has raged some*
> *hours, soon allays it.*   *

Rain

There seems to be no logic here.

> *Marry the rain to the wind,*
> *and you have a calm.* ✱✱

In certain frontal systems, especially cold fronts, this maxim rings true. Equally there are occasions when it does not occur.

> *A small rain may allay a*
> *great storm.*

To use the verb 'may' renders any saw as useless.

> *If it rains when the sun shines,*
> *it will rain the next day.* ✱✱✱✱✱

> *If it rains when the sun is*
> *shining, the devil is beating*
> *his grandmother. He is*
> *laughing, and she is crying.*

> *Sunshine and shower,*
> *rain again tomorrow.* ✱✱✱✱✱

> *If it rains when the sun shines,*
> *it will surely rain the next day*
> *about the same hour.* ✱✱

> *A sunshiny shower*
> *Never lasts half-an-hour.* ✱✱✱✱

> *Sunshiny rain*
> *Will soon go again.* ✱✱✱✱

The fourth saw hails from Suffolk, fifth Bedfordshire and sixth Devon. All are true. Showers are brief periods of rain, hail or snow caused chiefly by convective cumulus or cumulonimbus clouds and by definition are scattered. Therefore sunny intervals often occur between them. A showery airstream can last or indicate an unsettled weather pattern and the 66 percent result for rain the next day is a good figure. The Suffolk saying only emerged with 28 percent.   66/101 (66)
28/101 (28)

Rain

After rain comes sunshine. ***

If this saw literally means rain and not showers then it is not necessarily true.

*There is usually fair weather
before a settled course of rain.* ***

Again this is correct in some synoptic situations but not in others.

*Wet continues if the ground
dries up too soon.* ****

For a wet surface to quickly dry it presumably experiences a strong drying wind (of low humidity) or strong sunshine. Both are more often associated with short dry settled spells.

*Who soweth in rain,
he shall reap it with tears.*

*Who soweth in rain
Hath weed to his pain;
But worse shall he speed
That soweth ill seed.*

Good old fashioned farming lore.

*Although it rains,
throw not away thy watering pot.* ****

The weather is so changeable in England, what seems like a wet period soon becomes a dry spell.

*When the rain causes bubbles to
rise in water it falls upon, the
shower will last long.* ***

This Essex maxim is intriguing. For rain to cause water bubbles on rivers and lakes presumably it has to possess a fast downward velocity which only occurs in moderate or heavy rain or showers. As in previous saws in this chapter a sudden heavy rain soon passes over which tends to contradict this Essex saw.

Rain

It is raining heavens high.

It is raining heavens hard.

Yorkshire and Norfolk provide the first and second sayings. "Heaven" in this context is the region of the atmosphere where clouds are situated. The expression "the heavens opened" meaning a cloudburst or downpour is very similar and probably has the same meaning as the two above.

If the rain comes down slanting,
It will be everlasting. ***

"Slanting rain" is caused by strong low-level winds which can be associated with rain lasting for short or long periods.

In wet weather it rains
without half trying. ****

More subtle than it appears. In a long rainy spell or season the wet weather seems to painfully continue as if without asking. In meteorology once a long dry or wet sequence has become established its *persistence* is hard to break.

If it raineth when it doth flow,
Then take your ox and go to plough.
But if it raineth when it doth ebb,
Unyoke your oxen and go to bed. **

If it rains with the flow,
thee can go out to snow;
If it rains with the ebb,
thee can go back to bed. **

These two saws come from the Severn Estuary. Unfortunately there is no scientific or meteorological reason why tidal changes should affect the weather in a major way. The saws contain little truth. But the ebbing and flowing of the sea will always be believed by people to influence the weather - it is so deep rooted.

Rain

*A poor man's rain
cometh at night.*

Presumably a rich man grows affluent with a perfect growing combination of daytime rain and sun, whereas a poor man collects only half of this at night.

It never rains but it pours. ***

A very famous phrase more connected today with the human experience of finding that events, usually misfortunes, have an uncanny way of suddenly all coming together around the same time. Weatherwise it only occurs with well-established depressions, active fronts or heavy showers.

*A sharp shower of rain
following a period of
light, but continuous,
rain or drizzle is a
sign that the weather
will soon improve.* ****

*Showers and sunshine, the two
in their turn,
Bring certain good weather
for which we do yearn.* ****
*But showers and sunshine, then
gloom overhead,
Will bring on more rain
for some hours, it is said.* ****

Two sharp country observations of rain, shower and sunny interval sequences that are absolutely correct. The first saw seems to apply to the passage of a cold front or one with a warm sector. The clearance behind the cold front has usually clearer weather sometimes with showers. The last part of the second maxim possibly indicates an extensive shower or trough of showers indicating prolonged rain.

Small rain can lay a great dust. *****

*If very light, short showers
come during dry weather, they
are said to "harden the drought"
and indicate no change.* *****

Rain

In a way these two are like the recent saw connected with drought or wet weather. A prolonged dry spell, especially inland in the summers of 1975 and 1976, builds up its own dryness factor on the ground with foliage and soil. Any attempt to rain or shower is checked or partially "dried out" through this reason.

CLOUDS

People tend to have difficulty in distinguishing all the different types of cloud. Before the days of official cloud classification, English cloud weather lore often used terms such as "mackerel sky" and "curly wisps" to describe the shape and construction of a particular cloud. Infact the sayings contain a wealth of beautiful descriptive prose as well as prophecy.

To understand clouds two items are important: the type and height of base. The type depends on whether the cloud is in a layer or heap. Height of cloud base determines into which of the three major cloud levels it belongs. When all put together the following list makes up the official cloud classification:

High cloud	16,500 - 40,000 ft	*Cirrus (Ci)* *Cirrocumulus (Cc)* *Cirrostratus (Cs)*
Medium cloud	6,500 - 23,000 ft	*Altocumulus (Ac)* *Altostratus (As)* *Nimbostratus (Ns)*
Low cloud	Surface - 6,500 ft	*Stratocumulus (Sc)* *Stratus (St)* *Cumulus (Cu)* *Cumulonimbus (Cb)*

CIRRUS

The high level or *Cirrus (Ci)* clouds consist of ice crystals and very low temperatures. *Cirrus* (from the Latin meaning a lock of hair, tuft of horsehair or bird's tuft) is often fibrous and white. Depending on its shape one can foretell much in future weather.

After a long run of clear weather the appearance of light streaks of cirrus cloud at a great elevation is often the first sign of a change.

****

Clouds

> *The longer the dry weather has lasted the less is rain likely to follow the cloudiness of the cirrus.* *****

These two saws are opposite in meaning, but as can be seen in the results the general trend is that this type of *Cirrus* presages rain - a 50 percent chance within one day and a 71 percent chance within two.

> *If cirrus clouds dissolve and appear to vanish it is an indication of fine weather.* ****

> *Cirrus of a long, straight, feathery kind, with soft edges and outlines, or with soft, delicate colours at sunrise or sunset, is a sign of fine weather.* ****

> *Curly wisps and brown-backed pieces are not a bad sign.* ****

Three maxims indicating good weather to follow. This is not really true as to remain fine for one day results give a 50 percent chance and for two dry days only 29 percent.

> *Trace in the sky the painter's brush,*
> *Then winds around you soon will rush.* ***

> *The cloud called 'goat's hair' or the 'grey mare's tail' forbodes wind.* ***

The second adage mentions the famous phrases "goat's hair" and "gray mare's tail".

> *If woolly fleeces strew the heavenly way,*
> *Be sure no rain disturbs the summer day.* ****

Clouds

This one hints of possible rain the same day.

Thin *Cirrus*	then	rain	within	one day		114/228	(50)
"	"	"	"	"	two days	163/228	(71)
"	"	"	"	"	three "	206/228	(90)
Thin *Cirrus*	then	dry	for	one day		114/228	(50)
"	"	"	"	"	two days	65/228	(29)
"	"	"	"	"	three days	22/228	(10)

Slightly undulating lines of cirrus occur in fine weather; but anything like a deeply indented outline precedes heavy rain or wind. ✶✶✶✶✶✶

When the cirrus clouds appear at lower elevations than usual, and with a denser character, expect a storm from the opposite quarter to the clouds. ✶✶✶

The last part of the initial saying describes dense *Cirrus* cloud with solid outline. Often these are the blown-off anvil tops from *Cumulonimbus (Cb)* cloud tops - hence the surety of violent showers in the forecast. The test provided an excellent 100 percent result.   22/22 (100)

When looking in a westerly or easterly direction, if the centre of the bank of cirro-velum is to the right of the point from which the edge, or the cirro-fillum outside the edge, is moving, the probability of bad weather is not nearly so great as if the centre was to the left of this point. But looking in a northerly or southerly direction if the centre lies to the right of the direction of motion of the bank, the ensuing weather will be worse than if it lies to the left. ✶✶✶✶

If the upper current of clouds

Clouds

> *comes from the north-west in the morning, a fine day will ensue.*   *

> *If clouds drive up high from the south, expect a thaw.*   ****

> *High upper clouds, crossing the sun, moon, or stars in a direction different from that of the lower clouds, or the wind when felt below, foretell a change of wind towards their direction.*   **

This long and complicated piece of Victorian prose comes from the Rev. Clement Ley. If an observer faces south and sees the *Cirrus* bank moving from the west (then the centre of the cloud will be to the right of the cloud's motion) poor weather will ensue. Basically the clergyman is just viewing the wind direction at *Cirrus* levels, in this case S.S.W. to N.N.W.

> *Feathery clouds, like palm branches or the fleur-de-lys, denote immediate or coming showers.*   ****

> *When the tails are turned downwards, fair weather or slight showers often follow.*   **

> *Cirrus clouds announce an easterly wind.*   **
> *If their undersurface is level, and their streaks pointing upwards, they indicate rain;*   *****
> *if downwards, wind and dry weather.*   *****

> *When the streamers point upward, the clouds are falling, and rain is at hand; when streamers point downward, the clouds are ascending, and drought is at hand.*   *****

Clouds

> *A large formation of murky*
> *white cirrus may merely indicate*
> *a backing of wind to an easterly*
> *quarter.* ✱✱

This type of *Cirrus*, especially in the form where the streaks point upward, strongly denote wind and rain. The upward streamers (ice crystals which have grown and fall out of the main *Cirrus* cloud) denote winds increasing with height (shear) through the cloud layer. Often this cloud progressively invades the sky and is the classic forerunner of rain and overcast conditions. The downward streamers denote fine and settled weather. The easterly wind in the third and fifth maxims is to be expected.

Dense *Cirrus*	then rain	within	one day		376/607	(62)
"	"	"	"	two days	516/607	(85)
"	"	"	"	three days	565/607	(93)
Dense *Cirrus*	then dry	for	one day		231/607	(38)
"	"	"	"	two days	91/607	(15)
"	"	"	"	three days	42/607	(7)

> *The barred or ribbed cirrus is*
> *considered, as good a danger*
> *signal as that given by a falling*
> *barometer.* ✱✱✱✱✱

The barred or ribbed *Cirrus (Cirrus vertebratus)* is a definite indicator of rain.

> *If the cirrus clouds appear to*
> *windward and change to*
> *cirrostratus, it is a sign*
> *of rain.* ✱✱✱✱✱✱

> *When cirrus merges into*
> *cirrostratus, and when cumulus*
> *increases towards evening and*
> *becomes lower, expect wet*
> *weather.* ✱✱✱✱✱✱

> *The cirrocumulus, when*
> *accompanied by cirrostratus,*
> *is a sure indication of a*
> *coming storm.* ✱✱✱✱✱✱

Clouds

All three sayings are excellent observations of bad weather. In fact rain within 24 hours yields a test result of 81 percent and the average time interval between the first appearance of the cloud and the first rain is 6.9 hours.

```
Ci and Cs clouds then rain within one day      13/16   (81)
 "    "   "    "      "    "     "   two days   14/16   (87)
```

Cirrus moving from north or north-east with high barometer is a sign of settled weather in summer, and of temporary fine weather in winter; with low barometer, it is a sign of marked improvements in the weather.

*****

Cirrus moving from east (a rare occurrence) is a sign of fine weather in winter, but of unsettled weather in summer.

*****

Cirrus moving from the south-east (which rarely occurs in a low or unsteady barometer) is a sign of improving weather in winter, and in summer frequently indicates coming thunderstorms.

*****

Cirrus moving from the south generally indicates unsettled weather, especially in summer.

*****

Cirrus moving from the south-west indicates unsettled, and sometimes stormy, weather in winter. In summer it often precedes thunderstorms; but with a high barometric pressure and a high temperature it frequently has no disturbing influence, and is then usually replaced by cirro-macula (cirrocumulus).

*****

Clouds

If cirrus comes from the west it is commonly in summer a symptom of fair weather, but is less so in winter.

*****

When cirrus comes from the north-west, when not tending to the form cirro-filum (thread-like cirrus), it is an indication of temporary fine weather, especially in summer.

*****

A V-point north in cirrus commonly indicates improving weather over and to the south, but distant atmospheric disturbances in the north and north-west.

*****

A V-point north-east in cirrus, expect temporarily settled weather, especially with high barometer.

*****

A V-point east in cirrus, expect settled weather in winter; in summer, with high temperatures, it sometimes indicates disturbances, which will be felt most to the south-west of the place of observation.

*****

A V-point south-east in cirrus, fine weather in winter, except when occurring immediately after heavy rain, when it is commonly followed by squalls. In summer it is almost invariably followed by thunder, with damp and sultry weather.

*****

A V-point south in cirrus with a fairly low barometer, after a fall of rain, indicates

Clouds

showery weather in summer, and rough, squally weather in winter, with south-west or west winds, especially if the cloud velocity is great. With a high barometer, it indicates in summer thunderstorms from the south-west, but in winter may be taken as a sign of favourable weather.   *****

A V-point south-west in cirrus, moderately fine weather.   *****

A V-point west in cirrus, fine weather in the warm months. The weather to the south and south-east of the observer is then normally dry and warm but to the extreme north-west unsettled. In winter it is a symptom of unsettled weather.   *****

A V-point north-west in cirrus is bad; when it occurs just after a rise in the barometer, it indicates a sudden fall, with wind and rain.   *****

A V-point between west-north-west and north-west, especially with rapid cloud movement, is always followed by unsettled weather.   *****

These closely observed rules of V-point cirrus are the sole work of the Rev. Clement Ley mentioned earlier in the chapter. In practice they describe the movement of cirrus cloud or the wind direction at these levels. The associated weather is true.

Cirrocumulus

Cirrocumulus (Cc) cloud is easily recognised by its regular pattern of fish scales. It often occurs with other types of *Cirrus* cloud and can be the sign of bad or good weather to come. The famous "**Mackerel sky**" of course refers to the mackerel's

Clouds

back resembling the dappled small white fleecy clouds of *Cc*. Sometimes very high *Altocumulus (Ac)* can be included as a mackerel sky. All 10 saws refer to the unsettled changeable weather to follow. Rain occurred within 24 hours 69 percent of the time.

    Mackerel sky then rain within one day   70/102 (69)
        "   "   "   "   "   two days   85/102 (83)
        "   "   "   "   "   three days 95/102 (93)

Cirrocumulus is commonly called 'mackerel sky'.

Mackerel sky and mares' tails
Make lofty ships carry low sails.   *****

A mackerel sky denotes fair
weather for that day, but rain
a day or two later.   *****

Mackerel sky, mackerel sky,
Never long wet and never
long dry.   *****

Mackerel clouds in sky
Expect more wet than dry.   *****

A mackerel sky
Is as much for wet as tis
for dry.   *****

Mackerel scales
Furl your sails.   *****

A mackerel sky,
Not twenty-four hours dry.   *****

Mackerel sky
Rain is nigh.   *****

Clouds

> *If clouds look as if scratched
> by a hen,
> Get ready to reef your topsails
> then.*   *****

> *Hen's scarts and filly tails.
> Make lofty ships carry low sails.*   *****

These two maxims mention "hen's scarts" or scratchings - a descriptive phrase referring to *Cc* cloud. Infact the same as a mackerel sky. The forecast is emphasized here for wind.

> *Cottony shreds, rounded and
> clear in outline, indicate
> dangerous disturbances.*   *****

> *Small floating clouds over a
> bank of clouds, sign of rain.*   *****

> *If in the north-west before
> daylight ends there appear a
> company of small black clouds
> like flocks of sheep, it is a
> sure and certain of rain.*   *****

> *Small white clouds like a flock
> of sheep, and red in colour,
> wind follows.*   *****

> *If the sky, from being clear,
> becomes quickly fretted or
> spotted all over with bunches
> of clouds, rain will soon
> follow.*   *****

> *Small white clouds, like a flock
> of sheep, driving north-west,
> indicate continued fine weather.*   **

Further country descriptions of the *Cc* cloud. The last adage differs in that it forecasts fine weather.

> *A curdly sky
> Will not leave the earth long
> dry.*   *****

Clouds

> *Curdled cirrus cloud often
> indicates the approach of
> bad weather.*   *****

> *A curdly sky
> Will not be twenty-four hours
> dry.*   *****

"Curdly" is a rough interpretation of *Cc* with rain to ensue.

> *Cirro-macula (speckle-cloud)
> nearly always occurs in warm
> weather, when the atmosphere
> at the earth's surface has but
> little lateral motion.*   **

> *A sky dappled with light clouds
> of the cirrocumulus form in the
> early morning generally leads to
> a fine and warm day.*   **

> *Before thunder, cirrocumulus
> clouds often appear in very
> dense and compact masses, in
> close contact.*   ***

> *A blue and white sky
> Never four-and-twenty
> hours dry.*   *****

The first sayings hail from the Victorian vicar, the Rev. Clement Ley, calling *Cc* a speckled cloud. Northamptonshire provides the last maxim which can just about be passed off as *Cc*.

Cirrostratus

> *In unsettled weather sheet
> cirrus (cirrostratus) precedes
> more wind or rain.*   *****

> *When a plain sheet of the wane
> cloud is spread over a large
> surface at evening tide, or
> when the sky gradually thickens
> with this cloud, a fall of*

> *steady rain is usually the*
> *consequence.*   *****

> *If long lines of cirrostratus*
> *extend along the horizon, and*
> *are slightly contracted in their*
> *centre, expect heavy rain the*
> *following day.*   ***

> *The waved cirrostratus indicates*
> *heat and thunder.*   ***

> *A high sheet of cloud spreading*
> *across the whole sky, and*
> *casting a general gloom over*
> *the countryside, presages*
> *rain and wind.*   *****

> *If the sky looks washed with a*
> *milky white,*
> *The rain is near though not yet*
> *in sight.*   *****

Cirrostratus (Cs) or sheet *Cirrus* nearly always covers the whole sky and is of a white milky colour. The sun can still be observed often with the famous $22°$ halo (see Halo chapter). Cs cloud is nearly always associated with jet streams (an upper core of maximum winds) and warm fronts. As a warm front approaches *Cs* is normally followed by *Altostratus (As)* then rain and lower cloud. Rain followed within 24 hours on 67 percent of occasions. Also 6.1 hours was the mean time interval between the first *Cs* and first rain. The last saw refers to *Cirrostratus undulatus* or undulating or wave *Cs* occurring where there are strong upper waves near jet streams.

    Cirrostratus then rain within 1 day   62/93 (67)
         "   "   "   "   2 days   93/93 (100)

ALTOCUMULUS LENTICULARIS

Altocumulus lenticularis (Ac len) (alto means height or upper air, cumulus means heap and lenticularis shaped like a lens or lentil) appears in the form of long cigar-shaped clouds at medium levels.

> *When the ark is out,*
> *North and south,*
> *In the rain's mouth.*   ****

Clouds

> *When the ark is out,*
> *Rain is about.* ****

> *A long stripe of cloud, sometimes*
> *called a salmon, sometimes a*
> *Noah's ark, when it stretches*
> *east and west, is a sign of a*
> *storm; but when north and south,* ***
> *of fine weather.* ***

> *This cloud is called in the*
> *Yorkshire Dales 'Noaship', and*
> *the old Danes called it*
> *'Nolskeppet'.*

> *The fish (hake) shaped cloud,*
> *if pointing east and west,*
> *indicates rain; if north and* ***
> *south, more fine weather.* ***

> *North and south, the sign of*
> *drought;* ***
> *East and west, the sign of*
> *blast.* ***

The fourth saw comes from Yorkshire and fifth Bedfordshire. The "ark", "Noah's ark", "salmon", "Noaship", "Nolskeppit" and "fish-shaped" from the saws *all* refer to the shape of *Ac len* cloud. When positioned north to south fine weather is forecast, when east to west rain. This almond-shaped cloud is directly connected with mountain lee-waves. For example when a westerly upper wind blows across the Welsh mountains waves on the lee-side occur. Sometimes clouds form in their wave crests at right angles to the westerly. So a north to south "Noah's ark" indicates medium level westerly winds which often bring rain. The test for all orientated *Ac len* gave a 55 percent chance of rain within one day after the cloud was sighted.

Ac len then rain within one day   31/56   (55)
"   "   "   "   "   two days   33/56   (59)
"   "   "   "   "   three days 38/56   (68)

Altocumulus

> *Long parallel bands of clouds*
> *in the direction of the winds*
> *indicate steady high winds to*
> *come.* ***

Clouds

The ordinary *Altocumulus* which is often seen offers a high 68 percent chance of rain within 24 hours.

```
Altocumulus then rain within one day      257/376  (68)
    "         "    "      "   two days    311/376  (83)
    "         "    "      "   three days  348/376  (93)
```

Cumulus

Cumulus (Cu) clouds are of course those cottony heap clouds varying from small "fair weather" *cumulus* to huge towering *Cumulonimbus (Cb)* clouds producing heavy sometimes thundery showers. Therefore two important distinctions are made. The first is obvious - the deeper the cloud the more showery its nature. The second is that the colder the cloud (a lower freezing level) the higher the risk of showers.

Cumulus clouds are called rain balls in Lancashire.

A round-topped cloud, with flattened base,

Clouds

> *Carries rainfall in its face.* ✸✸

> *The rounded clouds called
> 'water-waggons' which fly
> alone in the lower currents
> of wind forbode rain.* ✸✸

The first saw comes from Lancashire. The three suggest that *all cumulus* clouds produce rain or more correctly showers which of course are confined to the larger deeper ones. Records kept in Oxfordshire show that only 31 percent of *cumulus* cloud provided showers within 6 hours.   197/634 (31)

> *When clouds appear like
> rocks and towers,
> The earth's refreshed by
> frequent showers.* ✸✸✸

> *When mountains and cliffs in the
> clouds appear,
> Some sun and violent showers are
> near.* ✸✸✸✸

Towering *cumulus* or *cumulonimbus* clouds should be a safe bet for showers. It came as a shock to find that only 45 percent of occasions provided showers within 6 hours. On reflection a shower falls over a relatively small area and often many regions remain dry. Even so a better result was hoped for.
106/233 (45)

> *Clouds like globes at sunrise
> announce clear, sharp weather.* ✸✸✸

> *When the cumulus clouds are
> smaller at sunset than they
> were at noon, expect fair
> weather.* ✸✸✸

Global cloud possibly denotes morning *cumulus* which usually accompanies clear sharp weather or an unstable cool airstream. The second adage follows the normal daily sequence of *cumulus* as it disperses around sunset - as air temperature falls inland the thermal activity to maintain the cloud is lost.

Clouds

*The formation of cumulus clouds
to leeward during a strong wind
indicates the approach of a
calm with rain.*   ***

*When cumulus clouds become
heaped up to leeward during a
strong wind at sunset, thunder
may be expected during the
night.*   ***

The first saying is difficult to understand. It may relate a windy showery airstream which is quickly stabilizing or losing its ability to produce *cumulus*. This often happens in the evening but sometimes occurs when a ridge of high pressure precedes a warm front. Here earlier gales would quickly be followed by frontal rain and calm. The second adage presents no solution.

Stratus

Stratus (St) cloud (meaning to extend, spread or flatten out or cover with a layer) is a low sheet of cloud with a base ranging from the surface to about 1,500ft. It is very important to distinguish between two types of *stratus*. The first is associated with dry weather and more often forms at night and during the morning. It is grey and can be a complete sheet or broken. Normally in spring, summer and autumn it begins in the early morning as a sheet. As the temperature rises the cloud will thin and lift often with sun's outline visible. Finally it will "burn off" or disperse but can form into *cumulus* cloud. The second type is connected with stormy wet weather being a *ragged* dark cloud sheet.

*Stratus clouds have always been
regarded as the harbingers of
fine weather, and there are a
few fine days in the year when
the morning breaks out through
a disappearing stratus cloud.*   ***

Stratus is *not* always a forerunner of fine weather as explained in the previous paragraph. Tests over a year (1979) in Oxfordshire showed that with any amount of *stratus* and a base 1,000ft or less was followed by rain within 6 hours on 59 percent of all occasions.   541/918 (59)

Clouds

*Misty clouds, forming or
hanging on heights, show
wind and rain coming, if
they remain, increase, or
descend. If they rise or
disperse, the weather will
improve.*
*****
*****

*Clouds upon hills, if rising,
do not bring rain; if falling,
rain follows.*
*****
*****

The first saw has the best description of the two *stratus* types and their subsequent weather.

*If mists rise to the hilltops
and there stay, expect rain
shortly.*
*****

*When it gangs up i'fops,
It'll fa' down i' drops.*
*****

*When the clouds are upon the
hills,
They'll come down by the mills.*
*****

The second maxim hails from Northern England where "it gangs up i' fops means the cloud covers the hills. Hampshire provides the last saying where the second line refers to heavy rain which will fill springs and streams to run watermills. Test results give a high 68 percent rating for *stratus* covering hills followed by rain within 6 hours.   465/679   (68)

*When the Pendle's Head is free
from clouds, the people thereabout
expect a halcyon day, and those
on the banks of the Can in
Westmorland can tell what
weather to look for from the
voice of its falls.*
****

*When Firle Hill and Long Man
has a cap,
We at Aston gets a drap.*
*****

CLOUDS

When Wolsonbury has a cap,
Hurstpierpoint will have a drap. *****

If Bever hath a cap,
Your churls of the vale look
to that. *****

When Ladie Lift.
Puts on her shift,
She feares a downright raine; *****
But when she doffs it, you will
finde
The rain is o'er, and still the
winde,
And Phoebus shine againe. *****

If Riving Pike do wear a hood,
Be sure the day will ne'er be
good. *****

If Roseberry Topping wears a
cap,
Let Cleveland then beware of
a rap. *****

When Roseberry Topping wears a
hat,
Morden Carre will suffer for
that. *****

When Eston Nabbe puts on a
cloake,
As Roseberry a cappe,
Then all the folks on
Cleveland's clay
Ken there will be a clappe. **

When Bredon Hill puts on his
hat,
Ye men of the Vale, beware
of that. *****

When Hoar Down has a hat,
Let Kenton beware of a skat. *****

Old Mother Goring got her cap on
We shall have some wet. *****

Clouds

> *When Fairlie Down puts on his
> cap,
> Romney Marsh will have its sap.*   *****

These thirteen weather adages maintain the hill stratus theme with emphasis to a particular local hill or mountain often referring to it as being covered by a cap, hat, shift or hood of low cloud *(stratus)*. The first saw refers to Westmorland; Sussex claims the second and third; Leicestershire the fourth; Herefordshire the fifth where Ladie Lift refers to a clump of trees near Weobley; Lancashire the sixth; Yorkshire seventh, eighth and ninth; Worcestershire the tenth. A "skat" in the eleventh is a shower; Sussex claims the twelfth referring to Chanctonbury Ring, a tree clump on the South Downs on the Goring estate; finally Kent originates the thirteenth. The test results of the previous paragraph apply here.

Helm Cloud

> *A cloud, called the 'helm cloud',
> or 'helm bar', hovering about the
> hilltops for a day or two, is
> said to presage wind and rain.*   ****

The "Helm bar" is a nearly stationary slender roll of whirling cloud which rests along or just above the Crossfell Range in Westmoreland and Cumberland, especially east of the river Eden. It appears and forms in a strong cold North-East wind (the Helm wind) most frequently in late winter and spring. It is an example of a mountain lee-wave and appears above a point ½ to 3½ miles from the foot of the fell.

THUNDERSTORMS AND CUMULONIMBUS CLOUDS

Thunderstorms and hail are associated with the vigorous Cumulonimbus (Cb) cloud - a very deep vertical cumulus cloud often with an anvil-looking cirrus top. Terrific up and down currents control the cloud's life cycle. They occur in cool unstable polar Westerlies and in warm moist summer polar South-Westerlies. Sometimes Altocumulus Castellanus (Ac Cas) cloud can be responsible for thunderstorms. They are the medium-level deep convective cloud often with bases as high as 6,000 feet. Remember lightning is a discharge of static electricity which can be *seen*. Forked lightning is seen as an irregular fork, sheet lightning is a mass glow of light. Thunder is the sound *heard* produced by the violent expansion of the air along the path of the lightning flash. Since light (lightning) travels faster than sound (thunder) one can judge the distance of the lightning from the observer by counting the number of seconds between the flash and the thunder and dividing by five. This gives the distance in miles. Using this method one can plot the path of such a storm. Thunderstorms continue throughout the year but are most active from May to September with a summer peak in July.

Usually three conditions are required for a Cb or thunder cloud to form. Firstly a very deep vertical unstable layer with the cloud beginning as a cottony cumulus cloud vigorously growing into a hugh Cb with tops 25,000-40,000ft (6-8 miles deep). Secondly plenty of water vapour is needed at the surface to supply the rapid cloud growth. Finally a trigger action is required to set off the convection, often in England by high afternoon maximum air temperatures (insolation). Trigger action from sea and windward coasts is also available with constant high sea-surface temperatures. One of the favourite situations for thunderstorms are stationary depressions and troughs sometimes helped by the lifting action of mountains.

The thunderstorm of the season will come from the same quarter as the first one. **

This fanciful idea that all thunderstorm clouds in one season move from one general quarter is intriguing but false.

Thunderstorms

*First thunder in winter or
spring indicates rain and
very cold weather.*   *

*Thunder and lightning early in
winter or late in fall indicate
warm weather.*   *****

Lightning brings heat.   *****

*The air useth to be extreme hot
before thunders.*   *****

One saw indicates cold weather and two others warmth after a thunderstorm. They produce poor results but the forecast of warm weather hits the jackpot with 80 percent. Of course this is to be expected as the majority of thunderstorms are associated with moist mild unstable airstreams. Bacon's saw is last.

1st thunder in winter/spring then wet/very cold   2/16   (13)
" thunder in early winter/late autumn then warm   8/10   (80)

*Winter thunder,
The old folk death, to young
folks plunder.*   ***

Presumably this means winter thunderstorms bring on humid heat which used to kill off old people but suited others.

*The first thunder of the year
awakes
All the frogs and all the snakes.*

A poetic way of saying the first year's thunder (occurring any month January to April) *can* coincide with end of winter hibernation of the frog (February/March) or snake (April).

*When it thunders in the morning,
it will rain before night.*   *****

*Thunder in the morning denotes
winds; at noon, showers.*   *****

Morning thunders signify winds;

Thunderstorms

> noon thunders, rain; roaring
> thunders, rough wind; crackling
> thunders, wind and rain. ****

> Thunder in ye morning signifies
> wynde, about noon rayne, in ye
> evening great tempest. ****

> If there be thunder in the
> evening, there will be much
> rain and showery weather. ****

Bacon originated the second saw. Thunder or lightning or both occurring at any time of the day (except nightime) signify heavy showers of rain (sometimes hail) with strong gusts.

> If in a clear and starry night
> it lighten to the south-east,
> it foretelleth great store of
> wind and rain to come in from
> those parts. ****

> If there be sheet lightning and
> a clear sky in spring, summer
> and autumn evenings, expect
> heavy rains. *****

> The distant thunder speaks of
> coming rain. *****

If on fairly clear nights lightning is seen, especially to the S.E., it tells of heavy showers to come. The S.E. lightning denotes thundery activity in the English Channel or relevant coasts often denoting storms to arrive later.

> Forked lightning at night,
> The next day clear and bright. **

> Lightning without thunder after
> a clear day, there will be a
> continuance of fair weather. **

Opposite in meaning to previous maxims and basically incorrect. Only on very few occasions does the weather continue fine.

273

Thunderstorms

If it sinks from the north
It will double its wrath.
If it sinks from the south,
It will open its mouth.
If it sinks from the west,
It is never at rest.
If it sinks from the east,
It will leave us in peace.   ****

If the lightning is in the
colder quarters of the heaven,
in the north and north-east,
hailstones will follow; but
if in the warmer, as the south
and west, there will be showers
with a sultry temperature.   ****

Lightning under north star will
bring rain in three days.   *

Lightning in north will be
followed by rain in twenty-four
hours.   ****

Lightning in north in summer
is a sign of heat.   ***

When it lightens only from the
north-west, look for rain the
next day.   ****

Thunder from the south or
south-east indicates foul
weather; from the north or
north-west, fair weather.   ****

If from the south or the west
it lightens, expect both wind
and rain from these points.   ***

Lightning signifies the approach
of wind and rain from the
quarter where it lightens; but   ***
if it lightens in different
parts of the sky, there will
be severe and dreadful storms.   ****

Thunderstorms

*Thunder from the south or
south-east indicates long
storms; from the north or
north-west, short storms.* ********

These adages, with the first from Kent and second from Bacon's vigorous quill, are examples of very good observation and excellent forecasts. The main point to remember about thunderstorms is that they move or are steered by the wind at medium levels. For a Cb around 10,000-18,000ft. The surface wind in the vicinity of the thunderstorm would be under a barrage of violent up and down draughts causing it to experience *any* direction and speed. For example a Cb cloud can bodily move from the south to the north with east or west surface gusty winds.

Abundance depends on sour milk. *******

Every so often one comes across some vague weather saw which can be easily scoffed at and at first glance regarded as useless. This one intrigued the author. After a number of inquiries the true meaning appeared. (Never regard old country weather lore as ridiculous - they often hide subtle meanings.) This saw relates that thunderstorms aid crops. The increase in atmospheric electricity is supposed to oxidize the ammonia of the air forming nitric acid. In turn this affects milk - hence the "sour milk". Tests were conducted 1947-66 with very few cases.

Hay 3/6 (50)
Wheat 1/6 (17)

*When it thunders, the thief
becomes honest.*

If anyone has been very close to a lightning flash with its instant thunder, its terrific frightening explosive sound and suddenness, one will never forget it. Indeed it's enough to make a thief honest.

*Thunderstorms go round and
round the valley and cannot
escape.* ******

A quaint maxim hailing from the Thames Valley around Oxford. The saying isn't true as the valley is shallow (only deep mountainous valleys affect the tracking and life cycle of thun-

Thunderstorms

derstorms). If one is slow moving it means the medium-level steering speed is light. Often in these situations more than one thunderstorm joins together giving the impression that they remain in one area for a long time.

Some claim thunder is "God moving His furniture about."

An old country way of explaining why it thunders.

When a house-leek grows on the roof of a house, that house will never be struck by lightning.   *

Many wild flowers and plants have this non-lightning strike property. The house-leek is one of them. (Refer to the flower chapter for similar saws.)

It never thunders but it rains.   ****

After much thunder, much rain.   ****

Thunderstorms and heavy rain showers go together. One may hear thunder in the distance and escape rain, but this is the exception.

The sound of bells is supposed to dissipate thunder and lightning.   *

Although this looks like an intriguing maxim with a deep meaning, the author cannot see one.

HAIL

Hail is always associated with showers and Cumulonimbus (Cb) cloud and nearly always with thunderstorms. The latter occur all through the year but are most frequent from May to September peaking in England in July. If a large hailstone is cut the inside is similar to an onion with alternating layers of clear and opaque ice. In its early stages of development the hailstone gets caught up in vicious undraughts transfering it to the top of the Cb cloud where the temperatures are very low. Here the hailstone acquires a layer of opaque ice or rime. In its turbulent up and down journey it accumulates its multilayers finally descending to the ground.

Hail brings frost in the tail.   ***

*A hailstorm by day denotes
a frost at night.*   ***

Because hail is an ice phenomenon clearly the two saws associate it with cold weather and night frost. This is nearly always true in winter when hail is scarce. Summer hail is rarely followed by ground frost although often occurs with a cool airstream.

*If hail appears after a long
course of rain, it is a sign
that the weather will improve
very soon indeed, but showers
will follow if the wind is
westerly, and the stronger
the wind the sharper the
showers - which may be of hail.*   *****

This is a correct observation of the passage of a vigorous cold front, trough or line squall. The change from continuous rain to hail is caused by the transfer from stable cloudy weather to squally showers and partly cloudy weather. In *this particular* case it is true that the stronger the westerly wind the heavier the shower.

RAINBOW

*The old Norsemen called the
rainbow "the Bridge of the Gods".*

*When a rainbow is formed in an
approaching cloud, expect a
shower; but when in receding
cloud, fine weather.* *****

*When a rainbow appears in the
wind's eye, rain is sure to
follow.* *****

*If a rainbow appears in fair
weather, foul will follow;
But if a rainbow appears in
foul weather, fair weather
will follow.* *****

*The rainbow, after a long
drought, is the precursor of a
decided change to wet weather;
and it happens also that a
perfect bow, after an unsettled
time, is a precursor of fair
weather.* *****

*Rainbow to windward, foul falls
the day;
Rainbow to leeward, damp runs away.* *****

Before discussing the merits of the five saws it is best to state a few basic facts about a rainbow. There are sometimes more than one or the primary rainbow - they are the secondary and supernumary bows. Remember a rainbow can only appear to an observer when the sun is behind him and is illuminating raindrops *ahead* of him. The rainbow is made up of red, orange, yellow, green, blue, indigo and violet - easily remembered by the abbreviation ROYGBIV. The sun's rays of white light are refracted and reflected in the raindrop to produce the rainbow with the red on the outside. Also nearly all of the rainbows are connected with *showery* weather where short sunny showers provide the two vital basics for rainbow production. It becomes appar-

Rainbow

ent, for example, that in the morning with the sun in the SE a rainbow would form to the NW of an observer. If this is into wind then it is certain a shower is almost imminent. The reverse also applies.

A dog in the morning,
Sailor, take warning,
A dog in the night,
Is the sailor's delight.   *****

A rainbow in the morn,
Put your hook in the corn;
A rainbow in the eve,
Put your hook in the sheave.   *****

If there be a rainbow in the eve,
It will rain and leave;
But if there be a rainbow in
the morrow,
It will neither lend or borrow.   *****

A rainbow in the morning
Is the shepherd's warning;
A rainbow at night
Is the shepherd's delight.   *****

If the rainbow comes at night,
The rain is gone quite.   *****

The rainbow in the marnin'
Gives the shepherd a warnin'
The car' his gurt cwoat on his
back;
The rainbow at night is the
shepherd's delight;
For then no gurt cwoat will
he lack.   *****

A rainbow at night
Fair weather in sight.
A rainbow at morn,
Fair weather all gorn.   *****

The second adage hails from Cornwall, fifth from Suffolk and Wiltshire provides the sixth. A "dog" is a rainbow. Once the sun's elevation reaches above $42°$, rainbows cannot normally

Rainbow

form. So the main or primary rainbow occurs more frequent in winter than summer and is observed more often in the morning and late afternoon/evening time. It is impossible to see one in the middle of a summer's day. Based on the principle that most of our weather travels west to east, a morning rainbow seen in the west would signify showers and cloud to follow and an evening rainbow in the east clearer weather. Although no tests were carried out the result expected would be about 70 percent. Similar figures can be compared in the Rain Chapter.

When a perfect rainbow shows only two principle colours, which are generally red and yellow, expect fair weather for several days. ****

If the blue should predominate, the air is clearing. *****

If the green be large and bright in the rainbow, it is a sign of continued rain. If red be the strongest colour, there will be rain and wind together. After much wet weather the rainbow indicates a clearing up. If the bow disappears all at once, there will follow serene and settled weather. *****

When the rainbow is broad, with the primatic colours very distinct, and green or blue predominating, expect much rain the succeeding night. If the red colour is conspicuous and the last to disappear, expect both rain and wind. ****

If the rainbow forms and disappears suddenly, the prismatic colours being but slightly discernable, expect fair weather next day. *****

Rainbow

The general rule about rainbow colours is that the larger the raindrop (in a thunderstorm or heavy shower) the more vivid and beautiful the rainbow colours. A decrease in drop size produces a general fading of the colours. In fact in fog where the water droplets are so small, a rare fogbow is always white.

> *Whenever you observe the rainbow to be broken in two or three places, or perhaps only half of it visible, expect rainy weather for two or three days.* ****

> *When the rainbow does not reach down to the water, clear weather will follow.* **

These two maxims contradict each other. It would seem that a partial rainbow occurs in very windy and showery conditions leaving little time for the sun's rays to form the rainbow. It is therefore thought the first adage is the truest.

> *A bow low down on the mountains is a bad sign for the crop. If seen at a great distance, it indicates fair weather.* ***

Very small rainbows can only occur near the horizon extending from the ground to the cloud base.

> *Seven rainbows, eight days rain.* **

Just playing with numbers occurs here. Of course 7 rainbows would indicate an extremely showery if not thundery airstream.

> *A rainbow in spring indicates fair weather for twenty-four hours.* *

This is totally incorrect.

> *The bow in the morning, rain will follow; if at noon, heavy*

Rainbow

rain; if at night, fair weather. ✱✱✱✱✱
The appearance of double or
triple bows indicates fair for
the present, but heavy rain soon. ✱✱✱✱

A double rainbow contains the primary and secondary bows where the latter lies outside with reversed colour notation. A second rainbow does not indicate clearing weather, if anything the opposite.

WILD FLOWERS AND PLANTS

I find plant and flower weather lore one of the most pleasing chapters in this book. It must be the combination of the beautiful shapes and colours of the flowers with the mysteries of weather. Many plants are sensitive to humidity and sunlight changes and of course countrymen believe that in this lies the answer in forecasting weather. Flowers tend to close more when humidity increases, then the favourite forecast is rain but often moist air can naturally occur in dry periods in the evening and in mist and fog.

Most flowers close at night but some remain open. This can occur when overnight temperatures are high and humidity low, which also means a good breeze or cloud cover is present. This is often true when changeable weather is imminent.

Wood Anemone

The yellow wood anemone and the wind flower close their petals and droop before rain. ✱✱✱

The wood anemone never opens its petals but when the wind blows, whence its name.

The Wood Anemone is nicknamed the Wind Flower (which blooms from March to June) because its flowers nod and shake in the wind. Indeed the petals are very sensitive to disturbance. Certainly any strong increase of wind is always a sound forecast of rain to come, whether it be the downdraught of an oncoming shower or the first signs of a depression. It is interesting to note that its other nicknames are *Windflower* in Devon, Somerset, Hants, Glos, Bucks, N'thants, Warwicks and Cheshire; *Fairie's Windflower* in Dorset and *Wind Plant* in Lincs.

Bladder Campion

This is known as *Thunderbolt* in Kent and blooms from June to September.

White Campion

The flower is out between May and June and locally called *Thunderbolt* in Rutland and *Thunderflower* in Cumberland.

Chickweed

Chickweed expands its leaves boldly and fully when fine weather is to follow; but if it should shut up, then the traveller is to put on his great coat. **

The half opening of the flowers of the chickweed is a sign that the wet will not last long. **

Much early work in observing flowers and weather scientifically was done by Norman L. Silvester during the period 1917 to 1923 in London and Yorkshire. He observed flowers within 200 yards of his Stevenson screen (a purpose-built latticed enclosure for housing thermometers and other meteorological instruments) mainly in spring, summer and autumn. The common Chickweed flower, which is open all the year round, responds to temperature and humidity. Once above a soil temperature of $50°$ Fahrenheit ($10°$ Centigrade) *and* air temperature over $51°F$

Clover

(10.6°C) the flower answers to humidity, closing at 81 percent. Poor results of 22 percent occurred for rain to follow within 6 hours after the Chickweed flower closed.

26/120 (22)

Cinquefoil

*Expect rain if the flower of
the cinquefoil expands.* **

This is a North Riding of Yorkshire weather saw.

Clover

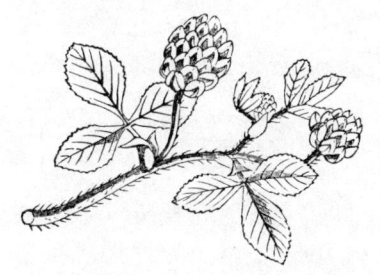

*Clover contracts its leaves
at the approach of a storm.* *

*Clover grass is rough to the
touch when stormy weather is
at hand.* *

*Expect rain if the stalks of
clover stand upright.* *

The third saying is from the North Riding of Yorkshire. Temperature and humidity do not seem to be controlling factors over clover movement. Silvester found the overriding reason for leaf closure was wind. On a 42-feet mast he found that in the daytime a wind gust of less than 20 m.p.h. left the leaf open; over 20 m.p.h. it nearly closed, shutting on reaching gale force (gusts of 49 m.p.h. or more). Poor figures evolved from a test of 11 percent success rate giving rain within 6 hours after the clover leaf closes. Also it was established that an increase in wind did not occur under similar circumstances.

1/9   (11)

Convolvulus

*The convolvulus folds up its
petals at the approach of rain.*   ******

This trumpet-shaped twining plant, flowering from July to September, is another sensitive type.

Cowslip

*The cowslip stalks being short
are said to foreshow a dry
summer.*   *****

This beautiful flower, blooming from April to May, will have short stalks due to poor weather conditions of the *previous* seasons.

Daisy

Dandelion

Although no weather lore can be found about the movement of the common daisy's flower (blooming from January to October) or leaves, humidity and temperature cause it to close its flower. Silvester found it opened only when the ground temperature ranged from 52°F (11.1°C) to 58°F (14.4°C) *with* relative humidity 64 to 82 percent. Once the last figure was reached the flower closed. The poor results relate to rain expected within 6 hours after the flower closed. 31/92 (34)

Ox-Eye or Moon Daisy

*The great white ox eye closes
before rain.* **

Another plant known as *Thunder Daisy* in Devon and Somerset which responds to humidity change. It flowers from June to August.

Dandelion

*When the down of the dandelion
contracts, it is a sign of rain.* *

*If the down flyeth off colt's
foot, dandelion, and thistles,
when there is no wind, it is a
sign of rain.* **

*The dandelions close their
blossoms before a storm.* **

*When the dandelion blooms early
in spring, there will be a short
season. When they bloom later   *
expect a dry summer.* ***

Silvester found that above 51°F (10.6°C) the golden Dandelion (which flowers March to June) always remained open. Below 46°F (7.8°C) they were completely closed. He further found that wind and humidity had no effect. The myth about the down or Dandelion "clock" of white fruits taking off before rain has no foundation. The flower is one of the first to bloom in March. The last weather maxim means that an early spring (very warm March) brings an overall cold or short-spring season and a cold March followed by a warm April or May portends a dry summer.

Gentian

A test of these last two statements proved negative.

                                                                                  8/105   (8)
                                                                                   12/29   (41)

Fern

It was anciently supposed that the burning of fern drew down the rain.   **

Another variation of the above saying occurred in 1636 when Charles I was due to visit Staffordshire. His Lord Chamberlain, Lord Pembroke, wrote to the county's High sheriff asking him not to burn ferns in case they should invoke rain for the expected royal party. The real connection lies deep in the mists of time. However, in very rare cases, the heat from forest fires in the ascending flames and smoke can cause a deep cumulus cloud to grow producing a rain shower.

Gentian

The gentian closes up both flowers and leaves before rain.   **

Whitlow Grass and Lady's Bedstraw

We may look for wet weather if the leaves of the whitlow grass droop, and if ladies bedstraw becomes inflated and gives off a strong odour.   **

Whitlow grass leaves drop because of increasing humidity, usually at its highest at night. Lady's Bedstraw provides a delightful illustration, when, in the evening or when the air is damp, its myrial flowers smell of honey and dry with a scent of hay.

African Marigold

If the African marigold do not open its petals by seven in the

Mistletoe

> *morning, it will rain or*
> *thunder that day. It also*
> *closes before a storm.* ∗∗

This means that in normal weather conditions the plant will open its petals by 7 a.m. If not then mist or cloudy conditions prevail which may lead to rain.

Cape Marigold

> *If the small Cape marigold*
> *should open at six or seven in*
> *the morning, and not close till*
> *four in the afternoon, we may*
> *reckon on settled weather.* ∗∗∗

The saw means that on a sunny day, the forecast of dry weather is a good bet.

Marsh and Common Marigold

> *The marsh marigold blows when*
> *the cuckoo sings.* ∗

> *The marigold that goes to bed*
> *with the sun,*
> *And with him rises, weeping.* ∗∗∗

Stillingfleet in Yorkshire's East Riding provides the first saw which proves difficult in producing a sensible meaning. The last saying is from Shakespeare's pen.

Mistletoe

> *Mistletoe hanging in a room*
> *affords protection against*
> *lightning.* ∗

This parasitic plant growing on trees, like many others, has thunderstorm protection properties originating in ancient folklore.

Scarlet Pimpernel

House Leek

Country people grew a house leek on their cottage roof to keep lightening away.   *

Houseleek with its pink flowers growing on walls and roofs is nicknamed the *Thunder Plant* in Somerset. The myth that it protected one from lightning originates from the Romans who called it *Jupiter's Plant*. One of the Roman god's emblems was lightning.

Scarlet Pimpernel

When the pink-eyed pimpernel (ploughman's weather glass) closes in the daytime, it is a sign of rain.   **

Pimpernel, pimpernel, tell me true
Whether the weather be fine or no;
No heart can think, no tongue can tell,
The virtues of the pimpernel.   ****** **

Now, look! Our weather glass is spread,
The pimpernel, whose flower
Closes its leaves of spotted red
Against a rainy hour.   **

Our pimpernel, whose brilliant flower
Closes against the approaching shower,
Warning the swain to sheltering bower
From humid air secure.   **

If the red pimpernel has its

Scarlet Pimpernel

> *flowers fully opened first thing in the morning, no matter what the barometer may indicate, it will be a sign to say that there will be no rain that day, and harvesting may proceed without fear. On the other hand, if the petals are still closed in the morning, then rain is on its way.*
>
> ******
>
> **

This is the most famous weather flower of all. It is better known as the Ploughman's Weather Glass. Its scarlet flowers bloom from May to September and are sensitive to temperature and air dampness change, often closing in wet and humid weather. Silvester found that the flowers stayed open for 8 to 9 hours even on the shortest lit day (normal time of opening $4\frac{1}{4}$ hours after sunrise and closing $1\frac{1}{3}$ hours before sunset). They never opened at night in all of his 247 observations. The controlling factor was relative humidity reaching a critical value of 80 percent when the scarlet gem was only partially open. By taking Silvester's data, average daylight and the Pimpernel's daily blooming time the following results evolved. With the flower closed in the daytime rain followed within 6 hours on only 17 percent of occasions. However an excellent figure of 81 percent was scored for dry weather to occur 6 hours after the flower opened.

Some of the countryman's weather nicknames for the flower make fascinating reading. *Change-of-the-Weather*, *Grandfather's Weatherglass* and *Old Man's Weatherglass* are all found in Somerset; *Ploughman's Weatherglass* in Wilts and Beds; *Poor Man's Weatherglass* in Somerset, Hants, N'thants, Warwicks, Cheshire and Cumb; *Shepherd's Calendar* in Devon; *Shepherd's Dial* in Middlesex; *Shepherd's Glass* in Norfolk and Rutland; *Shepherd's Warning* in Somerset and Lincs; *Shepherd's Weatherglass* in Devon, Somerset, Wilts, N'thants, Notts, Lincs, Yorks; *Weather Flower* in Dorset; *Weatherglass* in West Wilts, Bucks and Leics and *Weather-Teller* in Somerset.

24/139 (17)
87/108 (81)

Pitcher Plant

> *Expect rain if the flower of the pitcher plant turns upside down.*
>
> **

Another saying from Yorkshire's North Riding telling of

the unique weather change to this unusual plant.

Water Plantain

This plant which flowers from May to August is locally called *Great Thunderbolt* and *Umbrellas* in Somerset. The latter because of its wide leaves growing near the ground resembling open parasols.

Pondweed

> *Pondweed sinks before rain.* ✱✱

Pondweed is a special aquatic herb growing in still water and is not a general term for any number of water weeds. Presumably the maxim means that any freshening of wind (often a forerunner of rain) will disturb still water and agitate the Pondweed.

Poppy

> *English children believe that poppies should not be picked for fear of a thunderstorm and placing along the timbers under the roof warded off lightning.* ✱

Another flower blooming June to August which if placed in the house, especially in the roof timbers, repelled lightning. Many country children were too scared to pick the poppy in case a thunderstorm erupted. It seems curious that most large red flowers have some relationship with thunder or lightning, perhaps because the red colour traditionally has always been a sign of danger. The Poppy is also known as *Lightnings* in Northumbs; *Thunderball* in Warwicks; *Thunderbolt* in Devon, West England, Shropshire and Cheshire and *Thunder Flower* in Wilts.

Ragged Robin

Called in Yorkshire the *Thunder-Flower*, it blooms from May to June.

Sorrel

Purple Sandwort

> *Purple sandwort expands its
> beautiful pink flowers only
> when the sun shines, but closes
> them before the coming shower.*   ***
>   **

Another plant sensitive to weather changes.

Burnet Saxifrage

> *The burnet saxifrage indicates
> by half-opening its flowers
> that the rain is soon to cease.*   **

The Burnet Saxifrage probably reacts in humidity changes.

Seaweed

> *A piece of kelp or sea-weed
> hung up will become damp
> previous to rain.*   ***

At last we have the old favourite - the saying that every weatherman has his leg pulled about. Like the pine or conifer cones the seaweed reacts to humidity change. Many hours of high humidity moistens the kelp which can be caused by wet fogs (100 percent humidities), moist airstreams with no rain or occasionally in cases ahead of rain. The seaweed like many other sensitive plants is not a precursor of rain or sun but a crude instrument recording actual present weather conditions.

Sorrel

> *A species of wood sorrel
> contracts its leaves at the
> approach of rain.*   **

> *Expect rain if the flowers of
> the sorrel close.*

Star of Bethlehem

Another sensitive plant, flowering from April to May, reacting to humidity differences presenting itself as a natural hygrometer. The second saying hails from Yorkshire's North Riding.

Germander Speedwell

> *The germander speedwell closes*
> *its blue petals before rain,* **
> *and opens them again when it*
> *has ceased.* **

This sensitive flower is interestingly referred to as the *Strike-Fire* in N'thants.

Star of Bethlehem

> *The so called Star of Bethlehem*
> *has a star flower recalling the*
> *Nativity Star. They shut early*
> *in the day and always in dull*
> *weather.* ***

The Star of Bethlehem, so-called because the flower resembles the Nativity Star, normally closes around midday as can be seen from the following county nicknames. It is known as *Betty-go-to-Bed-at-Noon*, *Jack-go-to-Bed-at-Noon* and *Eleven O'clock Lady* in Somerset; *Noon-Peeders* in Wilts; *One O'clock* in Devon; *Twelve O'clocks* in Cornwall, Somerset, Dorset and Oxon and *Wake at Noon* in Wilts and the Isle-of-Wight.

Greater Stitchwort

> *The picking of the greater*
> *stitchwort provokes thunder.* *

The picking of the flower which blooms April to June is said to provoke thunder. In Dorset it is known as the *Thunderbolt* and *Thunder-Flower* in Cumberland.

Teasel

Trefoil

*Teasel or Fuller's thistle hung
up will open for fine weather,
and close for wet.*   ***

*Cut'em in June, they'll come
again soon;
Cut'em in July, they may die;
Cut'em in August, die they
must.*

Another sensitive humidity plant similar to the famous pine cones and seaweed, i.e. to open and shut on demand. The second Shropshire saying is perfectly true - an example of true nature observation.

Sow Thistle

*The non-closing of the flower
heads of the sow thistle warns
us that it will rain next day,*   **
*whilst the closing of them
denotes fine weather.*   ***

This Bacon saying proclaims another sensitive hygrometer; this time affecting the plant's stalk.

Trefoil

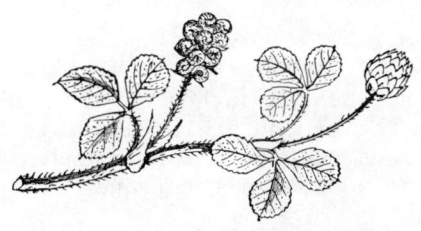

*The stalk of trefoil swells
before rain.*   *

Red Valerian

In Devon and Hants referred to as the *Scarlet Lightning*.

TREES

*Trees snapping and cracking in
autumn indicate dry weather.*

An observation of the obvious rather than a forecast. A long dry spell in autumn will often dry the land and plants, especially trees.

*When dry leaves rattle on the
trees, expect snow.* ******

Poetic turn of phrase, not always true.

*When the leaves show their
undersides,
Be very sure that rain betides.* *******

This is one of the more famous of tree weather lore. It seems that there can be two possible meanings to this saw; a period of damp air which softens leaf stalks and when strong winds manoeuvre the leaves. Both are supposed to be forerunners of rain.

*Dead branches falling in calm
weather indicates rain.* *******

A subtle meaning. Dead branches are often caused by disease. When they fall to the ground a wind aloft is indicated even-though calm conditions occur near the ground. This often is the first indication of a blow, a forerunner of rain.

Short boughs, short vintage. ********

Weather saw related to English wines.

*Plenty of berries indicate a
severe winter.* ******

Ash and Oak

This theme occurs throughout the chapter.

Ash

> *Avoid an ash,*
> *It courts a flash.*   ***

An ash tree, like the oak, is prone to lightning strike.

Ash and Oak

> *When the oak comes out before*
> *the ash, there will be fine*
> *weather in harvest; but when*   **
> *the ash comes out before the*
> *oak, the harvest will be wet.*   **

The series of saws to follow are related to the ash and oak. Luckily the author discovered records kept in Marsham in Norfolk of the first oak and ash leafing of the year from 1736 to 1935 by the Margery family. Of the 122 years actually observed 83 saw the oak leaf before the ash, 35 times the reverse and 4 when both leafed on the same day.

The first adage from the Midlands comes off poorly. The two results were tested for an August and September harvest. Averaged Norfolk data showed the oak to leaf on 24 April and ash 29th.

```
Oak before ash = fine weather in August harvest   23/83  (28)
 "      "   "  =    "       "    Sept     "       22/83  (26)
Ash     "  oak = wet         "    August   "       9/34  (26)
 "      "   "  =    "       "    Sept     "       12/34  (35)
```

> *When the ash is out before the*
> *oak,*
> *Then we may expect a choke;*   **
> *When the oak is out before the*
> *ash,*
> *Then we may expect a splash.*   **

> *When buds the oak before the ash,*
> *You'll only have a summer splash.*   **

> *The ash before the oak*
> *Choke, choke, choke;*   **

Ash and Oak

The oak before the ash,
Splash, splash, splash. ⁂

The first saw hails from Shropshire. "Choke" refers to a drought and "splash" a rainy, though not a torrential, period. Since both trees average leafing in late April, May was tested for a dry or wet month. The results are disappointing.

Ash before oak then a choke				9/34	(26)
Oak " ash " " splash				25/83	(30)

If buds the ash before the oak,
You'll surely have a summer
soak; ⁂
But if behind the oak the ash is,
You'll only have a few light
splashes. ⁂⁂

This saying is completely opposite to the normal oak and ash theme, and refers to flowering of the trees not their leafing. Note we have the first reference to "soak" or torrential wet periods.

If the ash is out before the
oak,
You may expect a thorough soak; ⁂
If the oak is out before the
ash,
You'll hardly get a single
splash. ⁂⁂

Here we have the usual phrasing of the legendary weather maxim. But poor results become evident.

Ash before oak then a soak (wet May)	11/34	(32)
Oak " ash " " splash (dry May)	30/83	(36)

Oak, smoke. ⁂
Ash, squash. ⁂

This brief Kentish saying recalls "smoke" as a hot summer and "squash" as a wet one. Poor results emerge.

Hot summer	14/83	(17)
Wet "	10/34	(29)

Beech

> *The oak before the ash,*
> *Prepare your summer sash;* ⁂
> *The ash before the oak,*
> *Prepare your summer cloak.* ⁂

Dorset provides this adage. A "sash" either refers to a scarf worn over the waist or around the collar or a window sash which would have to be freed in hot sticky summer weather. The test and results in the next maxim equally apply here.

> *If the oak is out before*
> *the ash,*
> *Twill be a summer of wet*
> *and splash;* ⁂⁂
> *But if the ash is before*
> *the oak,*
> *Twill be a summer of fire*
> *and smoke.* ⁂

This Hampshire variation of the popular theme also gains poor results.

                          Wet summer   33/83   (40)
                          Dry   "   10/34   (29)

Beech

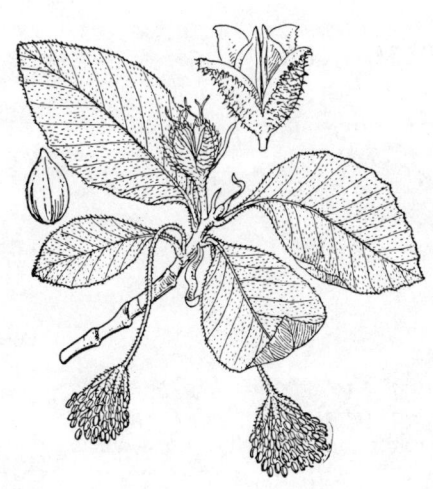

Broom

> *When the beech mast thrives well
> and oak trees hang full, a hard
> winter will follow, with much
> snow.*   ∗∗∗

Another "plenty of nuts, severe winter" type theme.

> *When beech nuts are plentiful,
> expect a mild winter.*   ∗∗∗

No records are available for plentiful beech nut years but the author thought that testing for early beech leafing years would be a reasonable substitute. Norfolk data for 1736-1926 were used. Records of 49 years of earliest leafing of the beech were judged to fall before its average date of 19 April. Poor results emerged.   Mild winter   21/49   (43)
            Hard   "   17/49   (35)

Broom

> *If the broom be full of flower,
> it signyfieth plenty.*   ∗∗

> *The broom having plenty of
> blossoms is a sign of a
> fruitful year of corn.*   ∗∗

The broom's yellow flower begins to bloom in May and June. Prolific growth is related to previous good weather seasons.

Dogrose and Whitethorn

> *If many whitethorn blossoms
> or dog-roses are seen, expect
> a severe winter.*   ∗∗

Dogwood

> *When the blooms of the dog
> wood tree are full, expect a
> cold winter; when the blooms
> are light, expect a warm winter.*   ∗∗

Elder

Excessive or deficient blooms again are only the result of previous good or bad growing seasons.

Elder

> *You may shear your sheep*
> *When the elder blossoms peep.*

Dangerous weather-cum-farming lore. Frosts can still occur after the elder tree blossoms.

Elm

> *When the elmen leaf is as*
> *big as a mouse's ear,*
> *Then to sow barley never fear.* *
> *When the elmen leaf is as*
> *big as an ox's eye,*
> *Then says I, "Hie, boys! hie!"* ***

> *When elm leaves are as big as*
> *a shilling,*

*Plant kidney beans, if to
plant-em you're willing;* ✶✶
*When the elm leaves are as big
as a penny,
You must plant kidney beans, if
you mean to have any.* ✶✶✶

The second saw comes from Worcestershire. If early leafing of the elm is accepted as a year when large leaves emerge then the tests are valid. The opposite applies to a small leaf or "mouse's ear". Early leafing occurs before 31 March and late leafing after 12 April. All poor results.

        Late leaf = good barley harvest   1/8 (13)
        Early " = poor   "   "   8/18 (44)

Hawthorn, May or Whitethorn

*It is always cold when the
hawthorn blossom.* ✶✶

This is not always true. Hawthorn mainly blossoms in May into June. The most frequent cold snap during this period is in the first two weeks of May when northerlies are dominant. The test provides terrible results.   8/28 (29)

Holly

*When the hawthorn has too many
haws
We shall have many snaws.* **

Usual balance maxim. Country folk believe nature provides abundant haws as food for the hungry birds in a forthcoming severe winter. Of course it is a measurement of previous good weather growing seasons.

*The leaves of the may tree
bear up, so that the underside
may be seen before a storm.* ***

Refer to the beginning of the chapter for the meaning here.

Holly

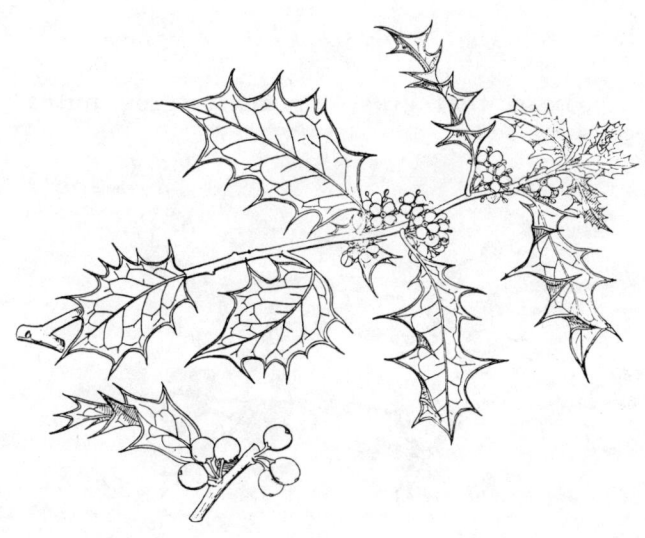

*Grow holly alongside your house
as it is considered to be a
protection against thunder and
lightening.* *

This adage is like the saw in the plant chapter connected with the houseleek. There may be some connection in that most of these thunder plants have *red* or *pink* flowers/berries which in itself is a sign of danger.

Oak

Mulberry

> *When the mulberry hath shown
> green leaf, there will be no
> more frost.*   ✳✳✳

Gloucestershire provides this saying.

Oak

There is no doubt that the old oak tree was connected with Thor the god of thunder. The oak is struck more by lightning than any other tree.

> *You must look for grass on the
> top of an oak tree.*

This adage means that grass only really grows quickly after the oak begins to leaf.

> *If the oak bears much mast, it
> foreshows a long and hard winter.*   ✳✳

Another "many berries, hard winter" type maxim which is all explained in similar saws in the September chapter.

> *When the oak puts on his
> gosling gray,*

Rowan

> *'Tis time to sow barley,*
> *night or day.*

The reasons for the underside of leaves to show can be seen at the beginning of the chapter.

Pine

> *Pine cones hung up in the house*
> *will close themselves against*
> *wet and cold weather, and open*
> *against hot and dry times.* ✸✸✸

A very famous saw which nowadays is used in conversation as a mocking phrase. There is no doubt that cones, pine in particular, close in high humidity and open with dry low humidities in the air. Unfortunately it is only a natural instrument for measuring *actual* conditions as they are, not the weather to come.

Rowan

> *Many rains, many rowans,* ✸✸✸
> *Many rowans, many yauns.* ✸✸✸✸

"Yauns" are light or poor crops. The rowan (mountain ash) probably refers to its berries in the saw. There seems to be a lot of common sense in the harmful and abundance effect of wet springs and summers.

Sloe or Blackthorn

> *When the sloe tree is white*
> *as a sheet,*
> *Sow your barley, whether it*
> *be dry or wet.*

The sloe tree or blackthorn when in full white flower bloom has always been regarded as a time for sowing of barley.

Sycamore

> *Before rain the leaves of the*
> *lime, sycamore, plane, and*
> *poplar trees show a great deal*
> *more of their undersurfaces*
> *when trembling in the wind.* ✸✸✸

GARDEN AND FARM PRODUCE

Plant the bean when the moon is light;
Plant potatoes when the moon is dark.

If apples bloom in March,
In vain for'um you'll sarch; ****
If apples bloom in April,
Well then they'll be plentiful; ****
If apples bloom in May,
You may eat'um night and day. ****

Onion's skin very thin,
Mild winter coming in; **
Onion's skin thick and tough,
Coming winter cold and rough. **

The first and second are old-style land and fruit farming maxims. The onion weather lore applies to *previous* good or bad seasons.

There gay chrysanthemums repose,
And when stern tempests lower,
Their silken fringes softly close
Against the shower. **

Poetic treatment of actual conditions.

Under the furze is hunger and cold,
Under the broom is silver and gold.

Possibly meaning the type of soil these two shrubs are found on. Furze prefers waste ground.

The tulip and several of the

Garden and Farm Produce

*compound yellow flowers close
before rain.*   **

For a comprehensive survey of closing and opening flowers before rain plough through the Wild Plant chapter.

*The sudden growth of mushrooms
presageth rain.*   *****

*If toadstools spring up in the
night in dry weather, they
indicate rain.*   ****

At last two true sayings. Sudden growth of toadstools, especially mushrooms, is caused by very warm *and* humid weather conditions by day *and* night. This is virtually always a forerunner of rain from late July through to early October.

*I find it will be a dear year;
the blade of the corn grow
withersones (contrary to sun's
course), and when it grows
sonegatis about (with the
course of the sun), it will be
a good cheap year.*   *

Another nonsense adage.

*Indian corn fodder dry and crisp
indicates fair weather; but damp
and limp, rain. It is very
sensitive to hygrometric changes.*   ***

Garden and Farm Produce

Ears of Indian corn are said to be covered with thicker and stronger husks before hard winters. ✱✱

A double husk on maize indicates a severe winter. ✱✱

An old farming maxim.

A beard of wild oats, with its adhering capsule, fixed on a stem, serves the purpose of a hygrometer, twisting itself more or less, according to the moisture of the air.

Abundant wheat crops never follow a mild winter. ✱

This saw is literally incorrect. In fact 16 "abundant wheat crops" followed 41 mild winters.

SUN, SUNRISE AND SUNSET

Red Sunset

This chapter contains some of the most beautiful weather lore of all. With the different colour hues of the cloud and sky in a setting or rising sun one cannot help but feel a romantic flavour entering the sayings. When the saws refer to a red *sky* at night or morning, clear and cloudy skies are both included. The setting or rising sun offers a longer distance for its own white light to travel to an observer. Now sunlight or white light is composed of seven basic colours (rainbow colours) red, orange, yellow, green, blue, indigo and violet (easily remembered by their initials ROYGBIV). Each colour component has its own wavelength with the red possessing the longest. Since the violet end of the sun's spectrum has the smallest wavelength, any dust particles in the lower atmosphere similar in size will scatter the violet colour. This will leave a mixture of the remaining six colours to be received by an observer. As larger atmospheric particles appear so other colours are scattered. So a red/orange light is seen when the remainder are deflected. When bigger particle sizes arrive beyond the red wavelength so much scattering occurs that the nett light received on the surface of the Earth is a dim white illumination. So the general theory is that the Earth's lower atmosphere between the setting or rising sun and an observer appears red due to scattering by dust particles or dry air. As most of England's weather systems traverse from west to east a red sunrise is indicating dry weather present or past (in the east), so rain should be expected soon. Conversely a red sunset hints of dry weather to come from the west.

Smoke or dust haze reflects sunlight diffusely producing a white sky - the thicker the haze the whiter the sky. So blueness of sky is a direct measure of the content, or lack, of atmospheric particles. Cloud colouring, say a red cloudy sunset, is the result of the red sun illuminating the underside of the cloud often with grey/white tops illuminated by the scattered blue of the sky.

Red sky at night,
Shepherd's delight;
Red sky in morning,
Shepherd's warning.

*****

*****

Sunset

*Sky red in the morning
Is a sailor's sure warning;
Sky red at night
Is the sailor's delight.*

*The skie being red at evening,
Foreshewes a faire and cleare morning;
But if the morning riseth red,
Of wind and raine we shall be sped.*

*A red sky in the morning
Is the shepherd's warning;
Though a red haze at night
Is the shepherd's delight.*

The red sun setting with distinct outlines, and with or without a red sky, is a sure sign of a fine day to follow, and the redness is caused by the dry dust in the air.

Red west at sunset, not extending up to the sky, and having no thick banks of black cloud, will be followed by a fine day.

Red clouds at sunrise foretell wind; at sunset, a fine day for the morrow.

Narrow, horizontal, red clouds after sunset in the west indicate rain before thirty-six hours.

Nobody is quite sure when the verse form was derived of "Red sky at night, shepherd's delight". It probably was influenced by the Shepherd of Banbury's adage "If the sun rise red and fiery - wind and rain", which dates at least back to the early 18th century and almost certainly way before. Of course the red sky can be found in the Old Testament of the Bible and throughout different literatures of the world. The test figures are the records of Spenser Russell who in London from October 1918 to September 1924 observed sunrise and sunset colours. He

Sunset

graded them into three main groups ; 1. reds or yellows, 2. predominance of red over yellow or vice-versa and 3. combination of both colours neither one being dominant. For a red sunset and a dry day to follow within 24 hours the tests produced an excellent 69 percent result.   111/161 (69)

> *If the sun in red should set,*
> *The next day surely will be wet;*
> *If the sun should set in grey,*
> *The next will be a rainy day.*   **

The first part of this saw is the only one found to be in "opposition" to the famous red sky at night theme. It yielded only 31 percent correct results.   50/161 (31)

> *If the sun set with a very red*
> *eastern sky, expect wind; if*
> *red to the south-east, expect*
> *rain.*   *****

The red eastern sky may be the purple or pink glow which occurs over the whole sky after sunset known as the First Purple Light. It could also be redness affecting the appearance of a steely-blue segment in the eastern sky at sunset which is the Earth's shadow thrown by the sun into the atmosphere. No observations are available.

Yellow Sunset

> *The weary sun hath made a*
> *golden set,*
> *And by the bright track of the*
> *fiery car*
> *Gives token of a goodly day*
> *tomorrow.*   ****

> *Clouds before sunset of an*
> *amber or a gold colour, and*
> *with gilt fringes, after the*
> *sun has sunk lower, foretell*
> *fine weather.*   ****

This Shakespeare quote means a dry day to follow a yellow sunset. Unfortunately only 49 percent were true.
   281/579 (49)

Sunset

When the sun sets with a golden yellow colour, with disc ill defined, and rays extending four or six degrees, a strong wind and much vapour exist at a considerable elevation, and rain usually occurs within twenty-four hours. ****

A bright yellow sky at sunset presages wind; a pale yellow, wet. ****

When the sun rises or sets of a golden yellow colour, with the disc ill defined, and rays extending four or six degrees, and strong winds and much vapour exists at a considerable elevation, and rain usually occurs within twenty-four hours, which will continue for some time if there are any opposing currents, whether direct or lateral. ****

Brassy-coloured clouds in the west at sunset indicate wind. ****

A yellow sunset to produce rain within 24 hours also gave unsatisfactory figures. The special conditions set out in the third saw relate to the upper air jet streams or upper levels of strong winds (often in excess of 100kt) which are almost always associated with mobile stormy weather systems.

298/579 (51)

Other Sunsets

After sunset if the western sky has a whitish yellow extending to a great height then there will probably be rain during the night or next day. After sunset if the western sky is gaudy or has unusual hues with hard definite outlined clouds then rain is foretold with probable wind. Before sunset if the sun is diffuse and brilliant white ****

***

Sunset

> *and the sky bright blue near
> the zenith then one forecasts
> fine weather.* ****

The second part fails miserably with only 33 percent. Its final part is very interesting. A bright blue sky and white sun at setting hints at very clean and clear air.   109/335   (33)

> *When the sun sets bright and
> clear
> An easterly wind you need not
> fear.* **

One would have thought that a clear sunset (usually associated with west, north-west or north airstreams) could easily turn to an east wind. Certainly with the same frequency as any other airstream experienced at sunset.

> *When the air is hazy, so that
> the solar light fades gradually,
> and looks wet, rain will almost
> certainly follow.* *****

> *If the sun goes pale to bed,
> Twill rain tomorrow, it is said.* *****

> *When the sun appears of a light
> pale colour, or goes down into
> a bank of clouds, it indicates
> the approach of a continuance
> of bad weather.* *****

> *When the sun sets in a bank
> A westerly wind ye shall not
> lack.* ***

> *A sunset and a cloud so black,
> A westerly wind ye shall not
> lack.* ***

> *Thy sun sets weeping in the
> lowly west,
> Witnessing storms to come, woe
> and unrest.* *****

Sunrise

The fifth adage comes from Yorkshire and sixth from Shakespeare's quill. The general rule is that any pale or grey sunset or sunrise denotes a moist atmosphere (dry air holding dust particles turns sunsets red, orange etc) and is a classic example for rain to occur within 24 hours. The sixth saying shows a watery sun which is the appearance of altostratus (As) cloud (a medium-level cloud sheet - see cloud chapter) which foreruns a warm front. Here rain can be expected within 1-3 hours.

Red Sunrise

If at sunrise small reddish-looking clouds are seen low on the horizon, it must not always be considered to indicate rain. The probability of rain under these circumstances will depend on the character of the clouds and their height above the horizon. It has frequently been observed that if they extend ten degrees, rain will follow before sunset; if twenty or thirty degrees, rain will follow before two or three p.m.; but if still higher and near the zenith, rain will fall within three hours. *****

When the sun at rising assumes a reddish colour, and shortly afterwards numerous small clouds collect, the whole day will soon become overcast, and rain may be expected in the course of a few hours. *****

*If red the sun begin his race,
Be sure the rain will fall apace.* *****

Red clouds in the east, rain the next day. *****

The first saying was introduced by a Mr C L Prince during the 19th century. His accurate observations proving that the higher the red cloud (cirrus cloud over 30° above the eastern

Sunrise

horizon) the nearer the rain and red low cloud rain within 24 hours. The principle involved is that red cloud between an observer and sunrise indicates dry air, which on the usual west to east weather pattern of changeable types indicates rain from the west. In fact within 24 hours rain occurred on 68 percent of occasions - a very good result indeed.   218/319 (68)

> *In the winter season, a red sky at sunrise foreshows steady rain on the same day. The same sky in summer betokens occasional violent showers, wind in both cases generally accompanying.* *****
>
> *****

To distinguish between winter and summer red sunrises is misleading. Excellent figures of 67 (winter) and 70 percent (summer) emerged for rain to fall within 24 hours. More red sunsets occurred in winter.   143/212 (67)
75/107 (70)

Grey Sunrise

> *A grey sky in the morning presages fine weather.* ***
>
> *Dark clouds in the west at sunrise indicate rain on that day.* ****

Similar in context to previous maxims but no figures are available for testing.

Gaudy Sunrise

> *A gaudy morning bodes a wet afternoon.* **

Poor results evolve for a wet afternoon after a gaudy sunrise.   51/230 (22)

General Sunrise

> *The morning sun never lasts the day.* ***

Sun

This is only true when the atmosphere is very clear and clean with visibility 30km or more. This indicates a polar airstream which is often unstable. So cumulus clouds form during the morning changing into showers in the afternoon obliterating the sun. Conversely a long settled spell often with haze (certainly in summer) sees little cloud formation.

Sunrise and Sunset

Rose tints at sunset and grey dawn, a fine day to follow.   *****

Evening red and morning grey, Two sure signs of one fine day.   *****

The evening red and the morning grey Are the tokens of a bonny day.   *****

An evening grey and a morning red Make the shepherd hang his head.   *****

If the evening is red and the morning grey, It is the sign of a bonnie day;   *****
If the evening's grey and the morning red, The lamb and the ewe will go wet to bed.   *****

Evening red and morning grey Help the traveller on his way;   *****
Evening grey and morning red Bring down rain upon his head.   *****

The fifth saying hails from just over the border into Scotland at Yarrow. All saws are in agreement and are an advanced extension of the basic "red sky at night and morning" theme by adding a grey dawn or evening. The results would be excellent and in the same high range as the red sunrise and sunset.

Sun

A red sun has water in his eye.   *****

Sun

A red sun only indicates rain when it rises.

> *When solar rays are visible in
> the air, they indicate vapour
> and rain to follow, and the sun
> is said to be "drawing water".* ***

These solar rays are called crepuscular (twilight) rays which include three types. The saw here applies to sunbeams that penetrate a low cloud sheet and appear luminous because of water or dust particles in the air. The phenomenon is known as the "sun drawing water" or "Jacob's ladder" (see Genesis).

> *If rays precede the sunrise,
> it is a sign both of wind and
> rain.* ****

> *A high dawn indicates wind.* ****
> *A low dawn indicates fair
> weather.* ****

The first maxim is taken from Bacon's pen. An interesting set of rules. A "high dawn" is when first daylight is seen over a bank of clouds and a "low dawn" occurs when streaks of light first appear on or near the horizon. Very sound and factual saws but no data were available to test them.

> *If the sun appears concave at
> its rising, the day will be
> windy or showery; windy if the
> sun be only slightly concave,
> and showery if the concavity
> is deep.* ***

Another Bacon saying which looks fascinating. Certain cloud types plus the sun's atmospheric refraction at sunrise can cause odd overall shapes of the golden orb.

> *Storms are said to decrease at
> the rising or setting of the
> sun or moon.* ****

Sun

If storms mean heavy showers then they do decrease or die-out *inland* after dusk. Any other interpretation is false.

Make hay while the sun shines. ★★★★

Hay should only be made when a few dry days are guaranteed. To make hay when the sun shines continuously would be better phraseology. Sunny intervals can indicate rain showers.

*If the sun's shining pale with
a watery eye,
Be sure the soaking ere
nightfall is nigh.* ★★★★★

Similar to the maxim containing a "weeping" sun in the sunset section.

HALO

Moon and Solar Halo

If there be a ring or halo around the sun in bad weather, expect fine weather soon. ***

A bright circle round the sun denotes a storm and cooler weather. ****

A white ring round the sun towards sunset portends a slight gale that same night; but if the ring be dark or tawny, there will be a high wind the next day. ****

If the sun or moon outshines the 'brugh' (or halo), bad weather will not come. ****

The circle of the moon never filled a pond; the circle of the sun wets a shepherd. *****

Halo

The third saw comes from Bacon's quill. Two sun haloes can be observed when looking at Cirrus (Ci) or Cirrostratus (Cs) cloud. They are the common 22° halo and the rarer 46° halo. They are coloured red on the inside with a white outer edge. Haloes are formed by the sunlight rays being deflected or *refracted* through thousands of randomly placed hexagonal *ice crystal* prisms in high cirrus clouds. These 60° and 90° edged ice crystals refract sunlight to produce the 22° and 46° halo. It is believed that sun haloes forecast rain. An investigation by Mr. J.P. Brain in Bristol from 1 January 1969 to 2 March 1971 came up with some very interesting results.

It has often been thought that sun haloes in Ci or Cs cloud are most frequently connected with warm fronts, i.e. the cirrus cloud lies well ahead of the surface warm front giving ample warning (usually 3-12 hours) of forthcoming rain. Brain's observations confirm this by showing that 30 out of 40 (75 percent) true haloes (including coronae) were associated with warm fronts, 6 with cold fronts and 4 on occlusions. Unfortunately he combined *all* halo phenomena (including mock suns/moons and sun pillars) to give one result in forecasting rain instead of separating them. However it must be inferred that a very high percentage (probably 70-80 percent) would be true for rain to follow a sun halo or moon corona within 48 hours. Brain's final figures are given at the end of this chapter.

Moon Corona

If the moon rises haloed round,
Soon you'll tread on deluged
ground.   ****

The moon with a circle brings
water in her beak.   ****

Double or treble rings round
the moon foreshadow rough and
severe storms, and much more
so if the circles are not
pure and entire, but spotted
and broken.   ****

A circle or halo round the moon
signifies rain rather than wind,
unless the moon stand erect
within the ring, when both are
portended.   ****

Corona

> *If the moon show a silver shield,*
> *Be not afraid to reap your field;* ****
> *But if she rises haloed round,*
> *Soon we are to tread on deluged ground.* ***

Bacon originated the third and fourth maxims. The moon ring is called a corona and strictly is not a halo. It is formed by moonlight being bent or *diffracted* by *water droplets* in Alto-cumulus (Ac) cloud. Sometimes it can be perceived in Strato-cumulus (Sc) cloud. (Refer to the cloud chapter for information on these types.) A corona is a very small ring centred around the moon possessing a blue colour on the inside and red on the outer. Sometimes two coronae can be seen side by side. It is also true that coronae can occur around the sun.

> *The bigger the ring, the nearer the wet.* *

> *Near ring far rain,* *
> *Far ring near rain.* *

> *Far burr near rain.* *

> *When the wheel is far, the storm is n'ar;* *
> *When the wheel is near, the storm is far.* *

The word "burr" occurring in the third adage means a moon corona. A "far burr" is therefore the largest ring. These four saws follow the popular theme "the bigger the ring the nearer the rain". Unfortunately it is completely false. The corona is largest with small cloud water droplets and smallest with big droplets. So a large ring means the Ac or Sc cloud is well-broken and dispersing - a sign of dry weather. A better saying would be "the bigger the ring the further the rain" or "far ring far rain".

> *The open side of the halo tells the quarter from which the wind or rain may be expected.* *

Mock Sun

> *Circles round the moon always*
> *foretell wind from the side*
> *where they break, and a*
> *remarkable brilliancy in any*
> *part of the circle denotes wind*
> *from that quarter.*   *

The last saw again somes from Lord Bacon. On the face of it both maxims look promising. On close inspection a gap in the cloud (where the corona is broken) only signifies that there is broken cloud. No truth occurs here.

Mock Sun

> *Dog before,*
> *You'll have no more;*   ***
> *Dog behind,*
> *Soon you'll find.*   ***

Most of the mock moon (paraselene) and sun (parhelion) saws are dealt with in the moon chapter but this one was kept aside for its individual charm. A "dog" is a sun dog or mock sun. The words "before" and "behind" probably refer to the mock sun occurring before the sun starts to rise too high and sets too low in the sky. Mock suns only exist when the sun is at a low elevation (usually below 20°) and can be observed at the intersection of the 22° halo and the sun's horizontal line. They can appear as one or two bright spots.

> *Eclipse weather is a popular*
> *term in the south of England*
> *for the weather following an*
> *eclipse of the sun or moon,*
> *and it is vulgarly esteemed and*
> *not to be depended upon by*
> *the husbandman.*   *

A common-sense attitude appears in this adage which is lacking in the majority of the sayings.

> *A dim or pale moon indicates*
> *rain; a red moon indicates wind.*   ****

> *Pale moon doth rain,*
> *Red moon doth blow,*   ****

Moon Colour

> *White moon doth neither rain
> or snow.*   ***

> *When the moon is darkest near the
> horizon, expect rain.*   ***

The different moon colours tend to follow the same explanation in the sunrise/sunset chapter.

> *In the decay of the moon
> A cloudy morning bodes a
> fair afternoon.*   ***

> *When the moon rises red and
> appears large, with clouds,
> expect rain in twelve hours.*   ****

These are more specific than the previous set of maxims. A red moonrise, which can occur during the day or night, begins in the eastern sky. As with the red sunrise the reasons and results will be the same, so the saws are true.

Results apply to all solar and lunar halo phenomena.

```
Frontal rain to follow within  6 hours   9/80  (11)
    "       "   "    "      "  12   "   20/80  (25)
    "       "   "    "      "  24   "   36/80  (45)
    "       "   "    "      "  36   "   43/80  (54)
    "       "   "    "      "  48   "   45/80  (56)
```

SKY AND AIR

The farther the sight,
the nearer the rain. ******

When the distant hills are more
than usually distinct, rain
approaches. *****

When the Lizard is clear,
Rain is near. *****

Is Lundy high?
It will be dry.
Is Lundy low?
There will be snow.
Is Lundy plain?
There will be rain. *****

When the Isle of Wight is seen
from Brighton or Worthing,
expect rain soon. *****

The third and fourth maxims hail from Cornwall, the latter from Boscastle on the north coast. Lundy is a rocky island 50 km or 34 miles due north in the Bristol Channel. The last saw tells us that the high point of the Isle of Wight is about 50 miles from Brighton and Worthing. Excellent visibility of 30 km or more is always associated with an airstream with a polar origin. This cold clear air is often unstable or showery, hence the wet flavour in the saws. The excellent test results (made in Oxon in 1980) show that rain or showers follow visibility of 30 km or more within 24 hours on 77 percent of occasions.

```
30km or more then rain/showers in 24 hours   366/476   (77)
 "    "   "    "   rain              "   "   "   150/476   (32)
 "    "   "    "   showers           "   "   "   216/476   (45)
```

When the landscape looks clear,
having your back towards the
sun, expect fine weather; but
when it looks clear with your
face towards the sun, expect
showery, unsettled weather. *****

Sky and Air

This means that a clear landscape with a hazy sun ("back to the sun") is associated with settled weather but a completely clear atmosphere relates to showery polar air.

This section refer to a cloudless sky.

> *A very clear sky without clouds*
> *is not to be trusted, unless*
> *the barometer is high.* *****

> *If the mountains are clear in*
> *the morning, there'll be*
> *fountains by evening.* *****

These maxims are similar to those at the beginning of the Air Section.

> *If the sky is of a deep, clear*
> *blue or a sea-green colour near*
> *the horizon, rain will follow*
> *in showers.* *****

> *If the sky in rainy weather is*
> *tinged with sea-green, the rain*
> *will increase; if with deep blue,*
> *it will be showery.* *****

> *A dark, gloomy blue sky is windy,*
> *but a light, bright blue sky*
> *indicates fine weather. When*
> *the sky is of a sickly-looking,*
> *greenish hue, wind or rain may*
> *be expected.* ****

A deep blue sky means no dust particles are present (the airstream has polar origins), in fact the air molecules scatter the sunlight to produce a blue sky. Sea green skies are often a forerunner of showers or heavier rain in already wet conditions. The results in the Air section readily apply here.

> *When as much blue is seen in the*

Sky and Air

*sky as will make a Dutchman's
jacket (or a sailor's breeches),
the weather will be clear.* ****

If taken literally the saw would only be half true. In showery weather blue patches of sky are often seen. This famous saw should strictly be applied to the passage of a cold front or trough where wet cloudy conditions are normally followed by partly cloudy weather as the trend passes to a drier airstream.

*If there be a dark grey sky
with a south wind, expect frost.* **

The dark grey sky (cloudless) is an indication of thick haze or mist. A southerly wind provides the clue that an anticyclone would be centred roughly over the Continent. The saw would be true in winter but wildly out from late spring to early autumn.

*If the sky should fall we should
be able to catch larks.* *

A quaint pleasant saying. Larks fly high in the sky, so if the sky fell one would catch them. In practice it may refer to when torrential rain and turbulence occur grounding any lark.

*From a cloudless sky a bolt may
break.* *

A phrase similar to a "bolt from the blue" meaning a complete surprise. Lightning which is associated with Cb clouds and is obviously the meaning of bolt rarely seems to occur in cloudless skies.

*The Carle sky
Keeps not the head dry.* ****

A "Carle sky" is an abbreviation for a "Carlisle sky". It refers to a stormy looking yellow sky over Carlisle in Cumberland looking from the area around Dumfries and Gretna (i.e. to the S.E.). A yellow sky is nearly always a forerunner of rain. Similarly an angry red sky is an indicator of excess water vapour in the sky and a "gentle rose" sky means dust particles.

SOUND

There are basically three good reasons why sound waves travel fast and far through air. First high air temperature; second increase of wind vertically with height; and finally a low-level temperature inversion often occurring at night.

A good hearing day is a sign of wet.   ****

*A sound in air presaged approaching rain,
And beasts to covert scud across the plain.*   ****

The ringing of bells is heard at a greater distance before rain; but before wind it is heard more unequally, the sound coming and going, as we hear it when the wind is blowing perceptily.   ****

*Sound travelling far and wide,
A stormy day will betide.*   ****

Bacon penned the third saying. These saws are mainly true. With wind increasing with height (often the conditions before rain and gales) sound waves travel long distances and if the temperature is high will move fast (velocity of sound is proportional to the square root of temperature degrees Absolute). Once strong winds arrive the turbulent atmosphere limits sound travel.

A murmuring or a roaring noise, sometimes heard several miles inland during a calm, in the direction from which the wind is about to spring up, and is known as calling of the sea.   ****

Sound

> *When the sea is heard to make*
> *a raking noise on the beach in*
> *the bay to the west of Saint*
> *Leonard's, the fishermen say they*
> *"hear the Bulverhythe Bells",*
> *and this is held to be a sure*
> *sign of bad weather from the*
> *westward. In winter, during*
> *frost, it is an indication of*
> *approaching thaw.* ***

The second adage hails from St Leonard's near Margate, Sussex. These two have been lumped together as sea examples of sound travel. The previous explanations apply here.

> *When Pons-an-Dane calls to*
> *Lariggan River,*
> *There will be fine weather;*
> *But when Lariggan calls to*
> *Pons-an-Dane*
> *There will be rain.* ****

The mountain and river in this true Cornish saw incorporate sound and geographical siting to forecast rain and fine weather.

> *In the collieries of Dysart, and*
> *in some others, it is thought by*
> *the miners that before a storm*
> *of wind a sound not unlike that*
> *of a bagpipe or the buzzing of*
> *the bee comes from the mines,*
> *and that previous to a fall of*
> *rain the sound is more subdued.* *****

This Welsh maxim from Dysart, Wales, has been included to show the dual role of atmospheric pressure and sound travel. Most old coal mines, in conditions when large pressure falls occur ahead of a depression, experience gas and air escaping from their underground crevasses. The falling atmospheric pressure forces them out. In fact the old miners said the released gases sounded like the buzzing of bees.

> *Sounds are heard with unusual*
> *clearness before a storm. The*

Sound

*railway whistle, for instance,
seems remarkably shrill.* ****

*It will be a good day, we can
hear the trains.* ****

The famous sound of the train whistle or its wheels racing over the track or line is frequently true for bad weather to come especially when the noises are heard over long distances. The reasons as explained before are mainly wind increasing with height and high temperatures. But sometimes at night the story can be different. In dry settled weather (often at night) low-level temperature inversions occur. For example the surface may record $7^{o}C$ and as ones travels upward to say 200-300ft above the ground it could rise to $15^{o}C$. Now travelling sound waves will be bent or reflected by this temperature inversion and together with effect of warmer temperature aloft will be able to send the waves over a number of miles. But as the reader can see these conditions are favourable for dry settled weather, so here the two adages are false.

SNOW

Snow cherisheth the ground and anything sown in it.   ***

Corn is comfortable under snow as an old man is under his fur coat.   ***

An eight day mantle of snow is like a mother to the earth, but if it lasts longer it is like a mother-in-law.   ****

    A foot deep of rain,
    Will kill hay and grain;
    But three feet of snow,
    Will make them grow mo.   ***

    A foot deep of rain
    Will kill hay and grain;

SNOW

> *But three feet of snow*
> *Will make them come mo.* ***

> *Three feet of snow will make*
> *the hay and corn come more.* ***

> *Snow is the poor farmer's muck.*

Bacon originated the first saying and the fourth hails from the West Country. A good depth of snow covering the country-side acts as insulation for ground seed and growth against hard air frost and biting cold winds. The soil temperature under these conditions should maintain a level around 0°C. However eventually, as hinted in the third maxim, persistent frosty days will harden the snow lowering the soil temperature and harming virgin vegetation. The fifth saw comes from Devon.

> *In winter, during a frost,*
> *if it begins to snow, the*
> *temperature of the air generally*
> *rises to thirty-two degrees*
> *Fahrenheit (or near it), and*
> *continues there whilst the snow* ****
> *falls, after which, if the*
> *weather clear up, expect severe*
> *cold.* ***

Snow in England usually falls under two separate conditions. Any showers or general falls of snow from the NW, N, NE or E direction are frequently associated with persistent cold weather. Snow from the W, SW, S or SE more often than not instigates a thaw. When tested the first part of the maxim provided quite good results (62 percent correct). Unfortunately the last section yielded a poor figure (46 percent) from records kept in Oxfordshire over winters from January 1971 to February 1980.

69/111 (62)
51/111 (46)

> *If the snowflake increases in*
> *size, a thaw will follow.* *****

> *When the snow falls dry, it*
> *means to lie;*
> *But flakes light and soft*
> *bring rain oft.* *****

Snow

These observations are perfectly true. Snow falling as minute ice crystals and dry occurs with air temperatures well below $0^{\circ}C$ but as the snowflakes become larger the temperature rises nearer to $0^{\circ}C$. In these latter conditions a thaw often occurs, whether short or long, showing the saws to be true.

> *If the first snow sticks to the trees, it foretells a bountiful harvest.* *

I'm afraid this type of weather saying is ridiculous. One certain type of snowstorm cannot possibly rule the year's harvest.

> *A heavy fall of snow indicates a good year for crops, and a light fall the reverse.* **

The poor results for barley, hay and wheat can be seen in a similar saying in the Season's chapter.

> *Snow coming two or three days after new moon will remain on the ground some time, but that falling after new moon will soon go off.* *

> *As many days old as the moon is at the first snow, there will be as many snows before crop-planting time.* *

Further foolish moon and snow maxims.

> *The number of days the last snow remains on the ground indicates the number of snow storms which will occur during the following winter.* *

A number of these type of saws occur in the Monthly and Season's chapters - all of no avail.

Snow

*If the snow that falls during
the winter is dry, and is blown
about by the wind, a dry summer
will follow. Very damp snow
indicates rain in the spring.* ***

These balance themes - dry winter snows bring a dry summer and wet winter snows a wet spring - when tested were no good.

```
Dry winter snows = dry summer    20/53  (38)
Wet    "      "  = wet spring    13/34  (38)
```

*When in the ditch the snow
doth lie,
Tis waiting for more by-and-by.* ***

*If snow hangs about (along
ditches and hedgerows), then
it is waiting for more.* ***

Unfortunately this well-known saying is not entirely true as the test figures show.

```
Further snow after 1 day    70/140  (50)
   "      "    "   2 days   34/140  (24)
   "      "    "   3 days   13/140   (9)
   "      "    "   4 days    6/140   (4)
```

*When the snow falls in the mud,
it remains all winter.* **

This infers that snow falling in November, December or January on mud will be followed by a severe snowy winter. There is no way of forecasting a severe winter. The author has spent many fruitless hours trying to find the magic formula to forecast such a winter. Previous winter cycles over 300 years; wet, dry, cold or warm previous seasons and months and even sunspot cycles have all been tried but in vain. In this saw a mild wet October, November or December singly or collectively were tested but results were useless.

*Walk fast in snow,
In frost walk slow,
And still as you go,
Tread on your toe.*

Snow

*When frost and snow are
both together,
Sit by the fire and spare
shoe leather.*

*Snow that lies flattens
the ground.*

Obvious meanings to snow and frost situations showing how dangerous it can be to the mortal foot.

FROST

> *A hoar-frost,*
> *Third day crost,*
> *The fourth lost.*   ******
>
> *A white frost never lasts more*
> *than three days.*   ******

The records were taken in Oxfordshire from October 1968 to December 1973 of ground frost, that is grass temperature falling below $0°C$. Hoar or white frosts are ice crystals deposited on surfaces by the air being cooled (usually at night). They are mainly composed of frozen dew droplets and ice formed from water vapour below $0°C$. The two sayings are very famous ones with the second hailing from Lancashire. The results are excellent with an 88 percent rating, which states that any ground frost will last for 3 successive nights and no more. As one would expect there are single and many continued night frosts but the peak is for three.   204/233 (88)

> *If hoar-frost come in mornings*
> *twain,*
> *The third day surely will have*
> *rain.*   ***

This saying, although not lacking in sense, has only average results. Frost is often associated with settled anticyclones of the autumn, winter and spring. They can either persist or be of a mobile nature.   102/227 (45)

> *Three frosts in succession*
> *are a sign of rain.*   ***
>
> *Light or white frosts are*
> *always followed by wet weather,*
> *either the same day or three*   ****
> *days later.*   ****
>
> *Three white frosts and*
> *then a storm.*   ****

335

Frost

Take this a stage further and more disappointing results become apparent.

    1 day of frost then rain   75/132 (57)
    3 days 108/216 (50)

Hoar-frost indicates rain.   *****

As a general statement hoar frost is a good indicator of rain to come.   156/233 (67)

Rain is sure to follow after frost that melts before the sun rises.   ****

When the frost gets into the air, it will rain.   ****

This is the situation when a hoar frost on the ground encounters increasing wind or cloud and becomes a *black frost*. The latter is not black ice which is a modern term for glazed ice or rain freezing on a road surface to form a layer of ice. Black is used not as the colour of the road or ice but as a danger term for pedestrians and motorists. Now a *black frost* is an invisible frost although the temperature is below $0°C$ and the air too dry or turbulent. *Black frost* so termed to distinguish it from white or hoar frost. For testing purposes a surface wind of 13kt or more and temperature less than $0°C$ was regarded as a *black frost*. Results of 64 percent showed that when "the frost gets into air" rain is a good bet.

    18/28 (64)

Three rimy frosts, and then it rains.   ****

Here we have a slightly different type of frost. Rime or rimy frost, not to be confused with a hoar frost, is caused when supercooled water droplets from fog/mist come in contact with solid objects with temperature less than $0°C$. A rough white ice crystal deposit is left which in windy areas accumulate on the windward side of an object looking like fingers or horizontal stalagmites. The saying however should still have about the same amount of success as the ice/rain adages.

Frost

*Hoar-frost and gipsies never
stay nine days in a place.* ✶✶✶✶✶✶

One of the author's favourite maxims, mainly for its flowery phrase and most excellent result. Virtually all successive nights of frost last less than 9 days. 231/233 (99)

Bearded frost, forerunner of snow. ✶✶✶✶

This type of frost frequently occurs when very low temperatures persist and the thickening deposits of hoar frost resemble matted hair or a beard. Any precipitation to follow would then be of snow or sleet.

*A single white frost is almost
a sure sign of a fine day. In
seventy-three cases, fifty-nine
times fine days succeeded, and* ✶✶✶✶
fourteen times rain. But if ✶✶✶
*the white frosts continue
several mornings, then rain
generally follows.* ✶✶✶

Mr E. J. Lowe in the Victorian era confidently thought that a fine day would occur 59 out of 73 times (81 percent) after a single frosty morning and therefore 14 times (19 percent) would see rain to follow. The author's exhaustive results showed 57 and 43 percent respectively. A quick glance at the results of rain following days of frost can be seen below.

Number of successive days of frost followed by rain.	Result
1 day	75/132 (57)
2 days	102/227 (45)
3 days	108/216 (50)
4 days	34/73 (47)
5 days	26/48 (54)
6 days	13/27 (48)
7 days	9/17 (53)
7 and 8 days	7/18 (39)

*If the first frost occurs late,
the following winter will be*

Frost

> *mild, but weather variable.*   ∗∗
> *If the first frost occurs early,*
> *it indicates a severe winter.*   ∗∗∗∗

> *Early frosts are usually*
> *followed by a long and*
> *hard winter.*   ∗∗∗∗

An old weather favourite. The test covers 1877-1964 and showed little in the final analysis. The first air frosts of the autumn/winter ranged from 29 September to 17 December. The early frosts were reckoned to occur before 21 Oct and late ones after 15 November.

    first air frost early then severe winter   14/28   (50)
     .. .. .. late .. mild   7/27   (26)

> *The first and last frosts are*
> *the worst.*

The first winter frost will damage late crops and late spring frosts young budding growth.

> *Black frost indicates dry,*
> *cold weather.*   ∗∗∗∗

Black frost is followed by dry weather on 53 percent of occasions.   39/74   (53)

> *A black frost is a long frost.*   ∗∗∗∗

> *Black frost, long frost;*   ∗∗∗∗
> *Hoar-frost - three days and*
> *then rain.*   ∗∗∗∗

A good result is obtained when at least two days of black frost occur.   45/74   (61)

> *Frosts end in foul weather.*   ∗∗∗∗∗

A slight difference from the previous sayings as all frosts are included in the figures.   188/289   (65)

Frost

*Frost suddenly following heavy
rain seldom lasts long.* ***

For frost to be short lived after heavy rain one would expect a mobile weather pattern to exist. Unfortunately this is not always the case. Heavy showers and moderate rain belts can initiate a long quiet period of frosty dry weather.

*It is observed, that so far as
the frost penetrates the earth
in winter, so far will the heat
in summer.* *

Another variation of the balance maxim where a severe winter (being a rough measure of deep earth frost penetration) is compensated by a warm hot summer.

         Severe winter followed by hot summer   6/52 (12)
         Cold   ..   ..   .. warm ..   9/56 (16)

Quick thaw, long frost. ****

One of the oldest pieces of English weather lore coming from the Anglo-Saxon period. In winter a persistent cold spell can be influenced by a short mild interlude but is often only a temporary feature.

*When the corn is over the crow's
back the frost is over.* ***

A Cheshire saw meaning that the frost season ends around April or May when winter corn is about 9 to 12 inches high (average height of a mature crow) and late spring is reached. The exception is after a mild wet winter when the corn can grow quickly and catch March/April frosts.

A frost hurts not the weeds.

Presumably weeds are hardy enough to withstand frost - of course fruit blossoms are affected.

Frost

Walk slow in frost.

The obvious reason is probably the main one, but these sayings have a knack of providing hidden subtle meanings.

*Heavy frosts are generally
followed by fine clear weather.* ✶✶✶✶✶

Heavy frost is taken as meaning the excessive crystal deposits of the hoar frost. This is helped by low temperatures, an indication of a well-established cold spell. The very good results (67 percent) prove this point. 93/138 (67)

MIST, FOG AND DEW

Mist and fog are composed of water droplets. Fog is internationally agreed to occur when visibility is less than 1,000 metres (1,100 yards) with relative humidity about 100 percent. Mist often occurs with visibilities 1,000-4,000 metres and contains smaller water droplets. Humidities tend to range from 90 to 100 percent. Haze is another matter made up of smoke and dust particles.

In summer-time, when the sun at rising is obscured by a mist which disperses about three hours afterwards, expect hot and calm weather for two or three days. *****

A white mist in the evening, over a meadow with a river, will be drawn up by the sun next morning, and the day will be bright. Five or six fogs successfully drawn up portend rain. **** *

When the fog falls, fair weather follows; when it rises, rain ensues. ****** *

Fogs are a sign of change. ***

The first set of test figures offer a 56 percent chance of an evening mist continuing into the morning (from second saw). There are 88, 75 and 61 percent chances of having 1, 2 and 3 dry sunny days respectively after a misty morning in summer. So the first maxim receives excellent results. The summer results were virtually identical with other seasons' figures.

```
1 dry day  after a misty summer's morning = 151/171  (88)
2   "  days   "   "    "       "          = 129/171  (75)
3   "    "    "   "    "       "          = 104/171  (61)
4   "    "    "   "    "       "          =  89/171  (52)
5   "    "    "   "    "       "          =  70/171  (41)
6   "    "    "   "    "       "          =  55/171  (32)
```

Mist, Fog and Dew

To achieve five or six successive fogs is fairly rare but in the 45 cases found rain took a long time to appear - rain appeared within 3 days with only a 47 percent chance. So the last part of the second saw is false.

5 or 6 successive fogs then rain within 1 day   7/45 (16)
" " "   "   " " " " 2 days 16/45 (36)
" " "   "   " " " " 3 " 21/45 (47)

If mist rises in low ground and soon vanish, expect fair weather. ******

Thin, white, fleecy, broken mist, slowly ascending the sides of a hill or of a mountain whose top is uncovered, predicts a fair day. ******

These two are similar to the previous adages and are true.

If there is a damp fog or mist, accompanied by wind, expect rain. *****

An originally dry fog that is becoming gradually damper indicates rain, and probably wind. *****

When wind and dampening fog occur the likely cause is the approach of a front or a moist airstream (say a S.W.1'y) - the classic forerunners of rain.

Light fog passing under the sun from the south to the north in the morning indicates rain in twenty-four or forty-eight hours. ***
  *****

A southerly flow to advect the fog occurs here. The results are very good giving a 70 percent chance of rain within 2 days.

A S.1'y wind with fog then rain within 1 day   47/103 (46)
" " " " " " " " " 2 days 72/103 (70)

Mist, Fog and Dew

*When the fog goes up the
mountain, you may go hunting;
when it comes down the mountain
you may go fishing. In the
former case it will be fair, in
the latter it will rain.*   *****

                                             *****

*When the mist is from the hill,
Then good weather it doth spill.
When the mist is from the sea,
Then good weather it will be.*   *****

                                             ***

In many cases fog and very low cloud often go together. The comments and test results for stratus in the Cloud chapter equally apply here. Mist from the sea can either be associated with warm moist air and rain (often in S.W.1'ys) or summer sea fog (for example sea fret or haar in an Easterly along the NE English coast) with warmth and sun just inland.

*Heavy fog in winter, when it
hangs below trees, is followed
by rain.*   *

Heavy or dense winter fogs below trees point to wind strength above tree level. Sometimes this limited vertical extent of fog indicates rain but tests do not bear this out.

```
         Winter fog then rain within 1 day   14/132  (11)
            "        "    "    "     2 days  34/132  (26)
            "        "    "    "     3  "    49/132  (37)
            "        "    "    "     4  "    63/132  (48)
            "        "    "    "     5  "    74/132  (56)
            "        "    "    "     6  "    84/132  (64)
            "        "    "    "     7  '    93/132  (70)
```

*A fog cannot be dispelled with
a fan.*   *****

*During a thick town fog a breath
of air on the face, followed by
a slight swirling, is generally
the first sign of a clearance.*   *****

True country observation. Fog and mist patches form with *no* wind - a gentle breeze is needed to "mix" or develop a widespread fog. So a "fan" would only help to maintain it. Strong winds lift or disperse fog.

Mist, Fog and Dew

*A curious phenomenon is
observable in the neighbourhood
of Cocking, west Sussex. From
the leafy recesses of the
hangers of beech on the
escarpments of the downs, there
rises in unsettled weather a
mist which rolls among the trees
like the smoke out of a chimney.
This exhalation is called
'foxes-brewings', whatever
that may mean, and if it tends
westwards towards Cocking,
rain follows speedily.
Hence the local proverb:
When foxes-brewings go to Cocking,
Foxes-brewings come back dropping.* *****

This unusual but quaint saying was taken from Lower's "History of Sussex". The village of Cocking lies immediately north under the steep escarpment of the West Sussex South Downs. Beech trees surmount these hills and when a moist S. or S.E. airstream appears (usually ahead of a warm front), low cloud will be seen to cover the heights and gradually put Cocking into fog. Rain nearly always follows such a phenomenon.

Black mist indicates coming rain.

Black mist is a rare phrase meaning low cloud. It refers to wet frontal cloud having a dark ragged appearance opposite to the white mists of summer and autumn in dry weather.

*Three foggy nights in a week;
then expect foggy days as well.* *****

It is unusual that the saw does not imply three successive foggy nights. Three random foggy nights in a week is fairly strong evidence for a quiet prolonged period; three in succession would be almost a certainty.

Dew

Dew is water vapour condensing in small drops on cool surfaces such as grass. Perfect conditions for dew formation are

DEW

a calm wind, clear skies and moist air. It therefore follows that these conditions also serve dry weather periods. Dewless nights are connected with wind and cloud often leading to rain. Dew-ponds are an interesting spin off. They are artificially constructed ponds high up on chalk downs with watertight bottoms of clay or mud. The idea was that during long droughts overnight dew collected in the dew-ponds helping to water the sheep. In fact there were once such people as professional dew-pond makers. In reality the dew-ponds do retain water longer than ponds at lower-levels but only because more rainfall occurs the higher one is situated above sea-level. Dew does aid the dew-pond water level but only to a small extent. In very long droughts dew-ponds become dry.

The dews of the evening
industriously shun;
They're the tears of the
sky for the loss of the sun.

A poetic introduction to the evening dew.

With dew before midnight,
The next day will sure be
bright. ******

Dew in the night
Next day will be bright. ******

Dew is an indication of fine
weather; so is fog. ******

When the dew is on the grass,
Rain will never come to pass. *****

The test shows that there is an 88 percent chance of a fine day after a dewy night and 54 percent for 4 fine days.

```
        Night dew then fine for 1 day    296/336  (88)
          "      "    "    "    2 days   251/336  (75)
          "      "    "    "    3  "     212/336  (63)
          "      "    "    "    4  "     180/336  (54)
          "      "    "    "    5  "     151/336  (45)
          "      "    "    "    6  "     127/336  (38)
          "      "    "    "    7  "     100/336  (30)
```

Dew

If there is a profuse dew in summer, it is about seven to one that the weather will be fine. ✱✱✱✱✱✱

A 7/1 or 86 percent chance of fine weather to follow a profuse summer is perfectly correct. In fact it yielded 88 percent.

226/258 (88)

If there is a heavy dew, it indicates fair weather; no dew, it indicates rain. ✱✱✱✱✱✱ ✱✱✱✱✱

*Heavy dews in hot weather,
Foretell fine weather;
No dew after sun,
Hot weather on the run.* ✱✱✱✱✱✱ ✱✱✱✱✱

If on clear summer nights there is no dew, expect rain the next day. ✱✱✱✱✱

*If nights three dewless there be,
Twill rain you're sure to see.* ✱✱✱✱✱

When there is no dew at such times as usually there is, it foreshoweth rain. ✱✱✱✱✱

Dewless nights occur for a number of reasons. Too much wind; cloud cover; dry (low humidity) airstream or combinations of these reasons. The theme was not tested but the chances of rain must be high.

SHEPHERD OF BANBURY'S WEATHER RULES

One of the first books entirely about weather lore was called *Shepherd of Banbury's Rules to Judge the Changes of the Weather*, published in 1744 and written by John Claridge (shepherd) who may have been this Banbury (Oxfordshire) shepherd. There are 26 rules which contain small to large saws and stupid to accurate ones. The complete set is laid out although certain ones are repeated throughout the book (refer to index for the appropriate pages).

Rule 1

    If the Sun rise red and fiery
    Expect wind and rain. *****

    If red the sun begins his race,
    Be sure that rain will fall
    apace. *****

Rule 2

    If cloudy and it soon decreases
    Certain for fair weather. ****

    A red evening and a grey
    morning
    Sets the pilgrims awalking. *****

Rule 3

    If clouds are small and round,
    like a dappley grey, with a
    north wind, expect fair weather
    for two or three days. ***

    If woolly fleeces spread the
    heavenly way
    Be sure no rain disturbs the
    summer day. ****

Rule 4

    If there are large clouds,

Shepherd of Banbury

        like rocks, expect great showers.   ***

Rule 5   If small clouds increase, expect much rain.   ***

Rule 6   If large clouds decrease, expect fair weather.   ***

Rule 7   If mists rise in low ground and soon vanish, expect fair weather.   *****

Rule 8   If mists rise to the hill tops, expect rain in a day or two.   *****

Rule 9   A general mist before the sun rises, near the full moon, expect fair weather.   ***

Rule 10   If there are mists in the new moon, expect rain in the old.   *

Rule 11   If mists in the old moon expect rain in the new.   *

Rule 12   Observe that in eight years time there is as much south-west wind as north-east, and consequently as many wet years as dry.   ***
   **

Shepherd of Banbury

Rule 13   When the wind turns to north-east and it continues two days without rain, and does not turn south the third day nor rain the third day, it is likely to continue north-east for eight or nine days, or fair; and then to come to the south again.   ******

Rule 14   If it turn out again out of the south to the north-east with rain, and continues in the north-east two days without rain, and neither turns south nor rains the third day, it is like to continue north-east for two or three months. The wind will finish these turns in three weeks.   ***

Rule 15   After a northerly wind for the most part two months or more, and then coming south, there are usually three or four fair days at first, and then, on the fourth or fifth day, comes rain, or else the wind turns north again, and continues dry.   ***

Rule 16   If the wind returns to the south within a day or two without rain, and turn northward with rain, and return to the south in one or two days, as before, two or three times together after this sort, then it is like to be in the south or south-west two or three months together, as it was in the north before. The wind will finish these turns in a fortnight.   ***

Shepherd of Banbury

Rule 17 — Fair weather for a week, with a Southern wind, is like to produce a great Drought, if there has been much rain out of the South before. The wind usually turns from North to South, with a quiet wind without rain, but returns to the North, with a strong wind and rain; the strongest winds are when it turns from South to North by West. When the North wind first clears the air (which is usually once a week) look out for Squalls. **** **** **** *****

Rule 18 — In summer or harvest, when the wind has been south two or three days, and it grows very hot, and you see clouds rise with great white tops like towers, as if one were upon the top of another and joined together with black on the nether side, there will be thunder and rain suddenly. *****

Rule 19 — If two such clouds arise, one on either hand, it is time to make haste to shelter.

Rule 20 — If you see a cloud rise against the wind or side wind, when that cloud comes up to you, the wind will blow the same way that the cloud came; and the same rule holds of a clear place, when all the sky is equally thick, except one clear edge.

Shepherd of Banbury

Rule 21   Sudden rains never last long: *****
          but when the air grows thick,
          by degrees, and the sun, moon,
          and the stars shine dimmer and
          dimmer, then it is like to rain
          six hours usually. *****

Rule 22   If it begins to rain from the
          south, with a high wind for
          two or three hours, and the
          wind falls, but the rain
          continues, it is likely to
          rain twelve hours or more,
          and does usually rain till a
          strong north wind clears the
          air. These long rains
          seldom hold above twelve hours,
          or happen above once a year. ****

Rule 23   If it begins to rain an hour
          or two before sunrising, it is
          like to be fair before noon,
          and so continue that day, but ****
          if the rain begins an hour or
          two after sun rising, it is
          like to rain all that day,
          except the rainbow be seen
          before it rains. ***

          A rainbow in the morning,
          Is the shepherd's warning; *****
          A rainbow at night,
          Is the shepherd's delight. *****

Rule 24   If the last eighteen days of
          February and ten days in March
          be for the most part rainy,
          then the spring and summer
          quarters are like to be so to;
          and I never knew a great drought
          but it ended in that season. ***

Shepherd of Banbury

Rule 25 — If the latter end of October and beginning of November be for the most part warm and rainy, then January and February are like to be frosty and cold, except after a very dry summer. **

Rule 26 — If October and November be snow and frost, then January and February are like to be open and mild. *

BIBLIOGRAPHY

Brain, J.P. (1972). Halo Phenomena - An Investigation. *Weather*, vol 27, pp 409-410.
Brazell, J.H. (1968). London Weather.
A Century of Agricultural Statistics of Great Britain, 1866-1966. (1968). H.M.S.O.
Claridge, John. (1744). Shepherd of Banbury's Rules to Judge the Changes of the Weather.
Davis, N.E. (1969). Diurnal Variation of Thunder at Heathrow Airport, London. *Meteorological Magazine*, vol 24, pp 166-172.
Davis, N.E. (1972). Classified Central England Temperatures and England and Wales Rainfall. *Met. Mag.*, vol 101, pp 205-217.
Folklore Guide to the Weather. No 1 in Handy Guide Series.
Inwards, Richard. (1898). Weather Lore.
Jackson, M.C. (1977). A Classificatio- of the Snowiness of 100 Winters - A Tribute to the Late L.C.W. Bonacina. *Weather*, vol 32, pp 91-97.
Lamb, H.H. (1972). British Isles Weather Types and a Register of the Daily Sequence of Circulation Patterns, 1861-1971. *Geophysical Memoirs no 116*.
Lower, M.A. (1870). A Compendious History of Sussex.
Margery, I.D. (1926). Marsham Phenological Record (Norfolk 1736-1925). *Quarterly Jnl of Royal Met. Soc.*, vol 52, pp 30-37.
Merryweather, Dr George. (1851). A Tempest Prognosticator.
Mirrlees, S.T.A. (1929). St Swithun's Day. *Met. Mag.*, vol 64, p 143.
Nicholson, G. (1969). Wet Thursdays. *Weather*, March 1969.
Russell, Spencer C. (1926). "A Red Sky at Night ---." *Met. Mag.*, vol 61, pp 15-17.
Silvester, Norman L. (1926). Notes on the Behaviour of Certain Plants in Relation to the Weather. *Quarterly Jnl of Royal Met. Soc.*, vol 52, pp 15-23.
The Standard Cyclopedia of Modern Agriculture and Rural Economy. (c1909). Editor Sir R.P. Wright.

DATA SOURCES

BARLEY records of cwt/acre cover 1885-1966 for England and Wales were taken from *A Century of Agricultural Statistics of Great Britain*. The figures were statistically weighted for 1941-66 and finally all were divided into three equal classes to give bad, average or good yields.

CATTLE survey by the author in Yorkshire during the summer of 1980 studying the standing and sitting habits in relation to sun, rain and wind.

CLOUD data covered all types (from high Cirrus to low Stratus) and their relation with forthcoming rain during 1979 in Oxon.

DAILY WEATHER of Great Britain bring different airstream directions with anticyclone or cyclonic connections. Each airstreams having its own temperature, rainfall and weather properties. Nearly 37,000 reports were used in Lamb's figures for 1861-1971. So the weather proverbs relating to St David's Day (1 March) or the 40-rain days of St Swithun (15 July- 23 Aug) could be easily tested.

DEATH numbers per 1,000 of the population in Oxford from 1871-1911 were used for Jan-March with no weighting. Final data were equally grouped into three giving a high, average and low death rate.

FLOWER records of Silvester were used. They were made in London and Yorkshire from 1917-23 (spring to autumn). The author introduced the average monthly daylight duration (sunrise to sunset) from March to November to acquire the final figures.

Air and ground FROST figures come from Oxon from Oct 1968 - Dec 1973. Also the year's first ground frost (usually in autumn) appears in Brazell's 1841-1964 data.

All sun and moon HALO records come from Brain's collection for Bristol from 1 Jan 1969 to 2 March 1971.

HAY figures are from the same source as BARLEY ones covering 1885-1966. No weighting was necessary.

MILK data covers 1941-62 using two weighting periods 1941-51 and 1951-62. The same source as the Barley records apply. Final figures were divided equally into three classes.

MOON phase dates were taken for the U.K. from 1959-71.

PIG records again were the same source as those in the Barley section covering 1866-1966. 1916-20 and 1941-52 were ignored (due to poor production during the two world wars and their post-war recovery). 1866-1915, 1921-40 and 1953-66 were weighted with final numbers, as usual, divided equally into three.

POTATO data as the Barley source covering 1884-1966. Weighting introduced for 1959-66. Final division by three occurred.

RAINFALL figures came from Davis' England and Wales monthly and seasonal collection of 1727-1971. No weighting needed and were divided into three equal classes, wet, average and dry. HOURLY RAINFALL for testing adages like "rain at seven, fine before eleven" were confined to Oxon in the non-winter period of 1978-9. WEEKDAY RAINFALL figures came from Nicholson's Teddington records of Oct 1953 - Sept 1968.

SHEEP data are the same as in the Cattle section.

SNOW records of daily significance were taken from Oxon in the winters Jan 1971 - Feb 1980. Longer-scale data came from Jackson's list of Bonacina's work covering the period 1875-1975 of snow in the U.K.

SUNSET/SUNRISE colour figures are used in Russell's London record from Oct 1918 - Sept 1924.

TEMPERATURE values from Davis' Central England collection covered 1698-1971. Here monthly and seasonal temperatures were divided into 5 equal classes (quintiles) of very cold, cold, average, warm and very warm.

TREE records were taken from the Margery Collection of 1736-1925.

Good VISIBILITY data was obtained from Oxon during 1980.

WHEAT records from the Barley source covering 1885-1966. The period 1948-66 was weighted with final figures equally divided into three to give good, average or poor wheat yields.

INDEX

Acorn, 27, 188.
Africa, 133; South, 159.
Afternoon, 154; dry, 128; fair, 128, 323; moon, 211; rainbow, 280; showers, 316.
Ale, 72.
Alexandria, 90.
All Fool's Day (1 April), 40.
All Saint's Day (1 Nov.), 86.
Altocumulus (Ac) cloud, 252, 260, 264, 265, 321; or "ark", 263, 264; or "Noah's ark", 82; or "Noaship", 264; or "Nol-skeppit", 264; or "salmon", 264.
Altostratus (As) cloud, 252, 263, 314.
America, North, 164; Indians, 82.
Ammonia, 275.
Anemone (Wind flower), Wood, 283; or "Fairie's Windflower", 283; or "Windflower", 283, or "Wind Plant", 283.
Angler, 143.
Anglia, East, 13, 152, 246.
Anglo-Saxon, 339.
Animal, 166-201, 243; barometer, 187; behaviour, 166-174, 176-183; crowding, 166, 170, 171; eating, 171, 173, 183; hibernation, 180; lying down, 171; noises, 167-170, 172, 173, 175, 183; seeking shelter, 166, 170, 183, 184; washing, 168, 169.
Ant, 189, 190, 198; worker, 189.
Anticyclone, 1, 3, 11, 14, 15, 25, 44, 53, 67, 68, 71, 75, 78, 80, 84, 112, 117, 118, 228, 232, 238, 239, 326, 335.
Apple, 58, 65, 122, 306; leaf, 25; tree, 51, 94.

April, 1, 3, 15, 37-45, 48, 49, 78, 298; apple blossom, 306; changeable, 39; cloudy, 1; cold, 39, 41; very cold, 39; cold and stormy, 38; cold and wet, 39; dew, 42; dry, 38; fog, 41; frost, 339; hoar frost, 40; mild, 79; full moon, 42, 43; northerlies, 38; rain, 31, 39, 46; showers, 29, 38, 39; snow, 39; thunderstorms, 40; warm, 40, 41, 287; wet, 28, 30, 38; 1st (All Fool's Day), 40; 1-3rd, 48; 6th (Latter Lady Day), 41; 11-14th (Buchan's 2nd Cold Spell), 42; 23rd (St George's Day), 42; 24th (St Mark's Day), 42; 25-28th, 42, 43.
"ark" see Altocumulus cloud.
Armagh (Ireland), 16.
Ascension Day, 104.
Ash, 297-299.
Ash and Oak, 297-299; with "choke", 297, 298; with "sash", 299; with "smoke", 298, 299; with "splash", 297-299; with "squash", 298.
Ash Wednesday, 100, 101.
Ass, 167.
Aston (Sussex), 268.
Atherston (Warwicks), 87.
August, 60-62, 65, 67-70, 103, 106, 297; anticyclones, 67; cold spell in, 69; dew, 67, 69, 70; dry and warm, 67; fog, 30, 31, 67, 68; great heat in, 61, 69; hoar frost, 69; mists, 69; poor, 27; storms, 67, 68; thundery spell in, 67; thunder, 45; thunderstorms, 68, 70; thistles, 295; wet, 68; 1st (Lammas or Loaf-mass Day);

68, 69; 1-7th, 69; 6-11th (Buchan's 5th Cold Spell) 69; 12-15th (Buchan's 2nd Warm Spell), 69; 15th (St Mary's Assumption Day), 69; 24th (St Bartholomew's Day),65,69, 70.
Autumn, 90, 104, 108, 112-114, 119, 121, 122, 155, 199, 326; anticyclones,335; clear, 112; cold, 113; cold spells in, 225, 229; dry, 70, 107; dry spell in, 296; Equinox, 75; flies, 195; flowers, 90; fog, 113, 119, 232; frost, 195; first air frost in, 76, 338; first ground frost in, 76; hot and dry, 106, 113; Indian summer in, 82; late, 90, 91; lightning, 273; mild spells in, 231, 272, 344; prosperous, 70; rains in late, 78, 110; serene, 121; south-easterlies, 113; south-westerlies, 89, 236, 237; storms, 67, 78, 84; thunder, 113; thunder and lightning, 99, 272; warm, 76, 112, 197; wet, 70, 107, 113, 119; windy, 121.

Bacon (1561-1626), Francis, 109, 114, 115, 130, 132, 135, 136, 142, 147, 151, 181, 203, 208, 211, 212, 219, 223, 225, 227, 230, 232, 272, 273, 275, 295, 317, 320, 321, 327, 331;
Balance see Weather balance.
Banbury (Oxon), 347.
Bank Holiday Act (1871), 96.
Barley, 4, 15, 28, 32, 39, 45-47, 54, 57-59, 61, 68, 72, 74, 78, 111, 116, 120, 133, 301, 302, 305, 332.
Barnabas, Joseph, 56.
Barometer see Animal barometer.
Bat, 167, 168.
Bean, 49, 206, 302, 306.
Bedfordshire, 54, 193, 212, 219, 247, 261, 291.
Bee, Honey, 12, 48, 55, 61, 75, 189-192; activity, 190; buzzing, 328; collecting nectar and pollen, 191, 192; "dance", 192; drone, 190; flight, 191; hive, 191, 192; life of, 190, 192; queen, 191, 192; swarm, 48, 55, 61, 191, 192; worker, 190.
Beech, 299, 300, 344; bud, 97; mast, 300; nuts, 86, 300.
Beetle, 192, 193, 196; clock, 192; Scarab, 193.
Bells, 276, 327.
Berries, many, 72, 296, 303, 304.
"Betty-go-to-Bed-at-Noon" see Star of Bethlehem.
Bever (Leics), 269.
Bible (Old Testament), 310.
Biological clock, 191.
Birds, 129-165, 303; congregating,132, 136, 138, 156. 158; dawn chorus, 129,eating; 161; eggs, 141; flight, 129-131, 134, 135, 138, 141, 142, 144, 145, 148, 150, 151, 156-161; flocks of, 136, 140; migration of, 132, 136, 140, 159, 164, 165; nesting, 129, 145, 154, 155, 160; "peck-order" of, 155; perching, 152, 163; roosting, 132, 137, 148; social life, 155; song or whistle, 2, 58, 115, 130-132, 136, 138, 142, 144-148, 150, 151, 153-158, 161-163, 165; "tides", 139; washing, 130, 135, 148.
Bittern, 141.
Blackbird, 130, 153.
"Blackfrost" see Frost.
"Black ice" see Ice.
"Black mist" see Mist.
"Black ram" see March.

Blackthorn, 41, 50, see Sloe.
Blackthorn winter, 41, 42.
Blossom, 44, 52, 106, 108, 206, 302, 339.
Bodgham Hole (Ashton Vale, East Kent), 218, 219.
"Bolt", 326.
Bone, 85, 135, 136, 140.
"Borrowed day", 115.
Borrowing Days (29-31 March), 36, 37.
Boxing Day, 96.
Brain, J.P., 320.
Brazell, J.H., 65.
Bread, 44, 46, 59, 68, 110, 118.
Bredon Hill (Worcs), 269.
Brighton, 324.
Bristol Channel, 324.
Broom, 300, 306.
"Brugh", 319.
Buchan, Dr Alexander, 21, 22; Buchan's 1st Cold Spell (7-14 Feb.), 21, 22; 2nd Cold Spell (11-14 April), 22, 42; 3rd Cold Spell (9-14 May), 50; 4th Cold Spell (26 June- 4 July), 59; 5th Cold Spell (6-11 Aug.), 69; 6th Cold Spell (6-13 Nov.), 89; 1st Warm Spell (12 -15 July), 64; 2nd Warm Spell (12-15 Aug.), 69; 3rd Warm Spell (3-14 Dec.), 92.
Buckinghamshire, 283, 291.
Buck's horn, 74.
Bull, 168, 243.
"Bulverhythe Bells" (Sussex), 328.
Burnet Saxifrage, 293.
Burning, fire, 288.
"Burr", 321.
Butter, 105.
Butterfly, 61, 193; White, 193.
Buys Ballot's Law, 221.

Calendar, present, 63, 64.
Camomile (flower), 157.
Campion, Bladder, 283; or "Thunderbolt", 283.
Campion, White, 283; or "thunderbolt", 284; or "thunderflower", 284.
Can (Westmorland), river, 268.
Canary, 147.
Candle, 16, 17, 223.
Candlemas Day (2 Feb.), 16-21, 88; bright and clear, 17, 20; calm, 21; cloudy with rain, 19; cold, 16; cold and wet, 19; easterly, 20; fine and clear, 17, 18; icicles, 20; mild and gay, 18; snow, 16, 20; stormy, 18, 20; "waddle", 19.
Candlestick, 17, 75.
"Cap" see Stratus cloud.
Carle or Carlisle sky see Sky.
Carlisle (Cumberland), 326.
Cat, 14, 168, 169, 177.
Cattle, 9, 10.
"Change-of-the-Weather" see Scarlet Pimpernel.
Charles I, 288.
Cherry, 120.
Cheshire, 283, 291, 292, 339.
Chickweed, 284, 285.
Childermas (28 Dec.), 98.
Chilterns, 219.
"Choke" see Ash and Oak.
Christmas, 76, 89, 94-98, 105, 114, 138; before, 94; cold, 97; dry, 97; frost, 94, 95; "green", 96; icy, 86, 88, 93, 97; full moon, 97; new moon, 97; snow, 76, 95, 96, 104; south-westerly, 89; thaw, 92; warm, 85; wet, 86, 88, 97, 104; windy, 21, 94, 95; 25th (Christmas Day and Night), 94-96; Thursday, 95; Monday, 95; Friday 95-96; 24-26th, 96-98.
Chrysanthemum, 306.
Churchyard, 44, 65, 114.
Churton or Church Pulverbatch

(Shropshire), 218.
Cicada Lava, 201.
Cinquefoil, 285.
Cirrocumulus (Cc) Cloud, 252, 256, 259-262; or "cottony shreds", 261; or "curdly sky", 261, 262; or "filly tails", 261; or "fish scales", 259; or "hen's scarts", 261; or "mackerel sky", 252, 259-261;
Cirro-filum, 258.
Cirro-macula, 257, 258.
Cirrostratus (Cs) cloud, 252, 256, 257, 262, 263, 320; milky white, 263; or "wane cloud", 262, 263; waved, 263.
Cirrus (Ci) cloud, 203, 214, 252-259, 314, 320; barred or ribbed, 256; or "curly wisps", 252, 253; dense, 254, 256; feathery, 253, 255, or "fleur-de-lys", 255; or goat's hair", 253; or "grey-mare's tail", 253; or "mare's tails", 260; or "palm branches", 255; streamers, 255, 256; "V-point", 258, 259; or "woolly fleeces", 253, 347.
Claridge, John, 347.
Cleveland Hills, 269.
"Cloake" see Stratus cloud.
Cloud, 203, 214, 252-277, 314, 321, 343, 347, 348; base, 252; colour, 309; high, 252; latin names (see individual cloud name); low; 27, 55, 128, 141, 218, 252, 315, 343, 344; medium, 252, 314; red, 261, 310, 314, 315; type, 252; yellow, 311.
Clover, 97, 285, 286.
Coal mines, 328.
Coast, 41, 68; East, 139, 164.
Cocking (West Sussex), 344.
Cockerel, 137, 138.
Cockle, 169.
Cold front, 237, 240, 247, 250, 277, 326.
Coltsfoot, 287.
"Comeback" see Guinea Fowl.
Comet, 215.
Cone, pine or conifer, 293, 295, 305.
Continent, 165, 326.
Convection, 271.
Convolvulus (Bindweed), 286.
Coat, 38.
Cornwall, 12, 54, 128, 155, 204, 215, 216, 226, 229, 230, 232, 294, 302, 304, 328.
Corona, 320.
Corpus Christi Day, 105.
"Cottony shreds" see Cirrocumulus cloud.
Cow, 46, 104, 105, 133, 166, 168-172, 176, 183, 226, 243.
Cowslip, 286.
Crane, 131.
Cream, 226.
Crespuscular rays, 317.
Cricket, 193, 194.
Crossfell Mountains (N.E. England), 270.
Crow, 42, 81, 131, 132, 158, 339; Carrion, 81, 132.
Cuckoo, 7, 57, 58, 132-134, 164, 165, 289; migration, 165; song, 58, 132.
Cuckoo Bush Hill (Gotham, Notts.), 134.
Cuckoo spit, 201.
"Cuff away", 206.
Cumberland, 270, 284, 291, 294, 326.
Cumulonimbus (Cb) cloud, 129, 247, 252, 254, 265, 266, 271-277, 326; up and downdraughts in, 277; see also under shower.
Cumulus (Cu) cloud, 126, 128, 247, 252, 256, 265-267, 271, 288, 316; like cliffs and mountains, 266; "fair weather", 265; or "global cloud", 266; or "rain balls", 265; like

rocks and towers, 266, 348, 350; or "water waggons", 266.
"Curdly sky" see Cirrocumulus cloud.
"Curly wisps" see Cirrus cloud.

Daisy, 108, 286, 287; Ox-Eye or Moon, 287; "Thunder Daisy", 287.
Damascas, Bishop of, 9.
Dandelion, 287, 288; "clock", 287.
Danes, 264.
Day, 126-128, 347, 351; cloudy, 266; cold, 126; dry, 153; fine, 126; flowers, 290, 291, 294; lightning, 273; lowering, 126; moon, 209, 211; rainbow, 279, 280; rainy, 243-247, 335; rough and stormy, 218; southerly during, 232; stormy, 327; thunder, 272, 273, 289; 1000-1400 local time, 127; 1200-1400 local time, 127, 128; warm and serene, 126; wind directions, 235.
December, 75, 83, 92-99, 117, 121, 122; depressions, 92; easterlies, 92, 98, 99; fine in, 92; fog, 68; frost, 5, 92, 93; ice, 93; late, 99; lightning, 99; "lion" in, 99; mild, 98; north-easterlies, 98; northerlies, 98, 99; rain, 92; snow, 333; southerlies, 92, 98, 99; storms, 92, 113; thaw, 92; thunder, 92, 98, 99; westerlies, 92, 98, 99; wet, 84, 98, 113; windy, 78; first Sunday in, 92; 3-14th (Buchan's 3rd Warm Spell), 92; 13th (St Lucy's Day), 92; 21st (St Thomas' Day), 92-94, 117; 24-26th and 25th see Christmas; 28th (Childermas or Holy Innocent's Day), 98; 31st, 98-99.
Deddington (Oxon), 90.

Deer's coat, 8.
Depressions, 1, 53, 60, 67, 71, 92, 119, 125, 218, 219, 221, 225, 227, 228, 232, 235, 237, 239, 271, 283, 328.
Derbyshire, 38, 171, 183.
Desborough, Lord, 22.
"Devil bird" see Swift.
Devon, 51, 52, 120, 123, 138, 155, 218, 235, 239, 247, 283, 287, 291, 292, 294, 295, 331.
Dew, 30, 31, 42, 47, 53, 55, 67, 69, 70, 75, 76, 119, 185, 119, 214, 335, 344-346.
Dew-pond, 345; makers, 345.
Diffraction, 321.
"Dirt bird" see Owl.
Divers, 135.
Dog, 172, 173.
"Dog" see Rainbow.
Dog Days (3 July-11 Aug.), The, 62, 63.
Dog rose, 300.
Dog star (Sirius), 63.
Dogwood, 300, 301.
Donkey, 167.
Dorset, 26, 210, 283, 291, 294, 299.
Dotterel, 134.
Dore, 148.
Dove (Derbyshire), River, 38.
"Drainage wind", 224.
Drizzle, 228, 236, 237, 244, 250.
Drought, 73, 110, 185, 205, 222, 235, 243, 250, 255, 264, 278, 345, 350, 351.
Dry periods see in all chapters.
Duck, 84, 86, 89, 93, 135, 136, 140, 223.
Dumfries, 326.
Dunpickle, 140.
Durham, 155.
Dust, 25, 26, 250, 310, 317, 326, 341.
"Dutchman's jacket", 326.
Dysart (Wales), 328.

Earth, 202, 206, 215, 309, 311.
Easter, 22, 96, 97, 100, 103-105; frost, 96, 104; late, 103, 104; snow, 97, 104; wet, 96, 104.
Easter Day (Sunday), 100, 102, 124; sunny, 103; wet, 102, 103.
Easterlies see Wind.
Eden (N.E.England),River, 270.
Eel, 175.
Elder, 301.
Electricity, 271, 275.
"Eleven O'clock Lady" see Star of Bethlehem.
Ellesmere (Shropshire), 208.
Elm, 302, 303.
England, Eastern, 239; Northern, 169, 238, 239, 268; North-Eastern, 343; North-Western, 238; South-West, 278, Western, 292.
English Channel, 226, 228, 273.
Essex, 248.
Eston Nabbe (Yorkshire), 269.
Evening, 148; bats, 167, 168; beetles, 193; cloud, 256, 262; cows, 170; dew, 345; flowers, 288, 289; grey sky in, 316; mist, 341; moon, 209; rainbow, 279, 280, 351; red sky in, 309, 310, 316, 347; sheep, 183; showers, 273; spider webs, 199; tempest, 273; thunder, 273; worm "casts", 185; wind, 224, 238-240.
Ewe, 316.

"Fairie's Windflower" see Anemone, Wood.
Fairlie Down (Kent), 270.
Famine, 110.
February, 2-4, 11-24, 29, 41, 48, 68, 114, 116, 184; anticyclones, 11; bees, 12, 192; cold, 11, 17, 22, 23, 79; very cold, 11, 14, 53; cold spell in, 16; cold and frosty, 87, 352; drought, 15; Fill-dyke, 12, 13, 15, 33; fine days in, 12; one fine week in, 11; fog, 11, 14; frost, 2, 11, 12, 14, 17, 19, 23; gnats, 11, 12; midges, 11, 12; mild, 79; mild and dry, 84; mild and open, 91, 352; northerlies, 11, 14, 15; snow, 16; much snow in, 15; spring in, 11; storms, 11; thunder, 13; warm, 12, 192; warm day in, 15; wet, 26, 33; 1st (St Bridget's Day), 16; 2nd (Candlemas Day), 16-21, see Candlemas Day; 6th (St Dorothea's Day), 21; 7-14th (Buchan's 1st Cold Spell), 21, 22; 14th (St Valentine's Day), 22; middle of, 22; 22nd (St Peter's Day), 22, 23; 24th (St Matthias' Day), 23, 24; 28th (St Romanus' Day), 24; late Feb. and early March, 33; 11-18th Feb. and 1-10 March, 33, 351.
Fern, 288.
Fieldfare, 136.
Fill-dyke see February.
"Filly tails" see Cirrus cloud.
Finch, 136.
Firefly, 194.
Fires, 288.
Firle Hill (Sussex), 268.
First purple light, 311.
Fish, 139, 142, 173-175, 234.
"Fish or hake" cloud see Altocumulus cloud.
Flammer's Hole (Dunstable, Beds.), 218.
Flax, 73.
Flea, 194.
Flood, 46, 73, 76, 115, 116, 120, 160, 176, 180, 212, 244.
Flowers, 26, 29, 38, 44, 57, 90, 191, 276, 283-295, 303, 307; sensitive to humidity,

283, 284, 287, 288, 291, 292, 294, 295; sensitive to sunlight, 283, 293; sensitive to temperature, 284, 287, 291; sensitive to wind, 283, 285; wild, 283-295.
Fly, 48, 94, 175, 195; harvest, 195; house, 195.
Fog, 3, 14, 15, 27, 41, 49, 67, 79, 80, 84, 111, 113, 117, 119, 120, 127, 128, 204, 212, 223, 232, 281, 283, 293, 336, 341-345; bow, 281; sea, 343.
Forty days of rain see Rain.
Fox, 175; bark, 81.
"Fox", 115.
"Foxes-brewings", 344.
Fowl, Sea, 139; domestic, 136-138, 140; water, 138, 139.
France, 13.
Franklin's Frost (20 or 21st May), 51, 52.
Freezing level, 265.
Fret, Sea, 343.
Friday, 62, 95, 123, 124, 209.
Frog, 38, 142, 186, 272; tree, 187; yellow, 186, 187.
Frost, 333-340 and most other pages; air, 76, 145, 331; "bearded", 337; "black", 336, 338; deep earth, 339; ground, 14, 76, 145, 277, 335; heavy or severe, 79, 118, 186, 207; hoar or white, 4, 34, 40, 49, 69, 70, 85, 335-338; hollow, 145, 224; rimy, 336.
Fruit, 8, 17, 25, 72, 94, 95, 98, 100, 104, 106, 108, 116, 117, 206, 222, 231, 306.
"Funnelling effect" see Wind.
Furniture, 234, 276.
Furze, 306.

Gales see Wind.
Garden and Farm produce, 306-308.

Genesis, 317.
Gentian, 288.
Germany, 187.
Gipsies, 337.
Glazed ice see Freezing rain.
"Global cloud" see Cumulus cloud.
Gloucestershire, 283, 304.
Glow worm, 195, 196.
Gnats, 11, 12, 196.
Goat, 175, 176.
"Goat's hair" see Cirrus cloud.
Good Friday, 100, 102, 124; wet, 102.
Goose, 17, 20, 34, 93, 135, 136, 139, 140.
"Goose summer", 87.
Gossamer, 87, 199.
"Grandfather's Weatherglass" see Scarlet Pimpernel.
Grapes, 2, 56, 158.
Grass, 15, 20, 23, 25, 38, 39, 50, 56, 87, 102, 103, 105, 122, 133, 171-173, 184, 199, 222, 304, 344, 345.
Gravel, 169.
Great Bear, 216.
Great Exhibition (London, 1851), 178.
"Great Thunderbolt" see Plantain, Water.
Greenwich, 7.
Gretna, 326.
"Grey mare's tail" see Cirrus cloud.
Grub, 181.
Guinea fowl, 138; or "Comeback, 138.

Haar, 343.
Habberley and Habberley Hole (Shropshire), 218.
Hail, 109, 146, 195, 222, 228, 241, 247, 271, 277; stone, 274, 277.
Halo see Moon or Sun halo.

Hallowmas (1 Nov.), 86.
Hampshire, 13, 29, 35, 47, 102, 160, 268, 283, 291, 295, 299.
Hare, 176; coat of, 81.
Harrier, Marsh, 140.
Harvest, 2-4, 13, 16, 26, 30, 31, 42, 49, 50, 53-57, 67, 72-74, 82, 96, 98, 103, 106, 108, 110, 111, 113, 117, 120, 122, 133, 134, 164, 291, 297, 302, 332, 350.
"Hat" see Stratus cloud.
Haws, many, 72, 303.
Hawthorn, May, Whitethorn or, 102, 300, 302, 303; haws, 303; leaf, 303.
Hay, 2, 4, 9, 11, 12, 15-18, 24, 30, 34, 36, 40, 42, 44, 46-48, 54, 55, 102, 103, 108-111, 134, 165, 167, 181, 186, 192, 275, 288, 318, 330-332; rick, 35.
Haze, 112, 118, 204, 309, 310, 313, 316, 325, 326, 341.
Hazel nut, 58.
Hedgehog, 176, 178.
Heifer, 172.
"Heigh-ho" see Woodpecker, green.
Helm cloud or bar, 270.
Hemp, 73.
Hen, 137.
"Hen's scarts" see Cirrocumulus cloud.
Herefordshire, 26, 101, 104, 211, 270.
Hertfordshire, 103.
Hibernation see Animal and Reptile.
Hilarius, 7.
Hoar down, 269.
Hoar frost see Frost.
Hog, 101.
Hollandtide, 87-89.
Holly, 303.
Holy Innocent's Day (28 Dec.), 98.
Holy or Maundy Thursday, 102.
Holycross or Holyrood Day (14 Sept,), 74.
Honey, 73, 288.
"Hood" see Stratus cloud.
Hopper, 22, 24.
Hops, 66, 95.
Hornet, 97.
Horse, 17, 18, 133, 176, 177; manger, 110.
Houseleek, 276, 290, 303; "Thunder Plant", 290; "Jupiter's" Plant, 290.
Huesca (Spain), 7.
Humidity, 234, 236, 248, 283, 284, 287, 291, 292, 294, 296, 305, 307, 308, 341, 346.
Huntingdonshire, 7, 41, 89, 102, 211.
Hurricane, 160.
Hurstpierpoint (Sussex), 269.
Husbandman, 5, 11, 12, 15, 23, 111, 112, 116.
Hygrometer, 294, 295, 307, 308.

Ice, 14, 20, 23, 84, 86, 88, 93, 97, 277, 335; "black", 336; crystals, 203, 252, 256, 320, 332, 335, 336, 340.
Ice Saints (St Mamertius, St Pancras and St Gervatius, whose days are 11-13 May), 50.
Icicles, 20.
Indian corn, 307, 308.
Indian summer, 82.
Insect, 161, 189-201; behaviour, 189, 190, 194, 196, 197; black, 193; eggs, 189; flight, 192, 193, 196; movement, 190, 199, 201; nests, 189, 190, 197, 200, 201; noise, 194, 195; scent, 190.
Insolation, 271.
Inversion, Temperature, see Temperature.

Isle of Wight, 293, 324.

Jackdaw, 142.
Jack Frost, 4.
"Jack-go-to-Bed-at-Noon" see Star of Bethlehem.
"Jacob's Ladder, 317.
January, 1-10, 55, 61, 62, 99; anticyclones, 1; bird song in, 2; cold, 13, 61; cold and frosty, 87, 352; dry, 2; "favourable", 1; flood, 5, fog, 3; frost, 1, 3; frosty period in, 1; grain, 2; "lamb", 99; March in, 1; mild, 1, 2, 78, 79; mild and dry, 84; mild and open, 91; snow, 333; little snow in, 2; very snowy, 4; sow oats in, 4; spring in, 2; storms, 1; sunny, 1; thaw, 3; thunder, 4; warm, 2, 5; wet, 2, 81; very wet, 2; 25 Dec-5 Jan., 5; 1st, 5, 6; 2nd, 6; 1-3rd, 6; 12th, 6; 13 or 14th (St Hilary's Day), 6, 7; 17th (St Anthony's Day), 7; 22nd (St Vincent's Day), 7, 8; 25th (St Paul's Conversion Day), 8, 9, 59; 25th (St Ananias' Day), 9; 26th, 10; 19-31st, 10.
Jet stream, 263, 312.
Judges, Circuit, 31.
July, 60-66, 68, 190; bees, 48, 61, 192; changeable, 64; great heat in, 60, 61; showers, 60, 62, 65; storms, 60; thistles, 295; thunder, 30, 60, 61; warm, 60; wet, 62-64, 66, 105; westerlies, 60; 1st, 62; first Friday in, 62; 2nd (St Mary's Day), 62; 10th, 63; 12th, 63, 64; 14th (St Processus' and St Martin's Day), 64; 12-15th (Buchan's 1st Warm Spell), 64; 15th (St Swithin's Day), 64, 65; 20th (St Jacob's Day), 66; 20th (St Margaret's Day), 66; 22nd (St Mary Magdalene's Day), 66; 25th (St James' Day), 66.
June, 27, 30, 44, 53-59, 121, 122; anticyclones, 53; bees, 48, 55, 192; blossoms, 302; calm, 53; clear, 38; cold and wet, 54; dew, 53; early, 55; frost, 15; hot, 53; northerlies, 55; rain, 30, 41; stormy, 53; thistles, 295; warm and damp, 54; westerlies, 53, 55, 56; wet, 28, 45, 54, 56, 57, 59, 105; wet, cool and stormy period in, 53; 8th, 56; 11th (St Barnabas Day), 56; 15th (St Vitus' Day), 156, 157; 21 and 24th, 57; 23rd (Midsummer's Eve), 57; 24th (St John's or Midsummer's Day), 33, 58; 27th, 59; 29th (St Peter's Day), 59; 29 June - 4 July (Buchan's 4th Cold Spell), 59.
Jupiter, 216.
"Jupiter's Plant" see Houseleek.

Katabatic Wind, 224.
Kelp, 293.
Kennington (Berks), 19, 21, 26.
Kent, 78, 120, 169, 275, 283, 298; East, 218, 219, 270.
Kenton, 269.
Kew, 7.
Kidney bean, 302.
Kingfisher, 142, 143.
Kite, 141.

Ladie Lift near Weobley (Herefordshire), 269, 270.
Ladies Bedstraw, 288.
Lady Day (25 March), 36.
Lamb, 25, 27, 28, 99, 184, 316.

Lammas or Loaf-Mass Day (1 August), 31, 68, 69.
Lancashire, 93, 215, 265, 266, 270, 335.
Lapse rate see Temperature.
Lariggan (Cornwall), River, 328.
Lark see Skylark.
Lastingham (N. Yorkshire), 32.
Latter Lady Day, 41.
"Lazy wind", 231.
Lee waves, Mountain, 264, 270.
Leech *(Hirudo Medicinalis)*, Medical, 177-179, 187
Leicester, 103.
Leicestershire, 270, 291.
Lent, 100, 101.
Leo (star), 60.
Ley, Rev. Clement, 255-259, 262.
Lightning, 78, 99, 102, 107, 230, 271-273, 275, 276, 289, 290, 292, 297, 303, 304, 326; forked, 271, 273, 274; sheet, 273.
"Lightnings" see Poppy.
Lime, 305.
Lincoln, 140.
Lincolnshire, 17, 31, 283.
Lion, 27, 28, 99.
Lizard (Cornwall), 324.
Long Man (Sussex), 261.
London, 284, 310.
Lord Pembroke, 288.
Louth (Ireland), 16.
Lowe, E.J., 337.
Lower's *History of Sussex*, 344.
Lundy Isle (Bristol Channel), 324.

"Mackerel sky" see Cirrocumulus cloud.
Magpie, 143, 144.
Maize, 308.
Manure, 39.
March, 1, 3, 11, 13, 14, 25-37, 40, 41, 48, 81, 85, 99, 121, 122; "adder's head" in, 27; apple blossom, 306; "black ram" in, 27; cloudy, 1; cold, 287; cold spell in, 32; cold and stormy, 25, 27; cold and wet, 33, 34; dew, 30, 31; dry, 26, 28, 30, 31, 35; dust, 25, 26, 31; early, 22; flowers, 26; fog, 29, 30; frost, 2, 29, 34, 37, 339; grass, 25; "lamb" in, 27, 28; "lion" in, 27, 28; mild, 2, 14; mist, 29, 34; northerlies, 14, 25; northeasterlies, 35; "peacock's tail" in, 27; quiet weather in, 25, 27; rainfall, 30; sleet, 37; snow, 21, 27, 37, 39; stormy, 33, 35-37; sun, 26; thaw, 14; thunder, 13, 14, 32; varied weather in, 25, 27; warm, 41; very warm, 287; warm and wet, 26, 27, 37; wet, 26, 27, 29, 30, 33; wet and windy, 25; windy, 26, 28, 29, 37, 45; 1st (St David's Day), 32; 2nd (St Chad's Day), 32; 3rd (St Winnold's or Winneral's Day), 33; 1-3rd, 32, 33; 1-10th, 33, 34; 10th, 34; 14th, 20; 17th (St Patrick's Day), 34; 19th (St Joseph's Day), 34; 21st (St Benedict's Day), 32, 34; c21st (Vernal Equinox), 35; 20-27th, 35, 36; 25th (St Mary's or Lady's Day), 20, 36; 29-31st (The Borrowing Days), 36, 37; late March and early April, 41, 42.
"Margaret's flood", 66.
Margate, 328.
Margery family, 297.
Marigold, African, 288, 289; Cape, 289; Marsh or Common, 289.
Marlborough Downs (Wilts), 140.
Marsham (Norfolk), 297, 300.
Martin, 144, 145; House, 145; Sand, 145.

Martinmas, 87-89; Eve, 87.
Maundy Thursday, 102.
May see Hawthorn.
May, 5, 18, 38, 39, 44-52, 55, 71, 192, 298; anticyclones, 44; apple blossom, 52, 306; bees, 48, 192; blossom, 44, 302; cold, 5, 47, 49; cold and wet, 47; cold spell in, 14, 49, 51; cool, 30; cool and damp, 46; cool and windy, 47; dew, 47; dry, 28, 45, 54, 71, 298; easterlies, 47, 51; end of, 52; fine, 28; fine and dry, 44; flood, 40, 46, flowers, 29, 38, 44; frost, 14, 29, 47; ground frost, 14; hoar frost, 49; hot, 44; merry month of, 44; mild, 44; mists, 53; northerlies, 44,302; rain, 46; shear sheep in, 49,50); showers, 26, 46; snow, 48; southerlies, 44; storms, 51; summers in, 52; sun, 28, 45; thunder, 45; thunderstorms, 45, 46; warm, 49, 287; westerlies, 44; wet, 38, 46, 54, 298; wet and warm, 49; wind, 47, 49; 1st (May Day), 44; 1st (St Philip and St James' Day), 49, 66; 8th, 50; 9-14th (Buchan's 3rd Cold Spell), 50; 11-13th 1st Mamertius', (St Pancras' and St Gervatius' Day – The Ice Saints), 50; middle of (11-20th), 50; 17-19th, 51, 139; 19th (St Dunstan's Day), 51; 17-23rd, 51; 19-21st, 51; 20 or 21st (Franklin's Frost), 51, 52; 24th (St Urban's Day), 52; 29th (Oak Apple Day), 77.
Maypole, 44.
Medieval England, 2, 22.
Merryweather, Dr George, 178, 179.
Meteor, 215.
Meteorological Society, Scottish, 21.
Michaelmas, 76, 77.
Middlesex, 289.
Midges, 11, 12.
Midlands, 74, 87-89, 297.

Midsummer's Day (24 June), 33, 57; Eve (23 June), 57.
Milk, 105, 169, 226, 275.
Mill, 268.
Miller, 221.
Mirrlees, S.T.A., 65.
Mist, 9, 27, 69, 111, 127, 128, 208, 209, 212, 268, 283, 289, 326, 336, 341-344, 348; "black", 344.
Mistletoe, 289; berries, 162.
Mock sun and moon see Sun and Moon.
Mole, 176, 178, 179.
Monday, 95, 123, 126.
Moon, 76, 125, 202-215, 255, 306, 322, 351; clear, 213; colours, 203, 204, 323; corona; 320-322; crescent points of, 80; daytime, 206; with easterlies, 204; with fog, 204; Friday, 209; with frost, 203, 206, 207; full, 42, 43, 80, 97, 203, 207-213; halo, 215, 319, 320; high, 205; large, 323; low, 205; midnight, 209; with mist, 208, 209, 212, 348; mock (paraselena), 202, 203, 320; new, 97, 204, 205, 207-209, 211, 212, 332, 348; old, 207, 211, 212, 348; orbit, 205, 206; pale, 204; phases or quarters, 204, 207-209, 211; red, 203, 322; reddish-brown, 204; rise, 207, 208; Saturday, 209, 210; shape, 207, 208, 211; with snow, 208; and storms, 317, 318; Sunday, 210; waxing and waning, 19, 206, 332, white, 323.
Moorhen, 145, 160.
Morden Carrie (Yorkshire), 269.

Morning, 126, 151, 152, 154, 156; animals in, 166, 172; birds, 155, 157; bright, 126; cloudy, 128, 316, 323; flowers, 288, 289, 291; fog, 232, 341; frost, 223, 335, 337; grey sky, 16, 347; high dawn, 317; low dawn, 317; misty, 126, 341, 348; moon, 209; rain, 127, 244-246; rainbow, 279-281, 351; red, 316; red sky, 309, 310; spider's web in, 199; thunder, 272; wet, 128; wind, 217, 240.
Moth, 168.
Mountain, 175, 270, 271, 281, 328, 342, 343.
"Mountain breeze", 224.
Mouse, 93, 173, 301; Field, 178.
Mulberry, 304.
Mule, 177.
Mushroom, 307.

Nativity star, 294.
Nectar, 190.
Night, 127; blustering, 127; mild, 185; sheep at, 183.
Nimbostratus (Ns) cloud, 252.
Nitric acid, 275.
"Noah's ark, Noaship or Nolskeppit" see Altocumulus cloud.
Noah's flood, 23.
Noon, 153.
"Noon-Peeders" see Star of Bethlehem.
Norfolk, 54, 138, 210, 244, 249, 291.
Norsemen, 278.
North-Easterlies see Wind.
North Pole, 216; Sea, 165, 235; star, 274.
North-Westerlies see Wind.
Northamptonshire, 124, 147, 262, 283, 291.
Northerlies see Wind.
Northumberland, 25, 292.

Northumbria, 32.
Norwich, 142.
Nottinghamshire, 291.
November, 72, 75, 84-91, 114, 199, 200; anticyclones, 84; cold, 84, 85; dry spell in, 86; early, 87; easterlies, 85; fog, 84; frost and snow, 91; hoar frost, 85; ice, 84, 86, 88, 89; lightning, 99; very mild, 91; full moon, 80; northwesterlies, 88; rain, 84; snow, 333; snow and frost, 352; south-south-westerlies, 88; south-westerlies, 88, 89; storms, 84; thunder, 85, 99; wet, 86, 88; wet and warm, 87, 352; 1st (All Saints Day or Hallowmas), 86; late Oct. and early Nov., 87, 352; 10th (Martinmas Eve), 87; 11th (St Martin's Day, Martinmas or Hollandtide), 87-89; St Martin's "little summer" in, 87, 88; 6-13th (Buchan's 6th Cold Spell), 89; 21st, 90; 22nd, 90; 23rd (St Clement's Day), 90; 25th (St Catherine's Day), 90.
Nuts (filberts), 57, 58, 120, 184, 300.

Oak, 5, 77, 81, 297-300, 304, 305; Apple Day (29 May), 77; leaf, 80; mast, 81.
Oats, 32, 48, 49, 72; wild, 308.
Occlusion, 320.
October, 71, 75, 78-83, 114; anticyclones, 78, 80; cold, 84; dry, 80; dry and mild, 86; fine, 78; fine with dry spells in, 82; fog, 79, 80; frost, 79; frost and snow, 78, 91, 352; heavy frost and wind, 79; gnats, 197; mild, 79; full moon, 80; "Old-wives summer"

in, 78; storms, 78, 81; thunder, 81; thunderstorms, 78; warm, 40, 79; wet, 78, 80; wind, 81; wind and rain, 81. 29 Sept. and 16 Oct. (St Gallus' Day), 81, 82; 18th (St Luke's Day), 82; St Luke's "little summer", 82, 88, 89; 28th (St Simon's and St Jude's Day), 82.
"Old Man's Weatherglass" see Scarlet Pimpernel.
Old Mother Goring (Chanctonburg Ring, South Downs, Sussex), 269, 270.
"Old-wives summer", 71.
"One O'clock" see Star of Bethlehem.
Onion, 277, 306.
Owl, 146, 147; Barn, 147; Little, 147; Long-eared, 147; short-eared, 147; Tawny, 147.
Ox, 20, 25, 46, 61, 83, 249, 301.
Ox-eye daisy see Daisy, Moon.
Oxford, 9, 44, 275.
Oxfordshire, 244, 266, 267.

Palm Sunday, 101.
Paraselena see Moon, Mock.
Parhelia, see Sun, Mock.
Parrot, 147.
Pastor Sunday, 104.
Pea, 19, 32, 35, 100, 206.
Pea-fowl, 138.
Peacock, 27, 147, 148.
Pear, 58, 120.
Pendle's Head (Westmorland), 268.
Pennines, 225.
Penny, 302.
Pentecost, 104, 105.
Persistence, Weather, 127.
Petals, 283.
Pheasant, 148.
Pig, 39, 181.

Pigeon, 149.
Pike, 175.
Pine, 293, 295, 305.
Pitcher plant, 291, 292.
Plane, 305.
Planet, 215, 216.
Plantain, Water, 292; "Great Thunderbolt", 292.
Plants, 102, 107, 283-296, 303, 307; "Umbrellas", 292.
"Plervets", 221.
"Ploughman's Weatherglass" see Scarlet Pimpernel.
Plover, 134, 149, 150.
Plum, 58, 117, 120.
Poitiers, Bishop of, 7.
Polar airstream, 126, 212-214, 225, 227, 237, 271, 316, 324.
Pollen, 48, 61, 190.
Pons-an-Dane (Cornwall), 328.
"Poorman's Weatherglass" see Scarlet Pimpernel.
Poplar, 305.
Poppy, 292; "Lightnings", 292; "Thunderball, Thunderbolt or Thunderflower", 292.
Potatoes, 10, 27, 40, 306.
Pressure; Atmospheric, 328; falls, 219, 237, 256, 259, 328; high, 257, 259 see Anticyclone; ridge of high, 219, 237, 267.
Prince, C.L., 314.
Purification of the Virgin Mary or Candlemas Day, 17.

Rabbit, 181, 182.
Rain, 1-352 especially 242-251; drops, 278, 281; from east, 243; 40 days of, 23, 57, 63, 64; 30 days of, 57; about 4 weeks of, 62; 7 weeks of, 63; freezing (glazed ice), 336; heavy, 46, 68, 97, 107, 166, 171, 172, 176, 184, 190, 200, 212, 236, 244, 248, 249,

254, 258, 263, 268, 273, 282, 325, 326, 339; moderate, 171, 172, 184, 248, 339; slight, 171, 172, 184, 242, 244; from south, 243; from south-west, 243; from west, 243.
"Rain balls" see Cumulus cloud.
"Rain beetle", 192.
Rain bird see Woodpecker, Green.
Rainbow, 278-282, 351; or "the bridge of gods", 278; colours, 278, 280-282, 309; day, 279-281; or "dog", 279; main or primary, 278, 280; partial, 281; secondary, 278, 282; small, 281; supernumary, 278, 282.
Ragged Robin, 292; or "Thunder-Flower", 292.
Rat, 178, 182.
Raven, 150, 151.
Redwing, 136.
Reflection, 278.
Refraction, 203, 278, 317.
Reptile, 186-189; behaviour, 187, 188; hibernation, 186, 189; food hunting of, 188; noises, numerous, 187, 188; in water, 188.
Rickmansworth (Herts), 145.
Rime, 118, 277, 336.
River, 41, 234, 248, 328, 341.
Riving Pike (Lancs), 269.
Robin, 151-153.
Romans, 290.
Rome, 22, 90.
Romney Marsh, 270.
Rook, 150, 153-155, 197.
Rookery, 155.
Roseberry Topping (Yorks), 269.
Rowan, 305.
Rowanberry, 164.
Russell, Spenser, 310, 311.
Rutland, 2, 16, 96, 167, 291.
Rye, 8, 26, 42, 55, 59, 60, 100, 105.

"Sailor's breeches", 326.
Saints' days; St Ananias (25 Jan), 9; St Anthony (17 Jan), 7; St Barnabas (11 June), 56; St Bartholomew (24 Aug), 65, 69, 70; St Benedict (21 March), 32, 34; St Bridget (1 Feb), 16; St Catherine (25 Nov), 90; St Clement (23 Nov), 90; St Chad (2 March), 32; St David (1 March), 32; St Dorothea (6 Feb), 21; St Dunstan (19 May), 51; St Gallus (16 Oct), 81, 82; St George (23 April), 42; St Gervatius (13 May), 50; St Hilary (13 or 14 Jan), 6, 7; St Jacob (20 July), 66; St James (25 July), 66; St John (24 June), 57; St Joseph (19 March), 34; St Lucy (13 Dec), 92; St Luke (18 Oct), 82; St Mamertius (11 May), 50; St Margaret (20 July), 66; St Mark (24 April), 42; St Mary (2 July), 62; St Mary or Lady Day (25 March), 20, 36; St Mary Magdalen (22 July), 66; St Mary's Assumption (15 Aug), 69; St Martin (11 Nov.), 87-89; St Matthew (21 Sept), 75, 76; St Matthias (24 Feb), 23, 24; St Michael or Michaelmas (29 Sept), 76, 77, 81, 82; St Pancras (12 May), 50; St Patrick (17 March), 34; St Paul's Conversion (25 Jan), 8, 9, 59; St Peter (29 June), 59; St Peter (22 Feb), 22, 23; St Philip and St James (1 May), 49, 66; St Processus and St Martin (13 July), 64, 65; St Romanus (28 Feb), 24; St Simon and St Jude (28 Oct), 82; St Swithin (13 July), 64, 65; St Thomas (21 Dec), 92-94; St Urban (24 May), 52; St Valentine (1 Feb), 22; St Vincent

(22 Jan), 7; St Vitus (15 June), 56, 57; St Winnold or Winneral (3 March), 33.
St Bride, 16.
St Bridget, 16.
St Catherine, 90.
St James, 63.
St John's Wort, 57.
St Leonard's (Margate, Sussex), 328.
St Luke's "little summer", 82, 88, 89.
St Martin's "little summer", 87, 88.
St Peter, 90.
St Peter's Weathervane (Norwich, 142.
St Swithin, 63.
St Vincent, 7.
St Vitus, 57.
"Salmon" see Altocumulus cloud.
Sand, 130, 136.
Sandwort, Purple, 293.
"Sash" see Ash and oak.
Saturday, 6, 123-125, 209, 210.
Scandinavia, 164.
"Scarlet Lightning" see Valerian, Red.
Scarlet Pimpernel, 290, 291; or "Change-of-the-Weather", 291; "Grandfather's Weatherglass", 291; "Old Man's Weatherglass", 291; or "Ploughman's Weatherglass", 290, 291; or "Poor Man's Weatherglass", or "Shepherd's Dial, Glass, Warning or Weatherglass", 291; "Weather Flower, Weatherglass or Weather Teller", 291.
Scattering, 309, 325.
"Scud", 206, 327.
Schneirla, T.C., 190.
Scythe, 56.
Sea, 68, 98, 138-140, 327, 328, 343.
Seagull, 138, 139, 155, 156.
Sea mews, 155.

Seasons, 106-119, 121, 332.
Seaweed, 293.
September, 6, 56, 61, 71-78, 97, 103, 106, 121, 122, 196, 197, 297; anticyclones, 71, 75; bees, 75; cold spell in, 72; dry, 54, 73, 74; dry and mild, 72; dry spells in, 70, 71; dry and warm, 47; dew, 75, 76; fair, 73; floods, 76; frost, 47; great heat in, 61; "Old wives summer" in, 71; moon, 76; rain, 71; southerlies, 76; stormy, 71; thunder, 45, 72; wet, 45, 71, 73, 74; windy spells in, 74; 1st, 83; 8th, 73; 14th (Holycross or Holyrood Day), 74; middle of, 74; 15th, 74; 19th, 74, 75; c21st (Autumn Equinox), 75; 20-22nd, 75; 21st (St Matthew's Day), 75, 76; 29th (St Michael's Day or Michaelmas), 76, 77, 81.
Severn estuary, 249.
Shakespeare, William, 86, 89, 147, 233, 236, 244, 289, 311, 314.
Sheaves or stooks, 73, 279.
Sheep, 20, 49, 50, 133, 166, 170, 171, 175, 176, 182-184, 261, 301, 345.
Shepherd, 183, 217, 228, 235, 279, 309, 310, 316, 319, 347, 251.
"Shepherd's Calendar, Dial, Glass, Warning or Weatherglass", see Scarlet Pimpernel.
Shepherd of Banbury (Oxon), 87, 91, 228, 235, 310, 347-352.
"Shift" see Stratus cloud.
Shilling, 301.
Showers, 29, 38, 39, 60, 65, 126-128, 141, 143, 172, 174, 191, 196, 213, 217, 225-227, 234, 237-240, 244, 246-248, 250, 255, 259, 265-267, 272-

274, 277-280, 283, 288, 290, 293, 306, 316-318, 324-326, 331; downdraughts in, 61, 109, 271, 275, 283; hail, 109, 238, 241, 348; heavy or violent, 32, 61, 107, 172, 217, 219, 222, 250, 254, 266, 273, 276, 277, 281, 315, 318, 339; meteor, 215; sleet, 229; snow 229.
Shrewsbury, 218.
Shropshire, 124, 133, 165, 208, 218, 292, 298; West, 46.
Shrove or Pancake Tuesday, 100.
Silk, 199.
Silvester, Norman L., 284, 285, 287, 291.
Simeon, 16.
Sirius (Dog star), 63.
"Skat", 269, 270.
Sky (cloudless), 325, 326; blue, 309, 313, 325, 326; blue and white, 262; steel blue, 311; Carle, 326; Carlisle, 326; clear, 345; colours, 309; sea green, 325; grey, 326; purple or pink, 311; red, 5, 309, 310, 326; gentle rose, 326; yellow, 326; white, 309.
Skylark, 156, 157, 326.
Sleet, 37, 226, 228, 229, 337.
Sloe or blackthorn, 72, 305.
Slug, 188, 198.
"Smoke" see Ash and oak.
Smoke, 309, 341.
Snail, 197, 198.
Snake, 26, 187, 188, 272; grass, 188; smooth, 188.
Snow, 2, 4, 9, 13, 15, 16, 18, 20, 21, 27, 33, 37, 48, 76, 78, 79, 95, 97, 113, 114, 118, 120, 140, 163, 170, 194, 207, 208, 214, 225-229, 247, 249, 296, 303, 324, 330-334, 337; insulation, 4, 13, 118, 120; severe or heavy, 21, 67, 81, 134, 332.

Somerset, 110, 283, 287, 290-294; West, 55.
"Sonegalis", 307.
Sorrell, 293, 294; Wood, 293.
Sound, 186, 276, 327-329; railway, 329; waves, 327, 329.
South Downs (Sussex), 344.
Southerlies see Wind.
South-easterlies see Wind.
South-south-westerlies see Wind.
South-westerlies see Wind.
Spaniel, 172.
Sparrow, 157, 158; Hedge, 158.
Speedwell, Germander, 294; or "Strike-Fire", 294.
Spider, 198-200; web, 87, 198-200.
"Splash" see Ash and oak.
Spring, 2, 15, 20, 22, 97, 101, 106-108, 111, 115, 118, 121, 122, 133, 140, 152, 159, 229, 326; anticyclones, 25, 335; blossoms, 106, 108; cold, 103, 287; cold and dry, 119; cold and dull, 107; early cold, 113; cold and wet, 33, 34, 106; cold spells in, 225, 229, dry, 35, 81, 82, 107, 108, 200; early, 107, 108, 133, 134; easterlies, 229, 231; flies, 195; fog, 232; frost, 11, 108, 120, 225; last frost in, 338; gnats, 197; late, 106, 108, 134; lightning, 107, 273; mild, 44; mild and wet, 120; north-easterlies, 270; northerlies, 25; rain, 333; heavy rain in, 107; short, 287; thunder, 107, 231; first thunder in, 107, 272; thunderstorms, 107; warm spells in, 23; varied weather in, 108; wet, 33, 106, 107, 121, 305, 351; wet and very cold in, 272; windy, 106; winter in, 108, 114.
Squall, 147, 219, 235, 243,

371

258, 259, 277, 350.
"Squash" see Ash and oak.
Squirrel, 184.
Staffordshire, 37, 288.
Star of Bethlehem, 294; or "Betty-go-to-Bed-at-Noon", 294; or "Jack-go-to-Bed-at-Noon", 294; or "Eleven O'clock Lady", 294; or "Noon Peeders", 294; or "One O'clock", 294; or "Twelve O'clocks", 294; or "Wake at Noon", 294.
Starling, 132, 158.
Stars, 214-216, 255, 351; dim, 351; "huddling", 214; numerous, 214, 273; shooting, 215; twinkling, 214.
Stevenson screen, 284.
Stillingfleet (Yorks), 289.
Stitchwort, greater, 294; or "Thunderbolt or Thunder-Flower", 294.
"Storm bird" see Woodpecker, Green.
"Storm cock" see Thrush.
Storms, (to be found on most pages).
Stratocumulus (Sc) cloud, 252, 321.
Stratus (St) cloud, 252, 267-270, 343; to "burn off", 267; "cap", 269, 270; "cloake", 269; "hat", 269, 270; "hood", 269, 270; night, 267; "ragged", 267, 344; "shift", 270.
Straw, 16.
Strawberry, 105.
"Strike fire" see Speedwell, Germander.
Suffolk, 26, 31, 212, 243, 247, 279.
Sugar maple, 13.
Summer, 3, 20, 52, 57, 101, 109, 112, 114, 121, 122, 129, 134, 152, 201, 229, 230, 253, 257, 258, 299, 347, 350; anticyclones, 112; cold and wet, 33,

34; cool, 111, 205, 224, 238; dew, 346; dry, 35-37, 51, 95, 109, 110, 117, 145, 201, 216, 286, 287, 299, 333; dry spells in, 112; very dry, 87, 352; drought, 73, 110; early, 20; fine, 15; flies, 195; flood, 73, 115, 116; flowers, 38; fog, 111; "good", 155; hail, 177; haze, 112, 316; heat, 150, 274, 339; hot weather in, 179, 298, 341, 350; hot and dry, 115, 116, 159, 160; very hot and dry, 110, 113; lightning, 273, 274; meteors, 215; mists, 111, 341, 344; north-easterlies, 229; north-westerlies, 239; of 1975 and 1976, 251; rain, 109, 110, 207, 228, 297, 298; rainbow, 280; rainfall, 30; serene, 121; settled weather in, 257; showers, 259; south-westerlies, 271; storms, 56; sunrise, 315; thunder, 215, 258; thunderstorms, 109, 110, 229-232, 257, 259, 271; high temperatures in, 258; "unproductive", 111; unsettled weather in, 257; warm, 197; warm spells, 229, 231; wet, 30, 33, 36, 51, 56, 98, 108, 109, 145, 200, 201, 216, 298, 299, 305, 351; winter in, 112.
Sun, (found on most pages), concave, 317; convex, 317; with coloured halo, 320; corona, 321; "drawing water", 317; halo, 215, 319, 320; $22°$ halo, 263, 320, $46°$ halo, 320; hazy, 325; mock (parhelia), 202, 320; pillar, 320; red, 310, 314, 316, 347; watery, 314, 318; white, 312; yellow, 312.
Sunday, 92, 104, 123-126, 210.
Sunlight, 309-318, 320.
Sunrise, 127, 345, 309-315,

322; cloudy, 253, 266; colours, 310; frost, 336; gaudy, 315; grey, 315, 316; misty, 212, 341; pale, 313; rainy, 246, 351; red, 309, 311, 314, 315; red cloudy, 314; red and yellow, 311; storms, 317, 318; yellow, 311.
Sunset, 119, 123-125, 127, 309-318, 322; bird song at, 161; clear, 313; cloudy, 253, 266, 267, 313; colours, 310, 314; gaudy, 312; grey, 311, 314; insects at, 196; moon, 203; orange, 314; pale, 313, 314; red sky at, 309, 311, 314; red cloudy, 309; red and yellow, 311; rose tints, 316; storms, 317, 318; halo, 319; temperature, 218; whitish yellow, 312; wind continuing at, 217; wind directions at, 240; wind subsiding at, 217-219; yellow, 311, 312; yellow and cloudy, 311.
Surrey, 12, 35.
Sussex, 19, 103, 209, 270, 328, 344.
Swallow, 111, 132, 153, 158-160.
Swan, 140, 145, 160.
Swarms, Bee, see Bee, Honey.
Swift, 159-161.
Swine, 181.
Swithin, 65.
Sycamore, 305, 306.

Teasel, 294, 295.
Teddington, 123.
Temperature, 185, 186, 189, 203, 214, 218, 224, 226, 240, 257, 258, 266, 271, 284, 287, 291, 332, 336, 337, grass, 335; ground, 287; high. 329; inversion, 112, 161, 217, 218, 327, 329; lapse rate, 240; low, 277, 340; maximum, 128, 218;

night, 283; soil, 185, 284, 331; water, 174.
Tempest Prognosticator, 178, 179.
Thames, River, 160.
Thames Valley, 275.
Thaw, 3, 14, 92, 180, 181, 183, 208, 255, 328, 331, 332, 339.
Thirty days of rain, 57, 62.
Thistle, 58, 287; Fuller's, 295; Sow, 295.
Thor, 123, 304.
Thorn, 102.
Thrush, Missel, 161, 162; Song, 161, 162.
"Thunderball, Thunderbolt or Thunder Flower" see Poppy.
"Thunderbolt" see Campion, Bladder.
"Thunderbolt or Thunderflower", see Campion, White.
see Stitchwort, Greater.
"Thunder Daisy" see Daisy Moon.
"Thunder-Flower" see Ragged Robin.
Thunder planet, 215, 216.
"Thunder Plant" see Houseleek.
Thunder plants, 303.
Thunder (storm), 4, 9, 13, 14, 40, 45, 46, 57, 68, 70, 72, 78, 85, 92, 98-100, 102, 107, 109, 110, 113, 116, 123, 129, 160, 161, 170, 172-174, 177, 187, 191, 215, 217, 226, 229, 230, 232, 243, 257-259, 262, 263, 265, 267, 269, 271-277, 281, 289, 292, 294, 303, 304, 350.
Thursday, 95, 123.
Tide, 202, 249; air, 327; atmospheric, 202; "bird", 139; spring, 139.
Tit, Great, 163.
Titmouse, 162, 163; Great, 163.
Toad, 188.
Toadstool, 307.
Tortoise, 188, 189.

Trees, 296-305; with dead branches, 296; flowering, 298; leaves rattle on, 296; underside branches of, 296; snapping, 296.
Trefoil, 295.
Tuesday, 126.
Tulip, 306.
Turbulence, 326, 327.
Turkey, 163, 164.
"Twelve O'clocks" see Star of Bethlehem.
Twilight, 127, 129.

Ultrasonic systems, 168.
"Umbrellas" see Plantain Water.

Valerian, Red, 295; or "Scarlet Lightning", 295.
Venus, 216.
Vernal Equinox (c21 March), 35.
Vineyards, 2, 71, 158.
Viper, 188.
Visibility, 341; clear, 324, 325.
Visibility, Good, see Polar airstream.
Vole, 142.
Vortex, 196.

"Waddle", 19.
"Wake at Noon" see Star of Bethlehem.
Wales, 328.
Wall, 200.
Walnut, 58.
"Wane cloud" see Cirrostratus cloud.
Warble fly, 172.
Warm front, 237, 263; sector, 267, 314, 320, 344.
Warwickshire, 283, 291, 292.
Wasp, 200, 201.
Water droplets, 321, 341; vapour, 271, 326.
"Water waggons" see Cumulus cloud.
Wave, Cold front, 237.
Waxwings, 164.
"Waxwing winter", 164.
Weald (Kent), 46.
Weather balance, 1, 3, 5, 31, 55, 69, 78, 79, 112, 115, 118, 242, 243, 300, 303, 304.
"Weather breeders" (Surrey), 112, 115.
"Weather Flower, Weatherglass or Weather-Teller" see Scarlet Pimpernel.
Weather glass, 219.
Web, Spider's, see Spider.
Wednesday, 123, 125.
Weeds, 339.
Weekdays, 123-126.
Welsh mountains, 264.
West Country, 231, 331.
Westmorland, 270.
Westerlies see Wind.
Wheat, 2, 9, 15, 24, 26-28, 31, 34, 36, 38, 39, 45, 46, 59, 61, 68, 72, 86, 93, 97, 111, 114, 116, 120, 134, 275, 308, 332.
Whit Monday, 102; Sunday, 103, 105.
Whitby (N. Yorks), 46, 178; Museum, 179.
Whitethorn, see Hawthorn.
Whitlow grass, 288.
Whitstable (Kent), 200.
Whitsuntide, 104, 105.
Willow, 97.
Wiltshire, 26, 29, 47, 134, 171, 178, 242, 279, 291, 292, 294; West, 291.
Winchester, 65, 126; Cathedral, 65.
Wind, (on most pages especially 217-241); backing, 219, 220, 235, 256; calm, 68, 87, 111, 119, 161, 190, 219, 223, 237,

247, 267, 287, 327, 343, 345; easterly, 20, 31, 47, 51, 85, 92, 98, 99, 174, 175, 200, 204, 222, 229-232, 236, 255, 256. 313, 331, 343, "funnelling effect" of, 218; gale force or strong, (found on most pages); gusts, 217, 222, 224, 240, 273, 275, 285; increase with height, 327,329; northerly, 11, 14, 15, 25, 38, 44, 55, 98, 214, 222-227, 230, 231, 234-237, 241, 331, 347, 348, 350; north-easterly, 35, 76, 98, 99, 118, 119, 207, 214, 222, 227-229, 236, 270, 331; north-westerly, 88, 118, 214, 222, 227, 237-241, 331; shear, 256; southerly, 44, 76, 92, 98, 99, 175, 204, 222, 223, 227, 228, 230-237, 243, 331, 342, 344, 348, 350, 351; south-easterly, 113,116, 331, 344; south-south-westerly,88; south-westerly, 88, 89, 155, 193, 207, 218, 222, 235-237, 241, 271, 331,343, 348, upper, 9, 256, 259, 263, 264, 312; veering, 219, 220, 235, 237, 240, 241; westerly, 1, 44, 53, 55, 56, 60, 92, 98, 99, 125, 218, 221, 222, 230, 234, 238-240, 259, 271, 277, 313, 331.

"Wind Flower and Plant" see Anemone, Wood.

Wine, 2, 7, 8, 46, 69, 75, 105, 296.

Winter, 3, 15, 19, 21, 62, 90, 101, 111, 112, 114-119, 121, 128, 146, 181, 186, 192, 200, 258, 259, 326, 333; anticyclones, 117, 118, 335; approaching, 195; cold, 85, 113, 114, 139, 185, 300, 339; cold and early, 190, 197; cold spell in, 205, 225, 229; late cold spell in, 32, 113, 114; cold and stormy, 109; cold and sunny with N.E. winds in, 76; early, 113, 116; easterlies, 231; ended, 21; fine weather in, 257; fog, 117, 343; frost, 129, 208, 212, 214, 224, 328, 331; first frost in, 337, 338; last frost in, 337; frosty, 31, 80, 106, 117, 118; gales, 108, 114; green, 114; hail, 277; haze, 118; long, 108, 112; mild, 44, 74, 75, 88, 113, 114, 119, 180, 300, 306, 308, 338; mild and cloudy, 236; mild and wet, 111, 197, 339; mild weather in, 238, 272; nearly over, 17; north-easterlies, 118, 119, 270, 348, 349; north-westerlies, 118, 129, 132; rainbows, 280; severe, 67, 69, 72, 80, 85, 86, 90, 93, 109, 110, 136, 140, 164, 165, 178, 180, 189, 296, 300, 303, 304, 306, 308, 333, 338, 339; sleet, 228; snow, 79, 114, 140, 183, 207, 227, 228, 332, 333; snowy, 67, 69, 80, 98, 113, 300, 333; Solstice (c21 Dec), 117; southerlies, 236, 326; south-westerlies, 236, 237; spring in, 108, 114; storms, 84, 92, 115, 151, 257; severe storms in, 237; warm storms in, 71, 84; summer in, 115; sunrise in, tail of, 50; thaw, 208; thunder, 116; first thunder in, 272; thunder and lightning, 99, 272; unsettled weather in, 259; warm, 108; warm and open, 115; "weather breeders" in, 115; wet, 84, 86, 89; wet and very cold in, 272; windy, 121, 238.

"Withershins, widdershins or withersones", 220, 307.

Wolsonbury (Sussex), 269.

Woodcock, 164, 165.
Woodlice, 201.
Woodpecker, Green, 148, 165.
"Woolly fleeces" see Cirrus cloud.
Worcestershire, 210, 270, 302; Vale, 209.
Worm, 180, 181, 185, 186, 231; "casts", 185.
Worthing, 324.

"Yaffel", 165.
Yarrow (Scotland), 316.
"Yaun", 305.
Year, 114, 119-122; cold, 119, 120; coldest day of, 7; good corn, 300; bad crop, 332; good crop, 332; dear, 307; dry, 119, 348; fair, 47; fertile, 15, 34, 36, 66, 85, 101, 105; foggy, 120; bad fruit, 108; good fruit, 107; snowy, 120; first thunder of, 272; thunderstorms in, 277; warm, 40, 79; wet, 119, 120, 122, 348; wettest day of, 7; windy, 122.
Yorkshire, 7, 17, 27, 35, 74, 113, 154, 155, 166, 170, 171, 183, 239, 249, 264, 270, 284, 291, 292, 314; Dales, 264; East Riding of, 132, 289; North Riding of, 6, 10, 20, 73, 285, 291, 294.